HELEN HALL LIBRARY
City of League City
100 West Walker
League City, TX 77573

DISCARD

D0952595

Oct 18

CONAN DOYLE

FOR THE DEFENSE

# CONAN DOYLE FOR THE DEFENSE

## The True Story of a Sensational British Murder, a Quest for Justice, and the World's Most Famous Detective Writer

MARGALIT FOX

RANDOM HOUSE
NEW YORK

DISCARD
HELEN HALL LIBRARY
100 Walker St
League City, TX 77573

Copyright © 2018 by Margalit Fox

All rights reserved.

Published in the United States by Random House,
an imprint and division of
Penguin Random House LLC, New York.

Random House and the House colophon are registered
trademarks of Penguin Random House LLC.

Published in hardcover in the United Kingdom
by Profile Books, London.

LIBRARY OF CONGRESS CATALOGING-IN-PUBLICATION DATA

Names: Fox, Margalit, author.
Title: Conan Doyle for the defense : the true story of a sensational British murder, a quest for justice, and the world's most famous detective writer / Margalit Fox.
Description: New York : Random House, 2018. | Includes bibliographical references and index.
Identifiers: LCCN 2017058151| ISBN 9780399589454 (hardback) | ISBN 9780399589461 (ebook)
Subjects: LCSH: Discrimination in criminal justice administration—Scotland—Glasgow | Murder—Scotland—Glasgow. | Criminal investigation—Scotland—Glasgow. | Forensic sciences—Scotland—Glasgow. | Vindication—Scotland—Glasgow. | Doyle, Arthur Conan, 1859–1930. | Detectives—Scotland—Glasgow. | BISAC: LAW / Forensic Science. | TRUE CRIME / Murder / General.
Classification: LCC HV9960.G72 G533 2018 | DDC 364.152/3094144—dc23

LC record available at https://lccn.loc.gov/2017058151

Printed in the United States of America on acid-free paper

randomhousebooks.com

2 4 6 8 9 7 5 3 1

First U.S. Edition

For D. J. R. Bruckner,
rationalist,
humanist,
stylist,
in memoriam

The fictitious world, to which Sherlock Holmes belonged, expected of him what the real world of the day expected of its scientists: more light and more justice. As the creation of a doctor who had been soaked in the rationalist thought of the period, the Holmesian cycle offers us for the first time the spectacle of a hero triumphing again and again by means of logic and scientific method. And the hero's prowess is as marvellous as the power of science, which many people hoped would lead to a material and spiritual improvement of the human condition, and Conan Doyle first among them.

—Pierre Nordon,
*Conan Doyle: A Biography*, 1966

For seventeen years I have met nobody here who knew me outside. Quite naturally I often feel I must shout "Forsaken, forsaken, forsaken I am as the stones of the street."

—Oscar Slater, in a
letter to his sister, 1926

I am the last and highest court of appeal in detection.

—Sherlock Holmes,
*The Sign of Four*, 1890

# CONTENTS

## BOOK FOUR: PAPER

# AUTHOR'S NOTE

IN THE REAMS OF PUBLISHED WRITING ON SIR ARTHUR Conan Doyle, he is referred to variously by the surnames "Doyle" and "Conan Doyle." In keeping with his biographer Russell Miller, who writes that his subject was "given the compound surname of Conan Doyle," I have accorded him both names here. (Conan Doyle's son Adrian does likewise in his slender 1946 memoir of his father, *The True Conan Doyle.*)

In the interest of linguistic economy, I have generally chosen in this book to forgo honorific titles—Dr., Mr., Mrs., and so on. There is one regular exception: Marion Gilchrist, the eighty-two-year-old Glasgow woman whose murder lies at the heart of the story. In previous accounts of the case, including Conan Doyle's, she is always "Miss Gilchrist," and I have decided, in deference to her time, place, and august age, that "Miss Gilchrist" she shall remain.

The currency conversions appearing in footnotes throughout this book, which translate early twentieth-century pound sterling values into contemporary pound sterling and contemporary U.S. dollars, reflect the historical inflation rate and the contemporary exchange rate of early 2018, when the book went to press.

A cast of characters appears on page 259, a glossary of Scottish vocabulary on page 263.

# INTRODUCTION

It was one of the most notorious murders of its age. Galvanizing early twentieth-century Britain and before long the world, it involved a patrician victim, stolen diamonds, a transatlantic manhunt, and a cunning maidservant who knew far more than she could ever be persuaded to tell. It was, Sir Arthur Conan Doyle wrote in 1912, "as brutal and callous a crime as has ever been recorded in those black annals in which the criminologist finds the materials for his study."

But for all its dark drama, and for all the thousands of words Conan Doyle would write about it, the narrative of this murder was no work of fiction. It concerned an actual case: a killing for which an innocent man was pursued, tried, convicted, and nearly hanged. This miscarriage of justice would, in Conan Doyle's words, "remain immortal in the classics of crime as the supreme example of official incompetence and obstinacy." It would also consume him—as private investigator, public crusader, and ardent nonfiction chronicler—for the last two decades of his life.

The case, which has been called the Scottish Dreyfus affair, centered on the murder of a wealthy woman in Glasgow just before Christmas 1908. The next spring, Oscar Slater, a German Jewish gambler recently arrived in the city, was tried and condemned for the crime. His very name became so notorious that for years afterward the phrase “See you Oscar” was Glasgow rhyming slang for “See you later”—as in “See you later, Oscar Slater.”

But as investigations by Slater’s handful of champions would uncover, the Slater case was rife with judicial and prosecutorial misconduct, witness tampering, the suppression of exculpatory evidence, and the subornation of perjury. It was, Conan Doyle declared, a “disgraceful frame-up, in which stupidity and dishonesty played an equal part.” A good cop sacrificed his career after he voiced deep misgivings about the conduct of the investigation and trial.

In May 1909, after a jury deliberated for barely an hour, Oscar Slater was found guilty and sentenced to death. But amid public unease at the verdict, his sentence was commuted to life at hard labor just forty-eight hours before he was scheduled to mount the scaffold. For the next eighteen and a half years he remained imprisoned, largely forgotten, on a barren, windswept outcropping in the north of the country, in a place that would one day be known as “Scotland’s gulag”: His Majesty’s Prison Peterhead.

Day after day, in bone-rattling cold and blistering heat, Slater hewed immense blocks of granite; endured a Dickensian diet of bread, broth, and gruel; and often languished in solitary confinement. Had he passed the twenty-year mark behind bars, he said, he would have taken his own life.

Then, in 1927, Slater was abruptly released; his conviction was quashed the next year. What set these events in motion was a secret message he had smuggled out of prison in 1925. That message—an impassioned plea for help—was directed at Conan Doyle.

Writer, physician, worldwide luminary, champion of the

downtrodden, Sir Arthur Conan Doyle had believed in Slater's innocence almost from the start. Joining the case publicly in 1912, he turned his formidable powers to the effort to free him, dissecting the conduct of police and prosecution with Holmesian acumen. But despite his influence and energy, Conan Doyle wrote, "I was up against a ring of political lawyers who could not give away the police without also giving away themselves." And so a conviction that, as one commentator remarked, rested on evidence so flimsy that in comparable straits "a cat would scarcely be whipped for stealing cream" endured for nearly two decades as one of the most tragically attenuated judicial farces of its time.

That the story did not end with Slater's death in prison owes chiefly to Conan Doyle. As investigator, author, publisher, and backroom broker in the loftiest corridors of British power, he is credited with having done more than anyone else to win Slater's freedom in a case that many observers deemed hopeless. "The Slater affair," one of Conan Doyle's biographers has written, "was to give Conan Doyle the chance to play a similar part in England to Zola's intervention in the Dreyfus affair in France."*

CONAN DOYLE REMAINS VENERATED today as a crime writer, but he is less well remembered as a crusader—"that paladin of lost causes," as one British criminologist memorably described him. By the time he died in 1930, at seventy-one, he had twice run for Parliament (without success) and had championed a

* In 1894, Alfred Dreyfus, a Jewish captain in the French army, was arrested on a spurious charge of treason amid a climate of roiling anti-Semitism. Convicted, he was sent to Devil's Island, the notorious prison in French Guyana. Among his staunchest public supporters was the novelist Émile Zola, whose outraged open letter, "*J'accuse . . . !*," published on the front page of a Paris newspaper in 1898, taxed the government with anti-Jewish bigotry and helped win Dreyfus a new trial. Dreyfus was pardoned in 1899 and fully exonerated in 1906.

string of causes, including divorce reform; the exposure of Belgian atrocities in the Congo; clemency for his friend Roger Casement, convicted of treason; and, in his later years, incongruous as it might seem for a man of such exquisite reason, the existence of the afterlife and the spirit world. Renowned as the creator of Sherlock Holmes, very likely the most famous character in Western letters, Conan Doyle was repeatedly beseeched by members of the public to solve real-life mysteries—deaths, disappearances, and the like—performing successful feats of amateur detection on more than one occasion.

By the time he cast his lot with Slater, Conan Doyle had helped right another notorious wrongful conviction, that of George Edalji, an Anglo-Indian lawyer imprisoned for maiming livestock. Conan Doyle's personal investigation of that case is the subject of a spate of nonfiction books and also inspired Julian Barnes's 2005 novel, *Arthur and George*.

But the Slater story, though it involves homicide, remains less well known, perhaps because the case is more complex than any other Conan Doyle tackled. For one thing, it lacks the stainless suspect and moral absolutes that the Edalji case presented. Where George Edalji was an educated professional man of unimpeachable character, Oscar Slater was an affable Continental rascal: a habitué of music halls and gambling rooms and, it was alleged (though never proved), a pimp. Conan Doyle himself thought Slater a blackguard: "a disreputable, rolling-stone of a man," he called him—seven words that speak volumes about the reflexive cultural assumptions of his era. In addition, Conan Doyle, creator of the ultra-rationalist Holmes, had become something of a laughingstock in the last decades of his life for his vigorous endorsement of spiritualism. As a result, press and public were inclined to regard any cause to which he attached himself, Slater's included, with skepticism if not outright derision.

Yet the case was Conan Doyle's last stand as a true-crime investigator, and a remarkable stand it was. The story of his long effort to free Slater throws into relief the singular temperament that let Conan Doyle light the age in which he lived: a readiness to wade into battle, a sense of honor so intense that it trumped personal antipathies, and a talent for rational investigation that far outstripped that of the police. Where today many wrongful convictions have been overturned through DNA analysis, Conan Doyle managed to free Slater with little more than minute observation and rigorous logic—precisely the kind of brainwork that had made his hero world famous.

*CONAN DOYLE FOR THE DEFENSE* tells a fourfold story. First, it is the tale of a condemned man exonerated without benefit of modern forensics. Second, it is a study of the singular method of detection that Conan Doyle used in the Holmes stories, applied by him to an actual murder. It is no accident that the man who saved Slater was both crime writer and doctor, for detection, like doctoring, is rooted in the art of diagnosis. That art, which hinges on the identification, discrimination, and interpretation of barely discernible clues in order to reconstruct an unseen past (a skill that Holmes memorably described as the ability to "reason backward"), animates Conan Doyle's approach to nearly every aspect of Slater's case.

The diagnostic imagination that Conan Doyle brought to the case had been instilled in him by his medical school professor Joseph Bell, the flesh-and-blood progenitor of Sherlock Holmes. Bell's tutelage would serve Conan Doyle brilliantly in a string of real-life mysteries, medical and criminal. "I have a turn both for observation and for deduction," Holmes tells Watson when they first meet. "From long habit the train of thoughts ran so swiftly through my mind that I arrived at the conclusion without being conscious of intermediate steps. There were such steps, however."

And so there were, too, for Conan Doyle in the Slater case. His published accounts and archived letters on the subject reveal a modus operandi that is truly Holmesian. His method entailed the search for small details whose significance other investigators had missed, the picking apart of logical inconsistencies on the part of police and prosecutors, an eye for negative evidence and the deep understanding of its value, and, as Holmes would have said, the ability to *observe* rather than merely to *see*. All this he would use to loosen, link by link, the chain of circumstantial evidence that had been tightened round Slater's neck.

Third, *Conan Doyle for the Defense* sketches a portrait of Slater himself, who in the few previous accounts of the case has been a conspicuous absence, a cipher at the center of his own story. This book seeks to fill the void by drawing on the moving series of letters, exchanged over nearly twenty years, between the imprisoned Slater—in many ways an immigrant everyman—and three generations of his loving family in Germany.

The letters yield a bittersweet bonanza. We see a thoughtful, soulful man struggling to hold on to his faith in a place where for much of the time he was the only Jew. We see a man torn between the need to resign himself to his fate and the need not to abandon hope altogether. We also see, hauntingly, a man who appears to be descending into madness. More haunting still is the fact that even after his release Slater would never see his family again: he had lost his German citizenship and could not readily return home. But as painful as this prohibition must have been, in the long run it may well have saved his life.

Fourth, *Conan Doyle for the Defense* explores a question that vexed many of Slater's advocates and which has persisted for more than a century: Why, when the Glasgow police knew within a week that Slater was innocent, did they continue to pursue him nearly into the grave?

The answer reveals much about the state of criminal investigation at the dawn of the twentieth century: Slater's case took place at a watershed moment in criminology, a state of affairs that ultimately worked against him. It also reveals much about the Victorian mindset, for the Slater story, which straddles the twilight of nineteenth-century gentility and the upheavals of twentieth-century modernity, is at its core a tale of Victorian morality. Though the case began in Edwardian times and extended into the Jazz Age, it is indisputably a product of what has been called "the long nineteenth century," which ran to the outbreak of World War I and perhaps even beyond.

The period saw sweeping social developments including the rise of modern science and medicine, the rise of the modern police force, and the rise of the modern literary detective—an era of which Conan Doyle could not have been more supremely representative had he been assembled by a committee. At the same time it looked longingly backward, to a time when the war's technologized carnage and other dubious attainments of science were unknown. With his simultaneous embrace of liberalism and traditionalism, and his simultaneous proselytizing for the scientific method and for the existence of a spirit world that many Victorians, amid modern insecurities, had begun to crave, perhaps no public person embodied this Janus-headed era more fully than he.

As it unspooled over two decades, the Slater story encapsulated much that was commendable about the ethos of the period—valor, fair play, and fealty to scientific reason—and much that was not: class bias, sexual prudery, xenophobia, nationalism, and anti-Semitism. Above all, the concern with honor, reputation, and gentlemanly behavior that permeated the age would govern the conduct, noble and otherwise, of many actors in the case, Conan Doyle and Slater included. Their intertwined narrative culminates in 1929, when the association between them, an otherwise curative convergence, ends in what Conan Doyle called "a painful and sordid aftermath," precisely over a matter of honor.

At bottom, *Conan Doyle for the Defense* is a story about class identification: those snap judgments, themselves dark diagnostic instruments, that in every age are wielded to segregate "us" from "them." In particular, Slater's case is about the ways in which such rude taxonomies—iconographies of otherness—reflect the tenor of their era and the fears of its majority culture. As it played out, his story is also about the manner in which these biases can be enfranchised by legislatures and the courts.

In its confluence of Victorian passions and prejudices, the case endures as a remarkable double-faced mirror of its time. What is more (a revelation I had not anticipated when I began work on this book half a dozen years ago), the Slater saga, with its foundational tension between reason on the one hand and the particularly insidious brand of unreason known as ethnic bigotry on the other—manifest in a social practice that has been called "the racialization of crime"—has become every inch a mirror of our own age.

# PROLOGUE: PRISONER 2988

On January 23, 1925, William Gordon, lately known as Prisoner 2988, was released from His Majesty's Prison Peterhead, a Victorian fortress on Scotland's raw northeast coast. Gordon would very likely have passed into history unremarked except for his possession of a vital anatomical feature: he wore dentures. Beneath his dentures that day, furled into a tiny pellet with a scrap of glazed paper rolled round it to keep it dry, he carried an urgent note from a fellow convict. Though prison officials had made a thorough search of Gordon before releasing him, no one thought to examine his gums. And so the message, which would culminate nearly three years later in Oscar Slater's release from life at hard labor, was spirited into the world.

Where earlier efforts to free Slater had been initiated by lawyers, this last, desperate stratagem was set in motion by Slater himself. He had slipped Gordon the note, written in pencil on a fragment of brown tissue paper, during a meeting of the prison debating society. A clandestine pellet like this was the safest means of communication between them: like most British prisons of its era, Peterhead maintained a regimen of enforced silence. Prisoners, supervised round the clock by armed guards, were allowed to speak to one another only in direct connection with their work. By 1925, Slater had already been disciplined for talking to a fellow convict through a ventilator between cells.

Slater's message, now fragile and faded, has been preserved in the archives of the Mitchell Library in Glasgow. Bearing many of the hallmarks of his idiosyncratic spelling, punctuation, and syntax, it reads:

> *Gordon my boy, I wish you in every way the best of luck and if you feel inclined, then please do what you can for me. Give to the English public your opinion regarding me, personally and also in other respects. You have been for 5 years in close contact with me and so you are quite fit to do so.*
>
> *Friend, keep out of prison but especially out of this God-forsaken hole. Farewell Gordon, we likely may never see us again, but let us live in hope, that it may be otherwise.*
>
> *Your friend*
> *Oscar Slater*
>
> *P.S. Please don't forget to write or see Connan D. . . .*

That Gordon carried out Slater's instructions can be gleaned from a second communication, an anonymous letter that reached Peterhead in mid-February. Addressed to Slater, it said:

> *Just a few lines to try to cheer you up. You have staunch friends in the outside world, who are doing their utmost for you so you must not lose heart. Sir Arthur Conan Doyle bids me say that you have all his sympathy, and all the weight of his interest will be put in the scale on your behalf. . . . We should like to get a line from you, if you are allowed to write. In the meantime keep up your heart & hope for the best, & rest assured we are doing our utmost for you.*

The letter, which prison officials strongly suspected came from Gordon, was suppressed on arrival. But though Slater did not know it, his anxious note had accomplished its purpose: it persuaded Conan Doyle, who had long sought, with immense energy but disheartening results, to commute his sentence, to take up the case one last time.

THE CRIME FOR WHICH Oscar Slater had barely escaped the hangman's noose was, in the words of a late twentieth-century writer, "a case of murder which has frequently been described as without parallel in criminal history." It was stunningly violent, its victim refined, wealthy, and more than slightly eccentric. Under pressure to solve the case, the police soon announced that they had a suspect: thirty-six-year-old Oscar Slater, who had arrived in Glasgow that year with his young French mistress, nominally a music hall singer but probably a prostitute.

In the eyes of Edwardian Glasgow, Slater was in every way a desirable culprit. He was a foreigner—a native of Germany—and a Jew. His dandified, demimonde life affronted the sensibilities of the age: Slater billed himself variously as a dentist and a dealer in precious stones but was believed to earn his living as a gambler. Even before the murder, the Glasgow police had been monitoring him in the hope of having him arrested as a pimp. (In the decorous diction of the times, the charge they sought to press was "immoral housekeeping.")

Slater's trial took place in Edinburgh in May 1909, with the case against him founded on circumstantial evidence and outright fabrication. "Circumstantial evidence is a very tricky thing," Conan Doyle wrote. "It may seem to point very straight to one thing, but if you shift your own point of view a little, you may find it pointing in an equally uncompromising manner to something entirely different." The words are Sherlock Holmes's, spoken in an 1891 story, "The Boscombe Valley Mystery." They stand as a precise augury of the Slater affair.

The jury deliberated for seventy minutes before finding Slater guilty, and the judge sentenced him to hang. The pronouncement had a terrible finality: there was no criminal appeals court in Scotland then. (Pardons, when they were occasionally granted, were by prerogative of the British monarch.) By the time, nearly three weeks later, that Slater's sentence was commuted to penal servitude for life, he had made arrangements for his own burial. Transported to Peterhead, he paced his tiny cell, hewed granite, and railed at his jailers for much of the next two decades.

IN LATE 1911 OR early 1912, Slater's lawyers asked Conan Doyle to lend his support to their cause. Though he deplored Slater's ungentlemanly life, Conan Doyle, a Scotsman himself, soon came to believe that the case was a stain on the British character. He trained his diagnostic eye on every aspect of the crime, manhunt, and trial; wrote *The Case of Oscar Slater*, his scathing 1912 indictment of the affair; penned a stream of letters to British newspapers; edited, published, and contributed a trenchant introduction to *The Truth About Oscar Slater*, the 1927 book by the journalist William Park; and lobbied some of the most powerful officials in Britain.

The reprieve came at last in November 1927. In 1928, after a criminal appeals court was established in Scotland—a development brought about partly by Conan Doyle's agitation—Slater's trial was reviewed and his conviction quashed. The hearing, which Conan Doyle covered for a British newspaper, marked the only time in their long association that he and Slater met face-to-face. Then, after the triumphant resolution, came the bitter, highly public rupture.

These developments form the long, painful sequel to an exceptionally strange event that occurred in Glasgow in December 1908, about a week before Marion Gilchrist's death—more than a week before Slater even knew of her existence. Though the fact would not be widely known for years, Miss Gilchrist told at least one person that week that she knew she was going to be murdered.

# BOOK ONE

---

# DIAMONDS

## Chapter 1

# A FOOTFALL ON THE STAIR

IN GLASGOW AT THE TURN OF THE TWENTIETH CENTURY, there lived an old lady whom few people liked. Her name was Marion Gilchrist, and on December 21, 1908, which was to be the last day of her life, Miss Gilchrist—an upright, formidable, churchgoing woman of robust health and impeccable breeding—was a few weeks shy of her eighty-third birthday.

The city in which she lived was a vast, forbidding place of cobblestones, soot, and damp. Industrialization had urbanized Glasgow, as it had much of the Western world. Cities, their skies black with coal, gorged themselves on the surrounding countryside; suburbs sprang up to which solid middle-class men could return after a day at the office; and men and women from the country, less well-heeled than these new suburbanites, thronged the cities in search of work. In 1900, Glasgow's population of more than three-quarters of a million made it, after London, the second-largest city in Britain.

By the late nineteenth century, as British cities teemed with new inhabitants, crime rates rose and more established residents came to be afflicted with a new, urban, and distinctly modern anxiety. For the middle and upper classes, it centered acutely on the protection of property, coalescing in particular around city dwellers who were not members of the bourgeoisie. These included the working class, the poor, new immigrants, and Jews, all of whom were viewed increasingly as agents of social contagion—a threat in urgent need of containment.

Newspapers and magazines of the period couched this anxiety in language that turned heavily on metaphors of invasion. In the spring of 1909, after Slater was convicted of Miss Gilchrist's murder, many publications decried his arrival on British soil in just such terms, one likening him to a vampire, a time-honored pejorative applied to Jews.

"Now an alien breed has come in," the *Bailie,* a respected Glasgow magazine, said that year. "Great Britain . . . opens her arms to the foreign scum . . . mole-ish blackguards are on the prowl in the community." The *Edinburgh Evening News* wrote that Slater's trial "has cast a lurid light on the dark places of our great cities, in which such wretches ply their calling. It shows a brood of alien vampires, lost to conscience, crawling in black depths and the basement of civilised society."

EVEN BY THE STANDARDS of a frightened age, Marion Gilchrist was a remarkably frightened woman. She was born in Glasgow on January 18, 1826, the daughter of James Gilchrist, a prosperous engineer. In later years, after her mother's death, Miss Gilchrist, who never married, remained at home to care for her father. Before he died, she appears to have persuaded him to leave the bulk of his estate to her; as a result, she wound up far wealthier than any of her siblings.

Miss Gilchrist had a bevy of nieces and nephews, though

she seemed not to care much for them, nor they for her. "Miss Gilchrist was not on good terms with her relations," her niece Margaret Birrell, who lived nearby, told the police after the murder. "Few if any visited her."

Among the rare people with whom Miss Gilchrist enjoyed a warm relationship was a former maid, Maggie Galbraith Ferguson, and her daughter, Marion Gilchrist Ferguson, named for her mother's old employer. On November 20, 1908, a month before she died, Miss Gilchrist altered her will. The previous version, which had been drawn up just six months earlier, had divided her estate—valued at more than £15,000* and including jewelry, paintings, furniture, silver, and considerable cash reserves—among various nieces and nephews. The new will left the balance of the estate to Maggie and Marion Ferguson.

FOR THIRTY YEARS BEFORE her death, Miss Gilchrist had lived in tasteful near-solitude in a large flat at 49 West Princes Street, a wide avenue that dips through north-central Glasgow from northwest to southeast. Lined with Victorian row houses and long home to middle- and upper-middle-class professionals, her neighborhood was at the turn of the twentieth century a quiet, elegant oasis. After her murder, as if to emphasize the exquisite inappropriateness of Miss Gilchrist as a victim, newspaper accounts took pains to describe the gentility of her part of town.

Miss Gilchrist lived alone except for her maid, a twenty-one-year-old Scotswoman named Helen Lambie. "A likeable, high-spirited, superficial and unreflective girl," as she has been

* Equivalent to about £1.3 million, or $2 million, in today's money.

called, Lambie, known as Nellie, had worked for Miss Gilchrist for three years. By all accounts the two women got on well, but it is striking that a previous employer, Agnes Guthrie, described her as "a very good domestic worker, but most illiterate, of rather a low mentality, very cunning and not at all trustworthy in her standards." Over the two decades that followed Miss Gilchrist's murder, Lambie's behavior suggested that she knew more about the crime than she would ever disclose—including, quite probably, the real killer's identity.

The southeast segment of West Princes Street, where Miss Gilchrist's home stood, was also called Queen's Terrace, and her address was sometimes rendered as 15 Queen's Terrace. Her building was a handsome three-story structure erected in about 1850; her flat took up the entire second story. The ground-floor flat (the "maindoor house," in the Scottish parlance of the day) was occupied by a family of musicians named Adams: a mother; her grown son, Arthur; and a flock of grown daughters. Their flat had its own door onto the street, 14 Queen's Terrace, which stood alongside Miss Gilchrist's. The third-floor flat, directly above Miss Gilchrist's, was, in the winter of 1908, vacant.

To reach Miss Gilchrist's flat, a visitor mounted a few steps from the pavement, passed through the street door of No. 15, and entered the vestibule-cum-stairwell known in Scotland as a "close." Inside the close, he ascended the staircase that led to the upper floors, climbing a single flight to the first landing, where Miss Gilchrist's front door stood. The door opened into a large entrance hall. To the left of the hall, its windows overlooking West Princes Street, lay the dining room, appointed, like the rest of the flat, with heavy Victorian furniture and paintings in lavish frames. To the right was the drawing room;

at the rear were the kitchen, parlor, two bedrooms, and a bathroom. Miss Gilchrist slept in the smaller of the two bedrooms, using the larger one as a combination spare room and dressing room. It was in this spare room that the drama of the Slater case first played out, for it was there that Miss Gilchrist stored most of her jewels.

For a woman of her time and class, Miss Gilchrist lived fairly unostentatiously except for one great indulgence: jewelry. Over the years she amassed an extensive collection, which included rings set with diamonds, emeralds, and rubies; bracelets of gold, silver, pearl, and turquoise; pearl and diamond necklaces; diamond earrings; and a great deal else. She seemed to have a particular fondness for brooches, and her collection contained a spate of them: brooches set with pearls, onyx, garnets, rubies, and topaz; a trio of star-shaped diamond brooches; and, fatefully for Slater, a crescent-shaped brooch set with diamonds. At her death, the collection, comprising nearly a hundred items, was valued at some £3,000.*

"She seldom wore her jewelry save in single pieces," Conan Doyle wrote in 1912. "It was a fearful joy which she snatched from its possession, for she more than once expressed apprehension that she might be attacked and robbed." To thwart robbery, Miss Gilchrist hid her jewels in curious places, forgoing the safe in her parlor for the wardrobe in the spare bedroom, where she secreted them between layers of clothing or in "a detachable pocket with a string on it," as the British journalist Peter Hunt wrote in his 1951 book on the case. She pinned other pieces behind the drapes and slipped still others into pockets of dresses.

* More than £250,000, or nearly $400,000, today.

She also turned her flat into a fortress. "Against . . . unwelcome intrusion, Miss Gilchrist had devised several formidable precautions," Hunt wrote:

> The back windows were kept locked. There were no less than three locks on the house-door; a common lock, patent lock and a Chubb. There were, in addition, a bolt and chain. When fully primed the door was virtually burglar-proof.
>
> Anyone visiting No. 15 would have to pull a bell, downstairs, outside the close door. There was a lever inside the hall of Miss Gilchrist's flat which operated the fastenings of the downstairs door. In this way Miss Gilchrist, on hearing the bell, could release the downstairs door from inside her own flat, open her flat door and see who was coming up the stairs. If the visitor looked sinister she had plenty of time, if she wished, to get back inside her flat and close the door on him. There is evidence to show that, when alone, she would admit no one except by pre-arranged signal.

Miss Gilchrist arranged another signal with her downstairs neighbors, the Adamses. If she were ever in distress and needed help, she told them, she would knock three times on the floor. On the evening of December 21, 1908, the Adamses would hear those knocks for the first and only time.

IN THE AUTUMN OF 1908, Oscar Slater—gambler, Beau Brummell, and happy-go-lucky world traveler—came to Glasgow. He had lived there at least twice before, in the very early years of the twentieth century; since leaving Germany as a youth, he had also lived in New York, London, Paris, and Brussels. In 1901, during his first documented Glasgow stay, he married a local woman, Mary Curtis Pryor, an alcoholic who was constantly after him for money.* Separated from her soon afterward, Slater resumed his travels, living under a series of aliases partly to confound her efforts to trace him. He was known to have lived briefly again in Glasgow in 1905 before pulling up stakes once more.

Slater arrived in Glasgow for what appeared to be the third time on October 29, 1908. A few days later he was joined by his mistress, Andrée Junio Antoine (known professionally as Madame Junio and familiarly as Antoine), and their maid, Catherine Schmalz. He spent the next few weeks settling in and, unwittingly, forging the first links in the chain of circumstantial evidence that would soon be drawn around him. Under the pseudonym Anderson, he rented a flat at 69 St. George's Road, a north-south thoroughfare in central Glasgow that crosses West Princes Street; the building was little more than five minutes' walk from Miss Gilchrist's home. That turned out to be the first link in the chain.

On November 10, Slater went to a hardware store and bought a set of inexpensive tools with which to fix up his new flat. Those tools—in particular the small hammer that came with the set—became the chain's second link. In early December, needing to have his watch repaired, he mailed it to Dent's, a London watchmaker. That would provide the third link.

By then, Slater had already visited a Glasgow pawnbroker, where, in exchange for an initial loan of £20, he left a crescent-shaped brooch set with diamonds. That was the fourth, and most damning, link of all.

* Archival records sometimes give Pryor's first name as Marie or May.

---

THAT AUTUMN, STRANGE THINGS had begun happening in and around Miss Gilchrist's house. In September 1908, her Irish terrier fell ill and died: Helen Lambie thought it had accidentally eaten something poisonous; the old woman believed that something far more deliberate was at work. Then, during the first three weeks of December, as more than a dozen local residents would later say, a man was seen loitering in West Princes Street. He seemed to be watching Miss Gilchrist's house.

"The 'watcher' was seen at irregular times and in varying types of clothing," Peter Hunt wrote. (As described by some witnesses, his attire included checked trousers, fawn spats, and brown boots.) "There was subsequently some confusion as to his appearance. One says he had a moustache; another says he did not; one says he did not speak like a foreigner; others say he looked like a foreigner."

In mid-December, about a week before Miss Gilchrist's murder, an agitated Helen Lambie paid a surprise visit to her ex-employer, Agnes Guthrie. As Guthrie later recalled, Lambie had much to say about recent goings-on in the Gilchrist home. "I was informed by her that she had some remarkable experiences at the house of Miss Gilchrist," Guthrie said. "She gave me a very long story about her peculiarities. Miss Gilchrist had a lot of jewellery and had taken unusual ways to secrete it in the house, under carpets, etc., and had told her that she felt sure there was a man coming to murder her, and that the dog had been poisoned."

The truly surprising thing, which Lambie implied in a later conversation with Guthrie—and confirmed outright to Miss Gilchrist's niece Margaret Birrell immediately after the murder—was this: It was no random stranger whom Miss Gilchrist feared but instead one or more people she knew very well.

ON THE AFTERNOON OF MONDAY, December 21, 1908, Miss Gilchrist left her flat to pay bills, returning at about four-thirty for tea. That night—a rainy evening—at five minutes to seven, one of the Adams sisters, Rowena Adams Liddell, was walking back to Queen's Terrace with her mother. As they approached their front door, she saw the "watcher" gazing up at the building. As she later testified for the prosecution at Slater's trial:

> Before I reached the door of the house I saw a dark form leaning against the railing, just under my mother's dining-room window. . . . I gave a good stare—almost a rude stare—and I took in the face entirely, except that I did not see his eyes. He had a long nose, with a most peculiar dip from here [pointing to the bridge of the nose]. You could not see that dip amongst thousands. He had a very clear complexion; not a sallow nor a white pallor, but something of an ivory colour. He was very dark, clean-shaven, and very broad in this part of the head [points to the cheekbone or temple]. He had a low-down collar. His cap was an ordinary cap, I think, of a brownish tweed. He was very respectable. . . . After I passed him I looked over my shoulder, and he glided from the railing and disappeared.

At a minute or two before seven, Helen Lambie left her mistress's house to buy Miss Gilchrist's evening paper. She planned, once she returned with it, to go out again to do the household shopping. From Miss Gilchrist, who sat by the dining room fire reading a magazine, Lambie obtained a penny for the newspaper and a half sovereign for the other purchases.* Taking the penny but leaving the half sovereign on the dining room table, Lambie left the flat.

"Lambie took the keys with her, shut the flat door, closed the hall door downstairs, and was gone about ten minutes upon her errand," Conan Doyle wrote. "It is the events of those ten minutes which form the tragedy and the mystery where were so soon to engage the attention of the public."

Directly below Miss Gilchrist's flat, Arthur Montague Adams, a forty-year-old flutist and musical instrument dealer, sat wrapping a Christmas present. At seven o'clock, Adams, his sister Rowena, and another sister, Laura, heard a loud thud from above. Three sharp knocks followed.

To reach Miss Gilchrist's flat, Adams had to exit his own front door at 14 Queen's Terrace and ring the bell of the close door at No. 15. Stepping outside, he was surprised to see the close door standing open. He climbed the stairs to Miss Gilchrist's landing and pulled the bell rope at her front door. "I rang hard—rude rings," Adams later testified. There was no answer. Listening for any sound from within, Adams heard something like splintering wood; he assumed, he said, that it was Lambie "breaking sticks in the kitchen" for kindling. Hearing nothing more, he returned to his flat and told his sisters that everything seemed to be all right.

The sisters, meanwhile, had been hearing noises so violent that they thought their ceiling "like to crack." More alarmed than ever, they sent Adams back upstairs. On the landing, he

* A half sovereign equaled half a pound. Its value in 1908 is equivalent to about £55, or $70, today.

pulled the bell again. He had his hand on the bell rope for another ring when, at about 7:10, he saw Lambie coming up the stairs with the paper. He was surprised to see her, as he had imagined she was in Miss Gilchrist's kitchen the whole time.

As she climbed the stairs, Lambie later said, she noticed a footprint, damp with rainwater, on each of two bottom steps; she was certain the prints had not been there when she went out. Reaching the landing, she was equally surprised to see Adams: "He was never a visitor at the house," she said, "and I was astonished to find him there."

As Lambie unlocked the door of Miss Gilchrist's flat, Adams told her about the fearsome noises. She seemed unconcerned. "Oh, it would be the pulleys," she said, implying that the clotheslines, which hung suspended in the kitchen by a set of pulleys, had fallen down. Adams told her he would stay there, just in case, and remained on the doormat.

After Lambie opened the door, Adams later recalled, she walked straight into Miss Gilchrist's entrance hall. (Lambie's memory differed: in her recollection, she remained on the doormat.) From wherever she stood, Lambie saw a well-dressed man come toward her from the direction of Miss Gilchrist's spare bedroom; the gaslight in that room, which had been off when she left the house, was now lit. The man left the flat, walked blithely past Lambie and Adams, and took to the stairs. As both she and Adams later told the police, his clothing bore no visible traces of blood.

"I did not suspect anything wrong for a minute," Adams later testified. "I saw the man walk quite coolly till he got up to me, and then he went down quickly, like greased lightning, and that aroused my suspicions." Lambie, meanwhile, went straight to the kitchen, checked the pulleys, and called out to Adams that they were fine. She then went into the spare bedroom.

"Where is your mistress?" Adams called out to her. Lambie stepped into the dining room. "Oh, come here!" she cried.

"The spectacle in question was the poor old lady lying upon the floor close by the chair in which the servant had last seen her," Conan Doyle wrote. "Her feet were towards the door, her head towards the fireplace. She lay upon a hearth-rug, but a skin rug had been thrown across her head. Her injuries were frightful, nearly every bone of her face and skull being smashed. In spite of her dreadful wounds she lingered for a few minutes, but died without showing any signs of consciousness." Miss Gilchrist had been beaten so savagely that autopsy photographs depict a face that looks as though it had never been human.

Adams rushed downstairs and out the close door. He saw a few people at the end of West Princes Street and ran toward them but could not spot the intruder. He was soon joined in the street by Lambie and his sisters. Adams next ran for a policeman and a doctor; Lambie ran a few streets to the west, to the home of Miss Gilchrist's niece Margaret Birrell. What Lambie told her that night—along with both women's later disavowal of the exchange—would haunt the case long afterward.

LAMBIE RETURNED TO MISS GILCHRIST'S flat later that evening. By then Adams had brought a doctor (coincidentally also named Adams) and a police constable. After examining Miss Gilchrist's body, Dr. John Adams surveyed the dining room, which was awash in blood. Looking for a weapon, he homed in on a heavy dining room chair whose back left leg dripped with blood. The chair's spindle-shaped legs, he observed, appeared to correspond to a set of odd, spindle-shaped wounds on Miss Gilchrist's body. "Dr. Adams surmised that that assault was committed by a number of heavy blows with the chair," Hunt wrote. "If the murderer was standing up, and on the body of his victim, he would be able to use great, but uncontrolled force. This would account both for the wide area of the wounds and the apparent lack of blood on the murderer himself, for he would be protected to some extent by the seat of the chair, interposed between himself and the body."

Throughout the evening, a string of Glasgow police detectives joined the scene. Noteworthy among them for their roles in advancing the case against Slater were Detective Inspector John Pyper, who arrived at 7:55, and a senior official, John Ord, superintendent of the Criminal Investigation Department of the Glasgow police, who arrived later that night.

Pyper took in the crime scene. Miss Gilchrist's reading glasses and her magazine lay on the dining room table. The half sovereign was on the rug beside her hand. No blood was found outside the dining room. There was no sign of a struggle in the entrance hall, nor had the flat door been forced. In the spare bedroom, a wooden workbox, of the kind Victorian women used to store sewing supplies, had been wrenched open. Its contents—papers—lay scattered on the floor. The killer, who had evidently lighted the gas in that room, had left his matches behind. The matchbox (bearing the ironically apt trade name Runaway) was not the brand used in the house. On a dressing table in the spare room was a dish that had held several pieces of jewelry, among the few Miss Gilchrist left in plain sight. While most of them, including a watch and some rings, remained untouched, Lambie told Pyper that a crescent-shaped diamond brooch, valued at £50, was missing.*

Pyper questioned Adams and Lambie about the man they saw leaving the flat. Adams, who was nearsighted and hadn't

* About £4,000, or $6,000, today.

been wearing his glasses, could describe him only generally as "well featured and clean-shaven," with "dark trousers and a light overcoat." Lambie said that she had not seen the intruder's face and would not be able to identify him. She described him as having worn a three-quarter-length gray overcoat and a round cloth hat.

At 9:40 that night, the Glasgow police department issued its first internal bulletin about the crime:

> An old lady was murdered in her house at 15 Queen's Terrace between 7 and 7-10 p.m. to-day by a man from 25 to 30, 5 feet 7 or 8, think clean shaven. Wore a long grey overcoat and dark cap.
>
> Robbery appears to have been the object of the murderer, as a number of boxes in a bedroom were opened and left lying on the floor: large sized crescent shaped gold brooch set with diamonds, large diamonds in centre, graduating towards the points, is missing and may be in possession of the murderer. The diamonds are set in silver. No trace of the murderer has been got. Constables will please warn Booking-Clerks at railway stations, as the murderer will have bloodstains on his clothing. Also warn Pawns on opening regarding brooch and keep a sharp lookout.

The next two days brought no leads. During this time, Oscar Slater, apparently oblivious of the crime, was preparing to leave town. In 1908, Glasgow, a city dependent on manufacturing and trade, was in the midst of a severe depression. Even for gamblers, times were hard. That autumn, after receiving a letter from an old American crony inviting him to San Francisco, Slater made arrangements to move there, via Liverpool and New York.

In the days before he sailed, Slater wrapped up his Glasgow affairs. He found a tenant to take over his flat on St. George's Road. He visited his barber to collect his shaving things—in those less hygienic times, many men kept their own razor at their barber's—and told the barber of his travel plans. He mailed a five-pound note to his parents in Germany as a holiday gift. To raise cash for his journey, he tried to liquidate some of his belongings, including the pawn ticket for his diamond crescent brooch.

ON WEDNESDAY, DECEMBER 23, two things happened that would affect the case for years. The first was the entrance into the investigation of a Glasgow police detective named John Thomson Trench. A highly respected officer, Trench would work on the Gilchrist case only tangentially. But as a result of his later condemnation of the investigation and trial, he would emerge, in Conan Doyle's words, "not merely as an honest man, but . . . as a hero."

The second event of December 23 would have repercussions lasting nearly two decades. That day, a local woman, Barbara Barrowman, told the police that her fourteen-year-old daughter, Mary, had seen a man fleeing Miss Gilchrist's building on the night of the murder.

Mary Barrowman was an errand girl for a bootmaker in Great Western Road, a major thoroughfare one block north of West Princes Street. Encouraged by her mother to come forward, she told detectives that shortly after 7:00 p.m. on December 21, as she was walking along West Princes Street on a job for her employer, she saw a man run out of the close door of Miss Gilchrist's building:

> He looked towards St. George's Road and immediately turned westwards. I wondered what was wrong, and turned round and watched him, following a few yards, and saw that he turned into West Cumberland Street, running all the time.
>
> I went and delivered my message and returned to the shop by Woodlands Road, and after leaving our shop at 8 p.m. I went to my brother's shop at 480 St. Vincent Street, and while going there I again passed along West Princes Street and saw a crowd opposite No. 49 and learned of the murder, and I then thought of the man I had seen running out of the close there. He was a man about 28 or 30 years of age, tall and slim build, no hair on face, long features, nose slightly turned to the right, dressed in a fawn overcoat-like waterproof, dark trousers, brown boots, and tweed cloth hat of respectable appearance.*
>
> I did not see any other person near the close or about, but I think I could recognise the man again, although I could not say that I ever saw him before.

Barrowman's description differed markedly from the one in the police bulletin. Where Lambie had described a man with a gray overcoat and round cloth hat, Barrowman spoke of a fawn-colored waterproof coat and a tweed hat of the kind, she later elaborated, known as a Donegal cap. As a result, the police now assumed that *two* men were involved. On Christmas Day, 1908, they issued a second internal bulletin:

* Slater was then thirty-six, stocky, of medium height, with a short mustache and a convex, or Roman, nose.

## Glasgow City Police

## MURDER

About 7 p.m. on Monday, 21st December current, an old lady named Marion Gilchrist was brutally murdered in a house at 15 Queen's Terrace, West Princes Street, where she lived, the only other occupant being a servant woman, who, about the hour mentioned, left the house to purchase an evening paper, and on her return in less than fifteen minutes afterwards found that her mistress had been brutally murdered in the room in which she had left her.

On her return with the paper the servant met the man first described leaving the house, and about the same time another man, second described, was seen descending the steps leading to the house, and running away.

### Descriptions.

(First) A man from twenty-five to thirty years of age, 5 feet 7 or 8 inches in height, thought to be clean shaven; wore a long grey overcoat and dark cap.

(Second) A man from twenty-eight to thirty years of age, tall and thin, clean shaven, nose slightly turned to one side (thought to be the right side); wore a fawn-coloured overcoat (believed to be a waterproof), dark trousers, tweed cloth hat of the latest make, and believed to be dark in colour, and brown boots. . . .

That day, Superintendent Ord placed a description of the two wanted men in the evening papers, and Glasgow soon blazed with rumor. "News of the dastardly outrage, so daringly executed in the heart of the city, thrilled the people of Glasgow and Scotland generally," the Scottish journalist William Park would later write. "The hue and cry for the murderer and his theft of a diamond brooch spread so widely as eventually to embrace the greater part of the civilized world."

On the evening of December 25, 1908, a Glasgow bicycle dealer named Allan McLean called at police headquarters. He told the police that a man he knew—a foreigner and a Jew—had been trying to sell a pawn ticket for a diamond crescent brooch. The man's name, he said, was Oscar.

## Chapter 2

# THE MYSTERIOUS MR. ANDERSON

McLEAN HAD NEVER BEEN TO OSCAR'S HOME, BUT he knew where he lived. On the evening of December 25, he led a Glasgow police detective, William Powell, to the building, 69 St. George's Road, a few blocks south of West Princes Street. Questioning residents, Powell learned that the man in the top-floor flat, who answered to the name Anderson and was said to work as a dentist, fit the description McLean had supplied. Powell reported his findings to Superintendent Ord, and at eleven-thirty that night he was dispatched to the building again, accompanied by two colleagues, with orders to arrest Anderson if the need arose.

The detectives climbed to the top-floor flat and rang the bell. The door was opened by a German maid, Catherine Schmalz. Her master was not home, Schmalz told them: he and "Madame" were on holiday in Monte Carlo. No, she said, no one named Oscar lived there.

The detectives searched the flat. They were looking for a pawn ticket, but what they found instead was just as damning. In a bedroom, they spied a piece of wrapping paper from a newly opened parcel: "Anderson" had mailed his watch to London for repairs, and the watchmaker had fixed it and sent it back. The wrapper read, "Oscar Slater, Esq., c/o A. Anderson, Esq., 69, St. George's Road."

The wrapper has been preserved in the collection of the National Records of Scotland, in Edinburgh. It weighs barely an ounce: I have held it in my hand. But on the strength of that ounce of crumpled paper, addressed in elegant turn-of-the-century copperplate, Oscar Slater would be pursued, tried, convicted, and very nearly hanged.

FOR THE FIRST TIME since Miss Gilchrist's murder, the police had the full name of the man who had pawned a diamond brooch. It was clear to them that Slater and Anderson were one and the same, a surmise that proved correct. From neighbors, they learned that Anderson and a woman had left shortly after eight that night, bound for the railway station. This seeming flight only heightened the appearance of guilt, and from headquarters, Ord issued instructions to watch all southbound trains. Thus the pursuit of Miss Gilchrist's killer, until now a diffuse affair, began to home in on Slater.

Next, the police sought the shop where Slater had pawned the brooch. They made inquiries in the local gambling clubs he was known to frequent—"marginal clubs, peopled by marginal characters," Peter Hunt has called them. From a friend of Slater's, a bookmaker's clerk named Hugh Cameron, they learned that he had left a diamond brooch at Liddell's, a pawnshop on Sauchiehall Street in central Glasgow. Cameron also asserted, the police said afterward, that Slater was not a dentist but rather an occasional dealer in jewelry and, even more damning, a pimp.

On the morning of December 26, Glasgow detectives

brought Helen Lambie to Liddell's to identify the brooch. It was the wrong one, she said immediately: Miss Gilchrist's brooch was set with a single row of diamonds, whereas Slater's had three. The pawnbroker said that Slater had left the brooch there on November 18, more than a month before the murder. It had been in the shop without interruption ever since.

As far as Slater's continued candidacy as a suspect went, this development should have been a "fiasco," as Conan Doyle pointed out. "Already the very bottom of the case had dropped out," he wrote. "The starting link of what had seemed an imposing chain, had suddenly broken.... The original suspicion of Slater was founded upon the fact that he had pawned a crescent diamond brooch.... It was not the one which was missing from the room of the murdered woman, and it had belonged for years to Slater, who had repeatedly pawned it before. This was shown beyond all cavil or dispute. The case of the police might well seem desperate after this, since if Slater were indeed guilty, *it would mean that by pure chance they had pursued the right man*."

But pursue him they did, for the police were anxious to produce a suspect, and in Slater—gambler, foreigner, Jew, and possible procurer—they had found a sublime one. "The trouble ... with all police prosecutions," Conan Doyle remarked with a caustic lucidity worthy of Holmes, "is that, having once got what they imagine to be their man, they are not very open to any line of investigation which might lead to other conclusions." That was precisely what transpired the moment the Glasgow police trained their sights on Slater.

ONE OF FOUR CHILDREN of Adolf Leschziner, a baker, and his wife, Pauline (also called Paula), Oscar Slater was born Oskar Josef Leschziner on January 8, 1872, in Oppeln, a town in Silesia, then part of the German Empire. He had a brother, Georg, and two sisters: Amalie, known as Malchen, and Euphemia, known as Phemie. The family favorite, Oskar was reared in Beuthen, a threadbare mining town in the region, near the Polish border. "I was educated very inadequately at the village school and never acquired any great proficiency as a scholar," a 1924 article in the British press quotes Slater as saying. "I liked to play truant."

For a footloose, high-spirited young man, Beuthen held few prospects. As a youth Oskar lighted out for Berlin, where he worked for a timber merchant, and later for Hamburg, where he was a bank clerk. But the celluloid-collared life was not for him. At eighteen, possibly to avoid conscription by the German army, he left the country, roaming over the European continent, Britain, and the United States. Keenly intelligent if not book-smart, he lived by his wits, earning income from card playing, billiards, and racetrack betting, along with modest dealing in secondhand jewelry.

Slater's family was poor. His parents were reported to live in "two or three well-kept rooms" in a "decayed tenement house" in Beuthen. Adolf, an invalid with spine disease, could no longer work by the time Oskar was a young man. Pauline was partly blind. Throughout his wanderings, Slater regularly sent them money. "I could not wish a better son for any parents," his mother told a reporter for the *Glasgow Herald* who had sought her out in Beuthen after Slater's arrest. "Eighteen months ago I had to undergo an operation for cataract in my eye. It cost twenty pounds and Oscar sent me ten pounds to help towards it. He was my son, my best son."

Slater first visited England in about 1895. There, to accommodate locals who struggled with "Leschziner" and its unwieldy clump of consonants, he began calling himself Oscar Slater.

Arriving in Glasgow for the first time about six years later, he became immersed in what one modern British writer has called an "underworld, peopled by strange denizens with Runyonesque monikers—the Moudie, the Soldier, the Acrobat, Willy the Artist, Little Wrestler, the Diamond Merchant. . . . A tricksy world of street-betting, whores and whoring, reset* or the harbouring of 'iffy' goods, playing the horses and the cards, and tickling the ivories or billiard-balls for money." In about 1904, Slater, separated from his Scottish wife, met the nineteen-year-old Antoine in London; she accompanied him on his subsequent travels.

Though Slater could be hotheaded and volatile, he was by all accounts not violent. His Scottish prison record notes two prior arrests, both for minor offenses. The first, in London in 1896, was for malicious wounding in what was apparently a pub brawl. (He was acquitted.) The second, in Edinburgh in 1899, was for disorderly conduct. (He received a sentence of 20 shillings or seven days in jail; knowing Slater, it is quite safe to assume that he paid the fine.)

Indeed, the "marginal world" in which Slater moved—a world that so horrified the straitlaced classes—was not one of violent felons but rather, as Hunt wrote, one of "men who, without being criminals, did not assess the moralities of a transaction, accepted jewellery as currency, were not above an ace up the sleeve, were accustomed to false names and designations." It was murky, perhaps, but by no means murderous, and a world in which many Jewish immigrants, lacking the education, acceptance, or capital needed to enter professional life, found themselves on coming to Britain.

* A Scottish legal term denoting the receipt or resale of stolen goods, or the illegal harboring of a criminal.

That Antoine was a prostitute seems likely; that Slater was a pimp is far less certain, though he was repeatedly tarred as such at his murder trial. But Slater's dubious livelihood—whatever it might have been—together with his foreignness, his Jewishness, and his dapper defiance of the class to which his birth should have consigned him, were more than enough to damn him, first in the public eye and later in court. For if Oscar Slater had succeeded at little else in life, he had managed to become a sterling embodiment of everything that post-Victorian Britain had been taught to fear.

IT WAS NO EASY THING to be a Jew in early twentieth-century Britain. What was more, Slater had arrived in Glasgow at a time of especially intense paranoia—and correspondingly intense anti-Semitism. Just three years before, the British Parliament had passed the Aliens Act of 1905: the first significant restriction of its kind in the country's peacetime history, it severely curtailed immigration from outside the British Empire. Though it did not say so overtly, the act was widely understood to have been aimed at Eastern European Jews, who in the late nineteenth century, fleeing pogroms and penury, had begun arriving in Britain in large numbers. Attitudes toward these new arrivals would vary over time and across the nation. But in the late nineteenth and early twentieth centuries, anti-Jewish bigotry permeated nearly every aspect of British life.

In England, Jews met with a long, deeply entrenched anti-Semitic tradition. During the Middle Ages, the belief that Jews engaged in usury and blood libel—the abduction and murder of Gentile children to use their blood in religious rituals—had wide currency. In 1190, in the deadliest pogrom in English history, a mob rampaged through York, looting Jewish homes, burning them to the ground, and murdering their occupants, resulting in the deaths of more than 150 Jews. In 1290, under King Edward I, the Jews were expelled from England, "the first ejection of a major Jewish community in Europe," as one historian has described it. Only in the mid-seventeenth century, under Oliver Cromwell, were Jews allowed, quietly, to return.

In the Middle Ages and afterward, Jews, like members of other marginalized groups, were denied many of the legal protections that England afforded the archetypal citizen: the free white native-born law-abiding Christian adult male. "The lay Englishman, free but not noble, who . . . has forfeited none of his rights by crime or sin, is the law's typical man," a pair of early twentieth-century historians write, discussing the medieval period. They continue:

> But besides such men there are within the secular order noble men and unfree men; then there are monks and nuns; . . . then there is the clergy constituting a separate "estate"; there are Jews and there are aliens; there are excommunicates, outlaws and convicted felons who have lost some or all of their civil rights; also . . . infants and . . . women, . . . and a word should perhaps be said of lunatics, idiots and lepers.

By the eighteenth and nineteenth centuries, the situation of English Jews had improved, though only in part: much depended on the degree of assimilation and class status that individual Jews had been able to attain. In London, a small handful of Jews could be found serving in Parliament from the late 1700s onward. Until the passage of Britain's Jews Relief Act in 1858, however, they were required to take the same oath of office that other MPs did, including the words "and I make this Declaration upon the true Faith of a Christian." The act let them omit that phrase.

Early Jewish MPs included David Salomons, a lawyer and member of an established banking family, who in 1855 became the first Jewish Lord Mayor of London. Also among them was Benjamin Disraeli, who would serve as prime minister through much of Victoria's reign, to date the only person of Jewish birth to hold that office.

By late Victorian and Edwardian times, British anti-Semitism was again on the rise. One provocation was the volume of Jewish settlement: between the early 1880s and the start of World War I, some two and a half million Jews left the European continent, and about 150,000 of them settled in Britain. In 1914, London had a Jewish population of 115,000—about 2 percent of the city as a whole. (Glasgow's the same year was much smaller: about 7,000, or just under 1 percent.) A second provocation was the increasing presence of poorer, less assimilated Jews.

In the late 1880s, for instance, with London terrified by the Ripper murders, it was barely a matter of weeks before they were connected publicly with the Jewish menace. "Following the discovery of the third ripper victim in 1888," the criminologist Paul Knepper has written, "rumours circulated that the killer had to be a *shochet,* a kosher butcher; crowds gathered in several parts of the East End to abuse and harass Jews. Sir Robert Anderson, head of [Scotland Yard's] Criminal Investigation Department, enflamed anti-Jewish furore by repeating his belief that 'Jack' was a Jew of Polish background. 'One did not need to be a Sherlock Holmes to discover . . . ,' Anderson said, 'that he and his people were low-class Jews.'"

By this time, Parliament was already considering the question of restricting Jewish immigration, first taken up formally in 1887 and culminating in 1905 in the Aliens Act. "Crime had become part of the rationale for restriction," Knepper said, adding: "At issue was not whether immigration led to an increase in crime rates, and if so, why, but rather *the kinds of criminal behaviour embedded in particular racial characteristics*." He added:

> Anti-alien and antisemitic agitators circulated leaflets linking Jews with prostitution, gambling, and other crimes. A typical circular . . . asked: "Why do we want an aliens Bill?" The answer appeared in block letters: TO SUPPRESS ALIEN CRIME, TO STAMP OUT ALIEN VICE. . . . Joseph Banister, an incandescent anti-Semite who published a flurry of booklets and brochures on the immigration issue, characterised foreign Jews as "thieves, sweaters,* usurers, burglars, forgers, traitors, swindlers, blackmailers, and perjurers."

SCOTLAND, AT LEAST IN earlier times, was less susceptible to the reflexive anti-Semitism for which England was known. "Scottish Protestants put great emphasis on the Old Testament and for them the Jews were the biblical people of the old covenant," Ben Braber, a historian of Scottish Jewry, has written. "Protestants . . . identified themselves as the people of the new covenant and as such they were rather benevolent towards Jews."

As in the rest of Britain, the acceptance of Jews by Christian Glasgow was furthered largely by class. The first Jews settled there in the early nineteenth century; by the mid-1800s, as the city's new middle class cultivated a taste for luxury goods, its

* Exploitative, low-paying employers—i.e., sweatshop operators.

small Jewish community, then about four dozen strong, rose up to fill the need. That community included an optician, a quill merchant, a jeweler, a furrier, and an artificial flower maker.

But in the late nineteenth century and afterward, the influx of large numbers of Jews, many of them destitute, met with a mixed reception even in Scotland. "A small group of Jews in Glasgow could be tolerated and individual Jewish businessmen . . . be admired and accepted into polite society," Braber writes. "The same tolerance, admiration and acceptance would not automatically be extended to the new immigrants."

The arrest and trial of Oscar Slater brought Scottish anti-Jewish feeling to the fore. The case centered on two foundation stones of anti-Semitic belief: blood and money. It also touched on an issue that for British bourgeoisie was a raw nerve: the supposed involvement of many new Jewish immigrants in criminal pursuits, particularly the scandalous vices of prostitution and pimping.

The knowledge that a Jew was sought underpinned the investigation from the start. Allan McLean, the bicycle dealer who put police on to Slater, made this clear. So did a Glasgow landlady named Ada Louise Pryne, who in January 1909 told police that the suspect's description resembled a former tenant, whose face, she declared, "was of a Jewish type."

Even Glasgow's Jewish community held Slater at arm's length. In the spring of 1909, after Slater had been sentenced to death, one of his few early champions, Rev. Eleazar P. Phillips, minister of Glasgow's Garnethill Hebrew synagogue, helped organize a campaign to commute the sentence.* Anxious not to

* Though he was an observant Jew, Phillips was called "Reverend" and held the title "minister." Those designations, applied to spiritual leaders who were not ordained rabbis, were in common use among British Jews in the late nineteenth century and afterward.

have their hard-won respectability tarred by association with a new immigrant of dubious livelihood, officers of the synagogue reprimanded him. If Phillips was to work on Slater's behalf, they told him, he must do so on his own.

BY THE LATE NINETEENTH CENTURY, urban anxieties had given rise to social institutions, and social practices, designed to protect the public from "undesirables." Foremost among these were the police departments that had sprung up in cities throughout Europe. The City of Glasgow police force, one of the first in Britain to be established by an act of Parliament, was inaugurated in 1800. At midcentury, an associated field of scholarship arose, known as criminology, which likewise sought to safeguard people and property. Its best-known practitioners—a cadre of anthropologically minded pseudoscientists—bestrode Europe in the 1860s and afterward, calipers in hand, attempting to codify the physical hallmarks of the criminal class. Their work, they asserted, would let members of the Victorian bourgeoisie spot criminals, and other marginal characters, at a safe distance.

The most famous of these pseudoscientists was Cesare Lombroso. An Italian doctor and criminologist, he devised an early-warning system (known as "criminal anthropology" or "scientific criminology") that sought to cloak racial, ethnic, and class bigotries in Victorian scientific garb. Criminals, he argued, were born, not made: they were compelled to commit crimes because they carried within them the legacy of primordial human ancestors. As a result, the criminal class could be spotted by atavistic features associated with primitive man: heavy brow ridges, small or oddly shaped skulls, asymmetrical faces, and the like. Lombroso's index of criminal physiognomy, long since discredited, now seems a flesh-and-blood forerunner of the aircraft silhouettes that civilians were urged to memorize in wartime. Both served the same function: to identify an alien invader before he got too close.*

Even Conan Doyle, humanist though he was, subscribed to scientific criminology, at least in part. Touring the United States in 1914, he visited Sing Sing, the venerable state penitentiary north of New York City. There, as he recalled in his 1924 autobiography, *Memories and Adventures,* he watched a group of prisoners being entertained by a visiting musical-hall troupe. "Poor devils, all the forced, vulgar gaiety of the songs and the antics of half-clad women must have provoked a terrible reaction in their minds," Conan Doyle wrote. "Many of them had, I observed, abnormalities of cranium or of features which made it clear that they were not wholly responsible for their actions. . . . Here and there I noticed an intelligent and even a good face. One wondered how they got there."

As Lombroso well knew, in turbulent times it is a comfort to put a face on nebulous fear. That face, it went without saying,

* Such taxonomies persisted well into the twentieth century. After the Japanese attack on Pearl Harbor on December 7, 1941, flyers purporting to instruct citizens in the art of telling Chinese Americans from Japanese Americans were ubiquitous in the United States. On December 22, *Life* magazine published an article headlined "How to Tell Japs from the Chinese." It began: "In the first discharge of emotions touched off by the Japanese assaults on their nation, U.S. citizens have been demonstrating a distressing ignorance on the delicate question of how to tell a Chinese from a Jap. Innocent victims in cities all over the county are many of the 75,000 U.S. Chinese, whose homeland is our staunch ally. . . . To dispel some of this confusion, *Life* here adduces a rule-of-thumb from the anthropometric conformations that distinguish friendly Chinese from enemy alien Japs." These were, the article went on to illustrate, (for the Chinese) "parchment yellow complexion," "higher bridge [of the nose]," "never has rosy checks," "lighter facial bones," "scant beard," "longer, narrower face" and (for the Japanese) "earthy yellow complexion," "flatter nose," "sometimes rosy cheeks," "massive cheek and jawbone," "heavy beard," "broader, shorter face." The article's strong implication was that while readers should refrain from beating up Chinese Americans, they need have no such scruples around Americans of Japanese descent.

must be sufficiently different from one's own—a face ideally belonging to a bogeyman specially constructed for that purpose. Once identified, he could be routed from the community, taking its worst fears with him. The historian Peter Gay calls this scapegoat the "convenient Other." In Glasgow in the winter of 1908–9, the face of that Other was coming increasingly to resemble Oscar Slater's.

ON DECEMBER 26, 1908, Superintendent Ord issued the first notice in which Slater's name appears. Based on descriptions by McLean and Cameron, and with a nod to the "Donegal cap" of which Mary Barrowman had spoken, it read:

> Wanted for identification for the murder at Queen's Terrace on 21st instant, "Oscar Slater," sometimes takes the name of Anderson, a German, 30 years of age, 5 feet 8, stout, square-shouldered, dark hair, clean shaven, may have few days' growth of moustache. Nose has been broken and is marked. Dressed when last seen in dark jacket suit, cap with flaps fastening with button at top; sometimes wears a soft "Donegal" hat; has a light and a dark-coloured overcoat, either of which he may be wearing.
>
> May be accompanied by a woman about 30, tall, stout, good-looking, dark hair, dressed usually in dark or blue costume, heavy set of furs, sable colour, and large blue or black hat with green feathers, residing till yesterday at 69 St. George's Road.

By this time Slater, who had gone not to Monte Carlo but on his long-planned trip to America, was far out to sea, blithely unaware of the dragnet that was starting to encircle him.

## Chapter 3

# THE KNIGHT-ERRANT

VICTORIAN FEARS WERE ON ABUNDANT DISPLAY IN THE detective novel, a genre that had its first great flowering in the late nineteenth century. Earlier crime fiction had concerned itself approvingly with the exploits of dashing brigands: heroes, heavily romanticized, were modeled on populist historical figures like Dick Turpin, the eighteenth-century highwayman who energetically robbed, plundered, and murdered his way across England. Villains were typically noblemen who had denied the masses their economic due or malevolent law officers seeking to snare the hero.

But by the Victorian era, with its metropolitan terrors, new middle class, and zeal for safeguarding possessions, the concerns of crime fiction had shifted markedly. Now property trumped populism in the foremost crime stories of the day, and the heroic rogue was replaced by the upright detective. This new fictional detective had a twofold role. His first task was to reassure. Lombroso had tried to convince upright citizens that criminals could be diagnosed at a glance and thus avoided. The detective novel, with somewhat more finesse, attempted to do the same: it sought to persuade the public that, as one scholar has described it, "the individual's traces were readable and could not be concealed in the crowd."

The detective's second function was scientific—even medical: to act, where prevention was impossible, as an agent of cure. If the Victorian age was about little else, it was about the coming of modern science: the world-shaking evolutionary theory of Darwin; signal advances in physics, chemistry, biology, and geology; the increased understanding of the structure and function of living cells and of the germ theory of disease; and, hand in hand with those discoveries, the professionalization of modern medicine.

These developments informed the era's preoccupation with crime and criminals. Crime was increasingly seen as a form of contagion—a kind of "social pathology"—and the new scientific method as a tool with which to track it down and wipe it out. By late Victorian times, criminals (especially foreign ones) were viewed as invading the populace in much the same way that germs invade the body. In the literature of the period, metaphors of invasion are everywhere: consider the blood-sucking antihero of Bram Stoker's *Dracula,* published in 1897, or the insidious Jewish hypnotist Svengali in George du Maurier's 1894 novel, *Trilby,* who co-opts the soul of his lovely young protégée.

The Holmes stories, too, bear witness to these fears, for their author, like many progressives of his era, was not immune to prevailing ideas about criminal physiognomy, about the glories of empire, and even—as some Holmes stories betray—about foreigners. (For his simultaneous embrace of ecumenical humanism and ardent fealty to Crown and country, the scholar Laura Otis has aptly described Conan Doyle as a "Liberal Imperialist.") While many of Conan Doyle's villains are Englishmen gone bad, the canon also contains its share of nefarious outsiders, like the vengeful American Jefferson Hope in *A Study in Scarlet,* or Tonga, the murderous Andaman islander from *The Sign of Four.* Conan Doyle, Otis writes, "depicts British society as permeated by foreign criminals, 'passing' as respectable citizens. . . . Sherlock Holmes, his hero, acts as an immune system . . . to identify them and render them innocuous."

The Slater case embodied the most potent concerns of its time. It is every inch about paranoia—highly personal on Miss Gilchrist's part, more general on the public's. It sprang from an act of invasion of the most terrifying kind: intrusion into a heavily fortified home. It involved a shadowy outsider who was not only a foreigner but also a Jew, a people long taxed, as Nazi ideology would soon trumpet, as being agents of the transmission of disease. Above all, it would require the use of sharp scientific reason to combat the willful unreason of police and prosecutors. How fitting, then, that Slater's greatest champion was both a medical doctor and the father of the literary figure who remains the supreme incarnation of the Victorian detective.

THE FIRST CITIZEN OF Baker Street, as Sherlock Holmes would be known, sprang fully and impeccably to life in Conan Doyle's novella *A Study in Scarlet.* First published in *Beeton's Christmas Annual* in 1887, it was reprinted in book form the next year. Though Conan Doyle would continue publishing Holmes stories until 1927, even the late works embody the Victorian sensibility to their core.

Holmes quickly became a global sensation, not only for his investigative prowess, unimpeachable morals, and ultra-rational mind but also for his embodiment of an age of Victorian gentility, and Victorian certainties, that was already slipping away.

JONATHAN CORUM

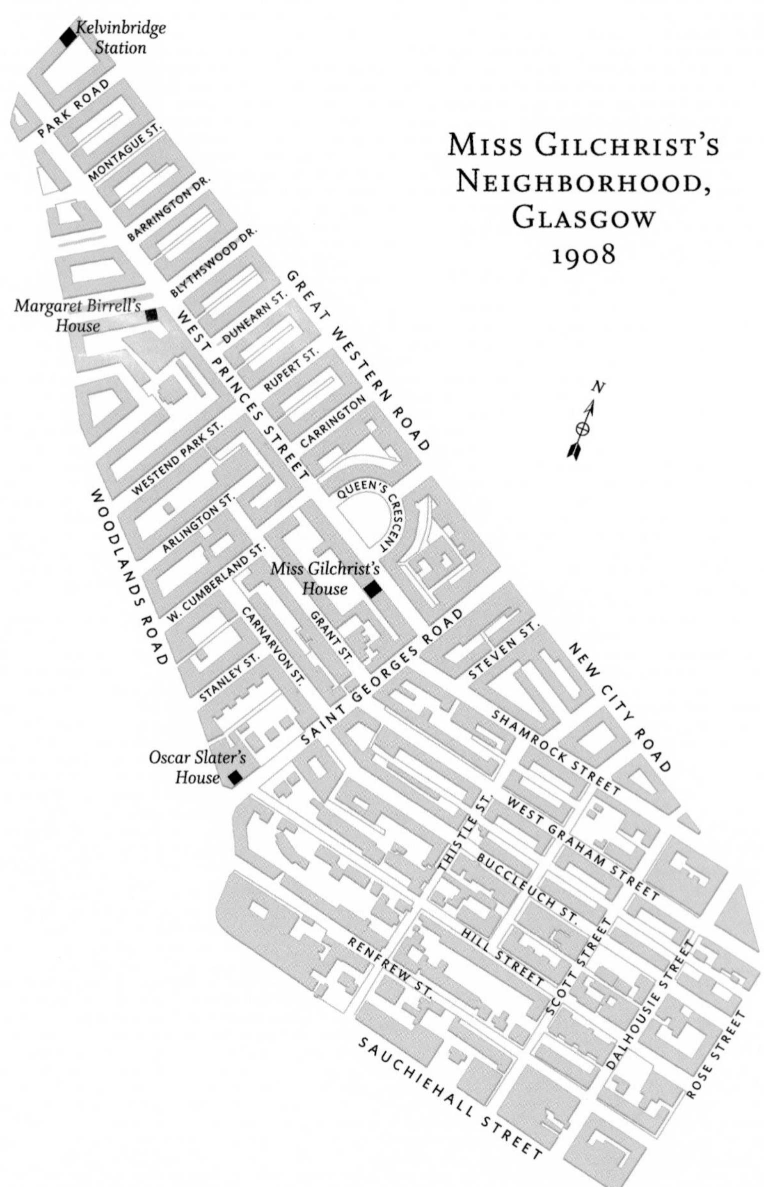


JONATHAN CORUM

# Miss Gilchrist's House

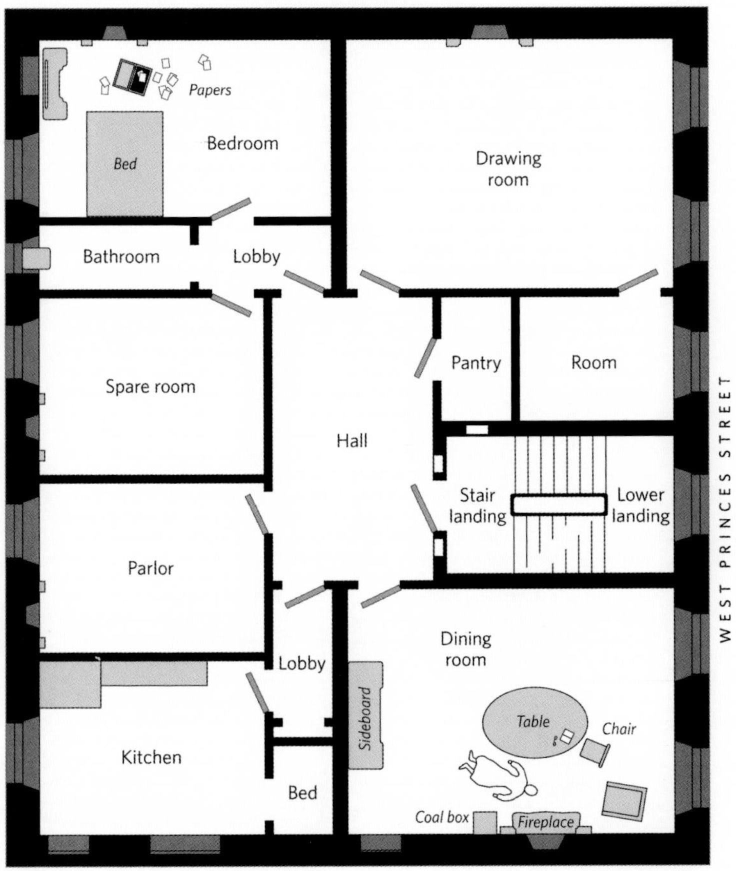


JONATHAN CORUM

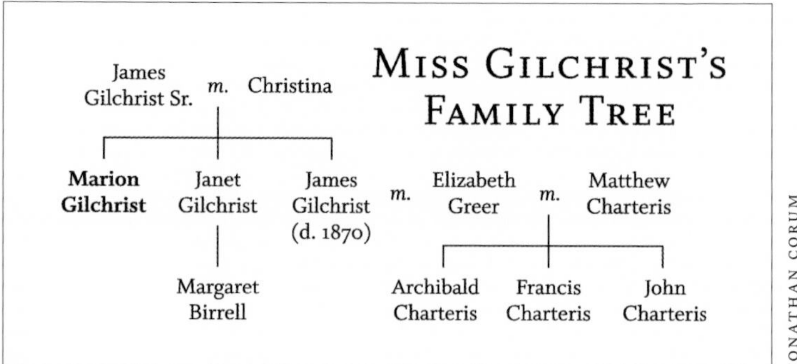


JONATHAN CORUM

Marion Gilchrist, in younger days and in old age

LEFT: PETERHEAD PRISON MUSEUM
RIGHT: WILLIAM ROUGHEAD, *TRIAL OF OSCAR SLATER* (1910)

TOP: West Princes Street. Miss Gilchrist's door is at left, the Adamses' at right.

BOTTOM: The stairs to Miss Gilchrist's flat bore two mysterious footprints.

BOTH: NATIONAL RECORDS OF SCOTLAND, HH15/20/1/6

TOP: Miss Gilchrist's entrance hall. Note the three locks on her front door.

BOTTOM: The dining room, the scene of Miss Gilchrist's murder

BOTH: NATIONAL RECORDS OF SCOTLAND, HH15/20/1/6

Jeweler's sketch of Miss Gilchrist's missing diamond brooch

NATIONAL RECORDS OF SCOTLAND, JC34/1/32/9

OSCAR SLATER,

*Dealer in Diamonds and Precious Stones.*

*33, Soho Square,*
*Oxford Street, W.*

Card printed with one of Slater's spurious business identities

NATIONAL RECORDS OF SCOTLAND, JC34/1/32/17

JC34/1/32/14/3

A. Anderson.

69 St. Georges Road,
Charing Cross,
Glasgow.

3 up right.

Another of Slater's cards, bearing one of his aliases

NATIONAL RECORDS OF SCOTLAND, JC34/1/32/14

Oscar Slater, Continental dandy, circa 1905

WILLIAM ROUGHEAD, *TRIAL OF OSCAR SLATER* (1910)

From the beginning, the tales conjured a comforting world of gaslight and empire, where problems could still be remedied through the combined palliatives of reason and honor.

"Marshall McLuhan . . . once observed that serious cultural change always comes masked in the familiar trappings of the preceding cultural norm," the critic Frank D. McConnell has written. "In this context, we can see that Doyle's invention of Holmes and Watson is a crucial survival myth for the modern era, the technologized and urban age. If Doyle had not invented Holmes, someone else would have had to."

The sea change to which Holmes bore witness was manifest in the scientific revolution then sweeping the West, of which Conan Doyle was an ardent adherent. Just as Thomas Henry Huxley (the distinguished nineteenth-century English biologist, Darwin acolyte, and grandfather of Aldous) had used his popular writings and lectures to bring the new scientific advances to the masses, Conan Doyle used Holmes to showcase their application to the investigation of crime. Holmes's rationalist approach differed from that of most earlier literary detectives, something his creator set out to ensure from the first.

"It often annoyed me how in the old-fashioned detective stories, the detective always seemed to get at his results by some sort of lucky chance or fluke or else it was unexplained how he got there," Conan Doyle said in a 1927 interview. "I began to think about . . . turning scientific methods . . . onto the work of detection."

Holmes resonated so deeply with the late Victorian public that people could scarcely countenance him as fictional. Readers requested his autograph and sent him pipe tobacco and violin strings. Women wrote to Conan Doyle, applying to be Holmes's housekeeper. An American tobacconist requested a copy of his putative monograph classifying 140 different varieties of ash. "Occasionally," a biographer has written, "when a certain 'pawky strain of humor' came over him, Conan Doyle would send a brief postcard in reply, expressing regret that the detective was not available. The signature, however, was calculated to raise eyebrows. It was: 'Dr. John Watson.' "

In 1893, Conan Doyle (who soon wearied of his hero and would rather have been known for the ponderous historical novels he also wrote) killed Holmes off in "The Final Problem." But so great was the public clamor for Holmes—and so correspondingly lucrative the prospect of renewed publication—that Conan Doyle found he could not leave him dead. He first revived his hero in flashback in the novel *The Hound of the Baskervilles,* serialized in 1901–2 but set in the years before Holmes's demise. In 1903, he brought Holmes fully back to life in "The Adventure of the Empty House," an act of resuscitation that prefigured his real-life rehabilitations of George Edalji and Oscar Slater. All three cases confirmed an essential truth that Conan Doyle had noted in childhood, after devouring boys' adventure stories: "It was easy to get people into scrapes," he observed, "but not so easy to get them out again."

IF OSCAR SLATER WAS the incarnation of late Victorian fears, then Arthur Conan Doyle embodied most of the era's sterling qualities: valor, thirst for adventure, love of manly competition in the boxing ring and on the cricket pitch, a passion for scientific knowledge, and a deep sense of fair play. To the systemic prejudices of Victorian Britain—his own included—he brought the unshakable counterweight of populist progressivism, for, like Slater, he had grown up poor, marginalized for his religion, and very much not an Englishman.

Arthur Ignatius Conan Doyle was born in Edinburgh on

May 22, 1859, the second child, and eldest son, of the seven surviving children of Charles Altamont Doyle and the former Mary Josephine Foley.* Theirs was an impoverished branch of an illustrious family: Arthur's paternal grandfather, John Doyle, an artist who drew under the name H.B., was a political caricaturist of renown in early nineteenth-century London; among his luminous acquaintances were William Makepeace Thackeray, Charles Dickens, and Benjamin Disraeli. Arthur's paternal uncles included James Doyle, author and illustrator of *The Chronicle of England;* Henry Doyle, manager of the National Gallery in Dublin; and Richard Doyle, an illustrator for *Punch.*

Arthur's father, a painter and illustrator, appeared to have been as gifted as his brothers. But he suffered from epilepsy, alcoholism, and, by the time Arthur was a youth, severe mental illness. When he was able to work, he earned a meager wage as a clerk in an Edinburgh municipal office. "We lived," Conan Doyle later wrote, "in the hardy and bracing atmosphere of poverty."

"Charles possessed the Doyle family charm in full measure, yet was frequently described as 'dreamy and remote,' 'apathetic,' 'naturally philosophic' or 'unworldly,'" the biographer Russell Miller has written. "When he was only 30 years old he suffered such a severe attack of delirium tremens that he was incapacitated and put on half pay for almost a year. Mary would later tell doctors that for months at a time her husband could only crawl, 'was perfectly idiotic [and] could not tell his own name.' . . . He became increasingly unstable, once stripping off his clothes and trying to sell them in the street." In 1881, Charles was committed to the first of the series of Scottish

* To honor a childless great-uncle, Michael Conan, Arthur and his elder sister, Annette, bore the dual surname Conan Doyle.

institutions that would be his home to the end of his life. He died in 1893, at sixty-one, at the Crichton Royal Lunatic Asylum in Dumfries.

Holding the family together in these years was Mary Doyle, the well-read daughter of an Irish doctor, who had married Charles in 1855, at seventeen. She was descended on her mother's side, or so she had been told, from English nobility. "Diminutive Mary Doyle . . . fiercely proud of her heritage, drummed into her son her fervent belief that they had aristocratic ancestors and schooled him in the traditions and lore of a bygone age, of chivalry and heraldry and knights in shining armour," Miller wrote, adding:

> She would frequently challenge him to emblazon heraldic shields and he could soon provide every detail. It was a welcome escape from the spartan conditions, anxiety and genteel poverty in which they lived. . . . Arthur never forgot sitting on the kitchen table while his mother busied herself cleaning the hearth and expounding on the past glories of her family and its connections with the Plantagenets, the Dukes of Brittany and the Percys of Northumberland: "I would sit swinging my knickerbockered legs, swelling with pride until my waistcoat was as tight as a sausage skin, as I contemplated the gulf which separated me from all other little boys who swang their legs upon tables."*

Arthur grew up curious, sturdy, literary—he began writing little stories as a child—and, when need be, bellicose. "I will say

* The interpolated quotation is from Conan Doyle's 1895 autobiographical novel, *The Stark Munro Letters,* about a young doctor.

for myself, however," he wrote, "that though I was pugnacious I was never so to those weaker than myself and that some of my escapades were in the defence of such." It was a trait that would define him to the end of his life.

The Doyles were Roman Catholics; as a youth Arthur, helped by well-to-do members of his extended family, was educated at Stonyhurst, a centuries-old Jesuit boarding school in Lancashire. He would remember it for its austerity, discipline, and frequent corporal punishment. "I can speak with feeling as I think few, if any boys of my time endured more of it," he later wrote. "I went out of my way to do really mischievous and outrageous things simply to show that my spirit was unbroken. . . . One master, when I told him that I thought of being a civil engineer, remarked, 'Well, Doyle, you may be an engineer, but I don't think you will ever be a civil one.' "

After leaving Stonyhurst in 1875, he studied for a year at a Jesuit school in Austria before returning to Edinburgh to start his university education. "I was wild, full-blooded, and a trifle reckless, but the situation called for energy and application, so that one was bound to try to meet it," he wrote. "My mother had been so splendid that we could not fail her. It had been determined that I should be a doctor, chiefly, I think, because Edinburgh was so famous a centre for medical learning."

Medical education in Scotland was then part of the undergraduate curriculum, and in 1876, at seventeen, Conan Doyle entered the University of Edinburgh to work toward a bachelor of medicine. He had already begun to part company with his religious beliefs, and the breach was widened by the scientific ideas to which he was exposed at university.

"Judging . . . by all the new knowledge which came to me both from my reading and from my studies, I found that the foundations not only of Roman Catholicism but of the whole

Christian faith, as presented to me in nineteenth century theology, were so weak that my mind could not build upon them," he wrote. "It is to be remembered that these were the years when Huxley, Tyndall, Darwin, Herbert Spencer and John Stuart Mill were our chief philosophers, and that even the man in the street felt the strong sweeping current of their thought, while to the young student, eager and impressionable, it was overwhelming." This loss of faith meant a corresponding loss of support from the well-heeled, observant branches of his family, both in his student days and afterward, when he was struggling to establish a medical practice. But he held firm to his newfound convictions.

At the university, Conan Doyle came under the sway of an eminent professor, Dr. Joseph Bell. "Bell was a very remarkable man in body and mind," he recalled. "He was thin, wiry, dark, with a high-nosed acute face, penetrating grey eyes, angular shoulders, and a jerky way of walking. . . . His strong point was diagnosis, not only of disease, but of occupation and character. . . . To his audience of Watsons it all seemed very miraculous until it was explained, and then it became simple enough. It is no wonder that after the study of such a character I used and amplified his methods when in later life I tried to build up a scientific detective who solved cases on his own merits and not through the folly of the criminal."

By the time Conan Doyle was twenty, he later wrote, "my father's health had utterly broken"—in his memoir, he refers to his father's decline with gentle diplomacy, never specifying the precise nature of his illness—"and I . . . found myself practically the head of a large and struggling family." To earn money, he began writing short stories. His first, "The Mystery of Sasassa Valley" (a non-Holmes tale set in Africa and regarded by modern critics as a pastiche of Poe and Bret Harte), was published in 1879 in *Chambers's Journal,* an Edinburgh literary magazine. The next year, also to ease family finances, he interrupted his studies to sign on as the medical officer of the whaling ship *Hope*. The seven-month voyage would be the first of his many dashing adventures.

Joining the ship, with its crew of fifty, Conan Doyle embarked from the port of Peterhead, the Scottish town where Slater would one day be incarcerated, bound for the Arctic. "The life is dangerously fascinating," he later wrote with characteristic Victorian understatement, and he soon found that its dangers applied to the doctor as well as the crew. More than once he was thrown overboard by a sudden swell, landing amid blocks of floating ice before regaining the ship. On another occasion he joined a party of harpooners in their little boat as they set upon a whale. "Its instinct urges it to get its tail to work on the boats, and yours urges you to keep poling and boat-hooking along its side, so as to retain your safe position near its shoulder," he wrote. "Even there, however, we found . . . that we were not quite out of danger's way, for the creature in its flurry raised its huge side-flapper and poised it over the boat. One flap would have sent us to the bottom of the sea." He added, with equally characteristic sentiment: "Who would swap that moment for any other triumph that sport can give?"

In 1881, Conan Doyle graduated from Edinburgh as a bachelor of medicine and master of surgery. That autumn, he took a post as a ship's surgeon on the steamer *Mayumba,* bound from Liverpool for the west coast of Africa. His account of that voyage betrays the best of Victorian valor and the worst of Victorian imperialism. On one occasion, he helped subdue an out-of-control fire aboard the ship, laden with a cargo of palm oil. On another, in Lagos, he fell seriously ill. "The germ or the mosquito or whatever it was reached me and I was down with a very sharp fever," he wrote. "As I was myself doctor there was no one to look after me and I lay for several days fighting it out with Death in a very small ring and without a second.... It must have been a close call, and I had scarcely sat up before I heard that another victim who got it at the same time was dead."

In his appraisal of the ship's African passengers, Conan Doyle does himself little credit. "There were . . . some unpleasant negro traders whose manners and bearing were objectionable, but who were patrons of the line and must, therefore, be tolerated. Some of these palm oil chiefs and traders have incomes of many thousands a year, but as they have no cultivated tastes they can only spend their money on drink, debauchery and senseless extravagance. One of them, I remember, had a choice selection of the demi-monde of Liverpool to see him off."

In 1882, Conan Doyle established a medical practice in Southsea, a suburb of Portsmouth in the south of England. Three years later, he married Louise Hawkins, familiarly known as Touie, the sister of one of his patients.* A daughter, Mary, was born in 1889; a son, Kingsley, in 1892. The marriage, which would last until Louise's death in 1906, was amicable, though it seemed based, as one scholar has noted, "more on affection and respect than on passion."

Conan Doyle was by all accounts a capable doctor, but he found solo practice a struggle. "I made £154 the first year, and £250 the second, rising slowly to £300, which in eight years I never passed," he later wrote. "In the first year the Income Tax paper arrived and I filled it up to show that I was not liable.

* Though her legal name was Louisa, she expressed the strong preference throughout her life for Louise.

They returned the paper with 'Most unsatisfactory' scrawled across it. I wrote 'I entirely agree' under the words, and returned it once more."

Between patients, he continued to write, selling the occasional story to magazines and completing a historical novel, *The Firm of Girdlestone,* which would not see publication until 1890. He began to dream of producing a set of stories that, unlike the popular serials of the day, would each be self-contained in a single issue yet leave readers clamoring for sequels.

"Poe's masterful detective, M. Dupin, had from boyhood been one of my heroes," Conan Doyle wrote. "But could I bring an addition of my own? I thought of my old teacher Joe Bell, of his eagle face, of his curious ways, of his eerie trick of spotting details. If he were a detective he would surely reduce this fascinating but unorganized business to something nearer to an exact science." For his hero, he considered various names—among them Sherrinford Holmes—before hitting on one whose steel-trap snap befit a detective whose acumen, logical rigor, and sense of honor would outstrip those of many real-life counterparts.*

For a time Conan Doyle plied his two trades in parallel: In 1891, after training briefly in Vienna as an ophthalmologist, he moved with his family to London, where he set up a practice. Before long, Holmes's success would let him relinquish medicine entirely, though his first vocation would stand in him good stead to the end. "Often, physicians who become serious writers abandon the clinic wholly or visit it only intermittently," Edmund D. Pellegrino, a doctor and bioethicist, has observed. *"But they retain the clinician's way of looking."*

* Conan Doyle's original name for the faithful Dr. John H. Watson was Ormond Sacker.

—

ONCE HOLMES MADE HIM FAMOUS, Conan Doyle had to spend a great deal of time denying that he was Holmesian himself. After a reviewer castigated him for letting Holmes disparage Poe's great detective, the chevalier Dupin, in *A Study in Scarlet*, he replied, charmingly: "Please grip this fact with your cérebral tentacle, / The doll and his maker are never identical." In fact, with his big bluff build, round face, and walrus mustache, Conan Doyle seemed far more the embodiment of Watson than of Holmes.

Yet the doll Holmes sprang from *somewhere*. Between his natural questing temperament and his supreme diagnostic training under Bell, Conan Doyle possessed a far more Holmesian cast of mind than he usually let on. "I have often been asked whether I had myself the qualities which I depicted, or whether I was merely the Watson that I look," he wrote. "Of course I am well aware that it is one thing to grapple with a practical problem and quite another thing when you are allowed to solve it under your own conditions. I have no delusions about that. At the same time a man cannot spin a character out of his own inner consciousness and make it really life-like unless he has some possibilities of that character within him."

He continued: "I . . . have several times solved problems by Holmes' methods after the police have been baffled. Yet I must admit that in ordinary life I am by no means observant and that I have to throw myself into an artificial frame of mind before I can weigh evidence and anticipate the sequence of events."

But according to Adrian Conan Doyle, a son from the author's second marriage, his father could perform feats of diagnostic logic with ease:

> In travelling through the capital cities of the world, it was one of my keenest enjoyments to accompany my father to any principal restaurant, and there to listen to his quiet speculations as to the characteristics, professions and other idiosyncrasies, all quite hidden from my eyes, of our fellow diners. Sometimes we could not prove the correctness . . . of his findings as the particular subject might be unknown to the head-waiter; but whenever those concerned were known to the maître d'hotel, the accuracy of my father's deduction was positively startling. As a footnote, here is a point that will intrigue Holmes enthusiasts. In the mind's eye, we surely visualize the Master complete with dust-red dressing-gown and curving pipe. But these were the accoutrements of Conan Doyle, and the originals are still in the family possession!

Conan Doyle's skill was evident not only in his powers of reasoning but also in his eagerness to amass the welter of empirical data—the *clues*—on which his rational mind could work. He had started down this empirical path in his university days. "I always regarded him as one of the best students I ever had," Bell said of him years later. "He was exceedingly interested always upon anything connected with diagnosis, and was never tired of trying to discover those little details which one looks for."

As a young doctor, Conan Doyle stood ready to challenge scientific opinion when he thought the facts did not bear it out. In November 1890, while practicing in Southsea, he traveled to Berlin to hear a lecture by the German doctor and microbiologist Robert Koch. Koch, who would receive the Nobel Prize in 1905, was already a titan, renowned for having isolated the bacilli that cause anthrax, cholera, and tuberculosis. By the late nineteenth century, he authentically believed that he had uncovered not only the cause of tuberculosis but also a cure, one of the most urgently sought grails in world health. This was the subject of his Berlin lecture.

Arriving the day before, Conan Doyle found the lecture so oversubscribed that he could not get a seat. "Undaunted," his biographer Russell Miller wrote, "he tried calling at Koch's home, but got no further than the front hall, where he watched a postman empty a sack of letters onto a desk. He realised, with a sense of shock, that they were mostly from desperately ill people who had heard about Koch's cure and believed he was their last hope. . . . Since Koch's findings remained to be verified it seemed to the sceptical Conan Doyle that 'a wave of madness had seized the world.'"

Returning to the lecture hall the next day, Conan Doyle befriended an American doctor who had gained admission, and who afterward shared his notes. Reviewing them—and spirited in by his American friend to tour Koch's clinical wards—Conan Doyle realized that the vaunted remedy was not all it appeared. "Observing the patients treated with Koch's tuberculosis 'cure,'" Laura Otis has written, "Doyle comprehended immediately that the treatment—which proved to be a tremendous disappointment—functioned not by killing the bacillus directly but by killing and expelling the damaged tissue in which the bacillus grew."

Conan Doyle outlined his conclusions in a letter in the *Daily Telegraph*. Koch's remedy, he wrote, "does not touch the real seat of the evil. To use a homely illustration, it is as if a man whose house was infested with rats were to remove the marks of the creatures every morning and expect in that way to get rid of them." His was a minority viewpoint, but over time it proved correct.

By the late 1890s, when Conan Doyle had forsaken medicine and Holmes was a vibrant worldwide presence, he was asked increasingly to turn his diagnostic skills to problems of another sort: real-life criminal mysteries. He would bring his "clinician's way of looking" to bear on each of them, including, in the most formidable case of his career, the conviction of Oscar Slater.

## Chapter 4

# THE MAN IN THE DONEGAL CAP

ON DECEMBER 21, 1908, THE DAY MISS GILCHRIST DIED, Oscar Slater received two letters from abroad. One was from a London friend, a man named Rogers, who wrote to warn Slater that his estranged wife, seeking money, was on his trail. Slater had already been planning to move to San Francisco at the behest of John Devoto, a friend from his American sojourn. Providentially, the second letter offered an answer to the problem described in the first. It was from Devoto himself, again urging Slater to come over and join him in business.

Slater promptly gave Schmalz, the maid, a week's notice. (To deflect inquiries on his wife's behalf, he instructed her to tell callers that he had gone to Monte Carlo.) It was during his last days in Glasgow that Slater, preparing for his move, did the two things that would put the police on his trail. First, he telegraphed Dent's in London to ask that his watch be repaired and returned at once. Second, to raise money for his passage, he began canvassing his cronies in Glasgow's gambling clubs, trying to sell the pawn ticket for his diamond crescent brooch. By 7:00 p.m. on December 21, he had returned to St. George's

Road and was, Antoine and Schmalz later testified, eating supper at home.

The next four days saw his continued preparations. At about 8:30 on Christmas night, he and Antoine left their flat, with hired porters carrying their ten pieces of luggage. At Glasgow's Central Station, they boarded the night train to Liverpool. Arriving at 3:40 a.m., they checked into the North-Western Hotel as Mr. and Mrs. Oscar Slater of Glasgow. At the hotel, Liverpool's chief detective would later confirm, "the chambermaid had a conversation with the woman, who told her that they were about to sail by the *Lusitania* for America."*

On December 26, Slater bought two second-class tickets aboard the *Lusitania,* leaving for New York that day. In an apparent effort to put his wife off the scent, he booked them in the name of Mr. and Mrs. Otto Sando. By now the Glasgow police, alerted by the Liverpool authorities, considered him a fugitive from justice, brooch clue or no brooch clue.

"The pawned brooch," Conan Doyle would write long afterward, "was one which belonged to Slater, and the police became aware of this fact . . . before Slater sailed for America." He added: "Slater, moreover, had been extremely open about his movements, he had made his preparations for going to America with the greatest deliberation, and carried them out in the same leisurely and open manner after the date when the crime was committed as he had done previously. . . . Such being the case, how is it that a cable was sent to New York to have him arrested on arrival?"

But just such a cable was sent by the Glasgow authorities:

* In May 1915, amid World War I, the RMS *Lusitania* would be torpedoed and sunk by a German U-boat, an event that generated worldwide headlines and sparked anti-German riots throughout Britain.

ARREST OTTO SANDO SECOND CABIN LUSITANIA WANTED IN CONNECTION WITH THE MURDER OF MARION GILCHRIST AT GLASGOW. HE HAS A TWISTED NOSE. SEARCH HIM AND THE WOMAN WHO IS HIS TRAVELLING COMPANION FOR PAWN-TICKETS.

On January 2, 1909, when the *Lusitania* steamed into the Port of New York, local police detectives boarded the ship and arrested Slater. That was the first, he said, that he heard the name Marion Gilchrist. Searching him, they found the pawn ticket for the diamond brooch: he had never been able to sell it. Antoine was dispatched to Ellis Island; Slater was confined in the Tombs, the gritty house of detention in lower Manhattan that still stands, to await extradition. From there, in February, he would write to his Glasgow friend Hugh Cameron—a shady underworld character known as "the Moudie."* Though Slater did not know it, it was Cameron who had pointed Glasgow detectives toward the pawnshop where he had left his diamond brooch.

"Dear Friend Cameron!" his letter begins:

*Today it is nearly five weeks I am kept here in prison for the Glasgow murder.*

*I am very downhearted my dear Cameron to know that my friends in Glasgow . . . can tell such liars about me to the Glasgow police. . . .*

*I hope my dear Cameron that you will still be my friend in my troubel and tell the truth and stand on my side. You know the best reason I have left Glasgow because I have*

* A Scottish dialect term meaning "the mole."

*shown to you the letter from St. Francisco from my friend, also I have left you my address from St. Francisco. . . .*

*The police is trying hard to make a frame-up for me. I must have a good trial, because I will prove with five people where I have been when the murder was committed.*

*Thanking you at present, and I hope to have a true friend on you, because every man is able to get put in such an affair and being innocent.*

*My best regards to you and all my friends—I am, your friend,*

*Oscar Slater,*
*Tombs, New York*

"It is a measure of Cameron's friendship," one modern British writer noted drily, "that he immediately showed this letter to the Police."

From this point on, the duplicity of the British authorities becomes truly naked. Between its social paranoia and its scientific advances, the Victorian era was preoccupied with identifying and vanquishing invaders of all sorts: microbes, criminals, foreigners. The Slater case, which sprang in large part from late Victorian ways of casting the convenient Other, would hinge crucially on questions of identification—identification that, as Glasgow officials would soon demonstrate, could be manufactured willy-nilly as the need arose.

On January 13, 1909, Detective Inspector Pyper and William Warnock, the chief criminal officer of the Glasgow sheriff court,* set sail for New York, accompanied by their three star

* "Sheriff" in this sense denotes a member of the Scottish judiciary who presides over a local court.

witnesses: Helen Lambie, Arthur Adams, and Mary Barrowman. They arrived on the twenty-fifth. At Slater's extradition proceedings, which began the next day, the British Crown would bring all needed mendacity to bear on its efforts to see him returned to Scotland.

THE HEARING FOR THE EXTRADITION of Oscar Slater, alias Otto Sando, opened in the Federal Building in lower Manhattan before John A. Shields, a United States commissioner for the Southern District of New York. Arguing for the Crown was an attorney named Charles Fox. Slater was represented by two American lawyers, Hugh Gordon Miller and William A. Goodhart. Because the Crown's case was slender, Slater's lawyers were confident he would prevail. As Goodhart wrote, "At the time of the arrest of Slater it was decided to resist extradition because . . . the pawn ticket constituted the Government's chief evidence and knowing that there was nothing to that, I advised a fight."

But the Crown was more than ready. Its strategy from this point forward would center not on the pawn ticket, which it knew to be worthless, but on witness identification of Slater as the man seen fleeing Miss Gilchrist's home. To hedge their bet, Glasgow officials showed Slater's photograph to Adams and Barrowman before the extradition proceedings started. They did not bother to show it to Lambie, who said she had not seen the suspect's face, though that story would soon change.

The first identification of Slater in New York took place before the extradition proceedings even began. As the hearing was about to start, Slater, flanked by two U.S. deputy marshals, was led down the hallway to Commissioner Shields's chambers. One marshal, John W. M. Pinckley, to whom he was visibly handcuffed, was six foot four. (Slater was about five foot eight.) The other wore a large badge marked "U.S.," adorned with red, white, and blue stars.

Standing in the hall as the three men passed were Mr. Fox, the Crown counsel; Inspector Pyper; and the three witnesses. As Marshal Pinckley would testify long afterward, when he passed the group with his prisoner, he saw Fox indicate Slater with his thumb and say to the witnesses something like "Is that the man?" or "That's the man."

Under questioning by Fox in chambers, Lambie offered suggestive testimony:

Q. Do you see the man here you saw that night?
A. One is very suspicious if anything.

Though she said she had not seen the intruder's face on the night of the murder, Lambie testified that she *had* noticed something peculiar about his walk—"he was sort of shaking himself a little"—a detail she had never mentioned before.

Q. Is that man in this room?
A. Yes he is, Sir.

After further questioning, she indicated Slater.

Another striking feature of Lambie's testimony was her account of what the intruder had worn. Just after the murder, her description of the man's clothing had differed markedly from Barrowman's—so much so that the police thought two men were involved. (Lambie had described the intruder as wearing a gray overcoat and round cloth hat; Barrowman spoke of a fawn-colored waterproof coat and a Donegal cap.) Now, at the extradition hearing, Lambie's description had dovetailed remarkably with Barrowman's: both young women testified that the man exiting Miss Gilchrist's flat had worn a fawn-colored waterproof and Donegal cap.

Next to testify was Barrowman, who reiterated her description of hat and coat. Asked whether Slater resembled the man she had seen in West Princes Street that night, she replied, "That man here is very like him," an assertion that would be considerably strengthened by the time the case came to trial. She repeated her claim that the man she had seen "had a slight twist in his nose." (Slater's nose, though somewhat convex, had no discernible twist.) She also admitted having been shown a photograph of Slater in Fox's office earlier that day.

Adams, to all appearances the only mature, reflective adult among the three witnesses, took the stand. He would say only that Slater was "not at all unlike" the man he had seen on Miss Gilchrist's landing. In glimpsing the intruder, he had noticed neither the peculiarity of walk described by Lambie nor the peculiarity of nose described by Barrowman.

The hearing continued for several days, with others testifying for the Crown and still others, including friends from his past American sojourn, for Slater. Slater himself, doubtless on the advice of counsel, who were concerned about his awkward, heavily accented English, did not testify on his own behalf. But his testimony may well have seemed unnecessary, for as the hearing unfolded, the Crown's case for extradition proved increasingly weak.

"I never doubted his innocence," Slater's lawyer William Goodhart wrote to Conan Doyle some years later. "It has always seemed to me, from my knowledge of the class of identification presented before our Commissioner at the extradition proceedings, that a grave doubt existed as to the identity of Slater as the man seen leaving the home of the victim on the night of the murder." Yet on February 6, 1909, as proceedings were about to reconvene for the day, Slater's lawyers announced that their client had chosen to waive the balance of the hearing. He would return to Scotland of his own volition and stand trial.

Slater's decision, amid proceedings that seemed almost certain to end in his favor, betrays several facets of his character. One is his mercurial temperament, a trait that would manifest itself repeatedly during his prison years and again after his release. Another was almost certainly a concern with finances: his modest reserves had already been exhausted in legal fees.

There appeared also to have been a third reason, one that more than any other attests to Slater's complex personality. Despite his decadent lifestyle, he was as concerned with reputation as any bourgeois of his era and wanted badly to clear his name. But beneath his foppish sophistication, Slater was in some ways breathtakingly naive. He knew full well he was innocent and so chose to put his faith in the Scottish justice system. A trial, he felt certain, would vindicate him once and for all.

# BOOK TWO

---

# BLOOD

# Chapter 5

## TRACES

IF YOU WANT TO SOLVE A CRIME, CALL A DOCTOR—BETTER still, a doctor who is a crime writer. Detection, at bottom, is a diagnostic enterprise: like many Victorian intellectual endeavors, medicine and crime-solving seek to reconstruct the past through the minute examination of clues. For if the nineteenth century was about the coming of modern science, it was also about the coming of science of a very particular type: reconstructive fields, like geology, archaeology, paleontology, and evolutionary biology, that let investigators assemble a record of past events through evidentiary traces, often barely discernible, that lingered in the present.

From a single bone, the French naturalist Georges Cuvier could induce the whole of an extinct animal. From ruins unearthed at Troy and at Knossos, the German archaeologist Heinrich Schliemann and the English archaeologist Arthur Evans conjured long-dead civilizations. "The foreteller asserts that, at some future time, a properly situated observer will witness certain events," Thomas Henry Huxley wrote in 1880; "the clairvoyant declares that, at this present time, certain things are to be witnessed a thousand miles away; the retrospective prophet (would that there were such a word as 'backteller!') affirms that so many hours or years ago, such and such things were to be seen. In all these cases, it is only the relation to time which alters—*the process of divination beyond the limits of possible direct knowledge* remains the same."

A goal of these new sciences was the creation of narrative—a narrative of things past, often long past, that could be assembled only through the close reading, painstaking analysis, and rigorous chronological ordering of what could be discerned in the present. Huxley evocatively called this process "retrospective prophecy."

"From a drop of water, a logician could infer the possibility of an Atlantic or a Niagara without having seen or heard of one or the other," one of the most famous nineteenth-century passages on retrospective prophecy runs. It continues:

> So all life is a great chain, the nature of which is known whenever we are shown a single link of it. Like all the other arts, the Science of Deduction and Analysis is one which can only be acquired by long and patient study. . . . Let the inquirer begin by mastering more elementary problems. Let him, on meeting a fellow-mortal, learn at a glance to distinguish the history of the man, and the trade or profession to which he belongs. Puerile as such an exercise may seem, it sharpens the faculties of observation, and teaches one where to look and what to look for. By a man's finger-nails, by his coat-sleeve, by his boots, by his trouser-knees, by the callosities of his forefinger and thumb, by his expression, by his shirt-cuffs—by each of these things a man's calling is plainly revealed.

The author of that passage, which is taken, we learn, from his celebrated essay "The Book of Life," is none other than Sherlock Holmes, as his very first adventure, *A Study in Scarlet*, reveals. For in creating Holmes, his fictional "scientific detective," Conan Doyle was evangelizing as vigorously for late Victorian rationalism as Huxley was doing in his essays and public lectures.*

Retrospective prophecy underpins both detection and doctoring, for in their modus operandi, the two have much in common. Both often start with a body. Both reason backward, from discernible *effect* (a clue, a symptom) to covert *cause* (a culprit, a disease). Both are deeply concerned with questions of identity, and both seek an elusive quarry: a criminal for the detective, a germ or other agent of illness for the doctor. Both bring about solutions through great learning, minute observation, and reasoned, carefully controlled leaps of imagination. Both are inherently moral enterprises, seeking to restore a state of order (safety, health) that has been disrupted. In the detective fiction of the late Victorian period, all these elements are exquisitely combined.

Ultimately, both disciplines seek to answer the most fundamental question there is: *What happened?* To do so, the investigator must gather evidence, but therein lies a basic challenge: neither detective nor doctor—nor any retrospective prophet—is apt to encounter the evidence in the chronological order in

* In preparing to write this book, I ordered a secondhand copy of Huxley's 1882 essay collection, *Science and Culture*. On arrival, the little volume, with its frayed binding and yellowed pages, fell open to a lovely, ghostly reminder of the reach of the author's scientific writings, which were aimed at the ordinary workingman. On the half title page, written in faded ink in impeccable nineteenth-century cursive, are the words "The Property of Fred P. Hopkins, Union Stock Yards, Chicago."

which it was laid down. It was not until the nineteenth century that medicine became fully cognizant of this problem, only then considering the patient's symptoms to be the last link in a narrative chain. With that conceptual shift, the diagnostic examination began to assume the form we recognize today.

"Throughout the 18th century, doctors based their diagnoses mainly on their patients' spontaneous verbal communications," the physician Claudio Rapezzi and his colleagues have written. "As diseases were categorised by symptoms, patients could communicate their symptoms verbally, or even by letter. Thus, doctors could effectively 'visit' a patient . . . by post." But by the nineteenth century, doctors who wished to discern, identify, and correctly order medical clues had to learn not merely to look directly but to "look feelingly," as Edmund Pellegrino has written. Precisely this skill was imparted to Conan Doyle by Joseph Bell.

By the end of the century, advances in microscopy had enabled doctors to look more precisely than ever. Likewise for detectives of the period, for whom seeing retrospectively was best accomplished by seeing minutely. "It has long been an axiom of mine that the little things are infinitely the most important," Holmes says confidently in "A Case of Identity," a story from 1891. A year later, Bell obliged Conan Doyle by furnishing the introduction to the 1892 edition of *A Study in Scarlet*. "*The importance of the infinitely little is incalculable,*" Bell wrote. "Trained as he has been to notice and appreciate minute detail, Dr. Doyle saw how he could interest his intelligent readers by taking them into his confidence, and showing his mode of working. He created a shrewd, quick-sighted, inquisitive man, half doctor, half virtuoso."

It is noteworthy, too, to recall that Conan Doyle trained as an eye doctor, for the Slater case is crucially about late Victorian ways of seeing—for good and, on balance, for ill. With its focus on identification, and its prejudices rooted in class and ethnicity, the case is at its core about visual diagnosis or, more accurately, misdiagnosis of a prolonged and pernicious kind.

RETROSPECTIVE PROPHECY DID NOT start with the Victorians, of course: the art has its roots deep in antiquity, born of the hunter's skill at tracking his prey by reading its traces. Before Holmes, one of the finest fictional exponents of this skill was Zadig, the ancient Eastern prince who is the title character of Voltaire's philosophical novella of 1747. In a passage that was an acknowledged influence on Conan Doyle, Zadig offers a masterly demonstration:

> One day, when he was walking near a little wood, he saw one of the queen's eunuchs running to meet him, followed by several officers, who appeared to be in the greatest uneasiness. . . .
>
> "Young man," said the chief eunuch to Zadig, "have you seen the queen's dog?"
>
> Zadig modestly replied: "It is a bitch, not a dog."
>
> "You are right," said the eunuch.
>
> "It is a very small spaniel," added Zadig; "it is not long since she has had a litter of puppies; she is lame in the left forefoot; and her ears are very long."
>
> "You have seen her, then?" said the chief eunuch, quite out of breath.
>
> "No," answered Zadig. "I have never seen her, and never knew the queen had a bitch." . . .
>
> The chief eunuch had no doubt that Zadig had stolen . . . the queen's bitch, so they caused him to be brought

before the Assembly of the Grand Desterham, which condemned him to the knout* and to pass the rest of his life in Siberia. Scarcely had the sentence been pronounced, when . . . the bitch [was] found. The judges were now under the disagreeable necessity of amending their judgment; but they condemned Zadig to pay four hundred ounces of gold for having said that he had not seen what he had seen. . . . Afterwards he was allowed to plead his cause. . . . He expressed himself in the following terms:

". . . I saw on the sand the footprints of an animal, and easily decided that they were those of a little dog. Long and faintly marked furrows, imprinted where the sand was slightly raised between the footprints, told me that it was a bitch whose dugs were drooping, and that consequently she must have given birth to young ones only a few days before. Other marks of a different character, showing that the surface of the sand had been constantly grazed on either side of the front paws, informed me that she had very long ears; and, as I observed that the sand was always less deeply indented by one paw than by the other three, I gathered that the bitch belonging to our august queen was a little lame. . . ."

All the judges marvelled at Zadig's deep and subtle discernment. . . . Though several magi were of opinion that he ought to be burned as a wizard, the king ordered that he should be released from the fine of four hundred ounces of gold to which he had been condemned. The registrar, the bailiffs, and the attorneys came to his house with great solemnity to restore him his four hundred

* A particularly savage whip or scourge.

ounces; they kept back only three hundred and ninety-eight of them for legal expenses.

It is clearly no accident that when the name "Zadig" is given a Germanic reading—with "z" pronounced "tz" and "g" pronounced "k," as it might be uttered by Yiddish-speaking Jews—it becomes "Tzaddik," the term, rooted in the Hebrew word for "justice," that denotes a spiritual master who possesses profound wisdom.

The first modern fictional detective, and every inch an heir to Zadig, was Edgar Allan Poe's cogitating protagonist, the chevalier C. Auguste Dupin. Dupin, who made his debut in 1841 in "The Murders in the Rue Morgue" and returned in "The Mystery of Marie Rogêt" and "The Purloined Letter," anticipates Holmes in several respects. He is a gentleman—brilliant, aloof, gothic, nocturnal, dissolute. He has a faithful companion who renders the tales of his exploits for the public. He is possessed of observational powers so minute, and a mind so rational, that he can induce a connected chain of contingencies from a single residual clue.

Dupin's skill at retrospective prophecy—"ratiocination," Poe calls it—can seem almost clairvoyant, as in a famous scene from "The Murders in the Rue Morgue." In it, Dupin correctly divines that his friend has been thinking about Chantilly, a petite, stagestruck local cobbler, from the way the friend stumbles in the street after a fruit seller bumps into him. "You were remarking to yourself that his diminutive figure unfitted him for tragedy," Dupin concludes. "The larger links of the chain run thus—Chantilly, Orion, Dr. Nichol, Epicurus, Stereotomy, the street stones, the fruiterer. . . . So far, you had been stooping in your gait; but now I saw you draw yourself up to your full height. I was then sure that you reflected upon the diminutive figure of Chantilly. At this point I interrupted your meditations to remark that as, in fact, he *was* a very little fellow—that Chantilly—he would do better at the *Théâtre des Variétés*."

BY 1887, WHEN SHERLOCK HOLMES made his debut, late nineteenth-century scientific method and the late nineteenth-century literary detective were poised for sublime convergence. In Conan Doyle's hero, the ratiocinative skills exhibited by Dupin would reach their apogee.* "The scientific method made the fictional detective possible and it made him popular," J. K. Van Dover, an authority on detective literature, has observed. "The detective offered himself as a special model of the new scientific thinker. . . . He promised to combine the most powerful method of thought with a fundamental commitment to traditional ethics (and, as a further attraction, to exercise his method . . . on the sensational matter of violent crime), and the public embraced him."

Conan Doyle was not the only crime writer of the period to combine detective and scientist into a single estimable hero. The British writer R. Austin Freeman (1862–1943) married detection and doctoring overtly in the character of John Thorndyke, a physician and crime-solving forensic analyst who starred in novels and stories published between 1907 and 1942. A master of "medico-legal practice," Thorndyke never traveled without the green canvas-covered box, "only a foot square by four inches deep," that contained his portable crime laboratory: "rows of little re-agent bottles, tiny test-tubes, diminutive spirit-

* Holmes's sneer to Watson, in *A Study in Scarlet*, that "Dupin was a very inferior fellow" was clearly an inside joke: Conan Doyle admired Poe immensely and throughout his career expressed his deep debt to the Dupin stories.

lamp, dwarf microscope and assorted instruments on the same Lilliputian scale." It came to his aid at many a crime scene.

But it was Holmes that the reading public embraced above all. His lightning-quick mind, unassailable logic, ironclad ethics, and genius for discerning patterns amid a forest of evidentiary noise equipped him spectacularly for the literary detective's most vital task: "The narrative of the detective story depends entirely upon [the hero's] ability to uncover the moral order of his world through a methodical observation and interpretation of its surfaces," Van Dover has written. "Those actions . . . must always allow two plausible readings, one erroneous and one true. *The first is the easy reading, the one toward which the inertia of our prejudices inclines us;* . . . the second is the hard reading, the one derived from the detective's thoughtful analysis."

It was the first reading, with its expedient conclusions and engineered results, that police and prosecutors nearly always pursued in the Slater case. It was the second, rooted in the subtle use of the diagnostic imagination, that Conan Doyle had learned to perform under the master, Joseph Bell.

Chapter 6

# THE ORIGINAL SHERLOCK HOLMES

If Holmes was the scion of the Chevalier Dupin, he was also the offspring of the flesh-and-blood diagnostic genius Joseph Bell. Bell (1837–1911) was born in Edinburgh to a long line of Scottish physicians. His grandfather Sir Charles Bell had identified the type of facial paralysis now known as Bell's palsy. An 1859 graduate of the University of Edinburgh, Joseph Bell began teaching there soon afterward. He quickly became renowned throughout the university, astounding students with a diagnostic ability that to the uninitiated appeared to verge on witchcraft.

In 1878, during Conan Doyle's second year of medical school, he was chosen to work as Bell's clerk. "For some reason which I have never understood," he wrote, "he singled me out from the drove of students who frequented his wards and made me his outpatient clerk, which meant that I had to array his outpatients, make simple notes of their cases, and then show them in, one by one, to the large room in which Bell sat in state surrounded by his dressers and students. Then I had ample chance of studying his methods and of noticing that he often learned more of the patient by a few quick glances than I had done by my questions."

Conan Doyle recalled one memorable case, in which Bell confronted a man he had never seen:

> He said to a civilian patient: "Well, my man, you've served in the army."
>
> "Aye, sir."
>
> "Not long discharged?"
>
> "No, sir."
>
> "A Highland regiment?"
>
> "Aye, sir."
>
> "A non-com. officer?"
>
> "Aye, sir."
>
> "Stationed at Barbados?"
>
> "Aye, sir."
>
> "You see, gentlemen," he would explain, "the man was a respectful man but did not remove his hat. They do not in the army, but he would have learned civilian ways had he been long discharged. He has an air of authority and he is obviously Scottish. As to Barbados, his complaint is elephantiasis, which is West Indian and not British."

In another case, a woman unknown to Bell entered the lecture hall with a small child in tow. "He greeted her politely," one of Conan Doyle's biographers wrote, "and she said good morning in reply." The following exchange ensued:

> "What sort of crossing did you have from Burntisland?" Bell asked.
>
> "It was guid," came the answer.
>
> "And had you a good walk up Inverleith Row?"

"Yes."

"And what did you do with the other wain?"* . . .

"I left him with my sister in Leith."

"And would you still be working at the linoleum factory?"

"Yes."

"You see, gentlemen," Bell told his students, "when she said good morning I noticed her Fife accent, and, as you know, the nearest town in Fife is Burntisland. You notice the red clay on the edges of the soles of her shoes, and the only such clay within twenty miles of Edinburgh is the Botanical Gardens. Inverleith Row borders the gardens and is her nearest way here from Leith. You observed the coat she carried over her arm is too big for the child who is with her, and therefore she set out from home with two children. Finally, she has dermatitis on the fingers of her right hand, which is peculiar to the workers at the linoleum factory at Burntisland."

BELL'S DIAGNOSTIC SORCERY WAS born of the potent combination of minute observation and rigorous scientific method. "Use your eyes, sir! Use your ears, use your brain, your bump of perception, and use your powers of deduction," one student, Harold Emery Jones, recalled his having said. "These deductions, gentlemen, must, however, be confirmed by absolute and concrete evidence." Jones, a classmate of Conan Doyle's, recalled Bell's greeting a new patient and, turning to his students, saying:

* "Wain" (or "wean") is Scots dialect for "child."

> Gentlemen, a fisherman! You will notice that, though this is a very hot summer's day, the patient is wearing top-boots. When he sat on the chair they were plainly visible. No one but a sailor would wear top-boots at this season of the year. The shade of tan on his face shows him to be a coast-sailor, and not a deep-sea sailor—a sailor who makes foreign lands. His tan is that produced by one climate, a "local tan," so to speak. A knife scabbard shows beneath his coat, the kind used by fishermen in this part of the world. He is concealing a quid of tobacco in the furthest corner of his mouth and manages it very adroitly indeed, gentlemen. The summary of these deductions shows that this man is a fisherman. Further, to prove the correctness of these deductions, I notice several fish-scales adhering to his clothes and hands, while the odor of fish announced his arrival in a most marked and striking manner.

Bell was so keen an observer that seemingly irrelevant details could acquire great significance for him alone—significance that might be confirmed only years later. More than three decades before Alexander Fleming isolated penicillin from mold in 1928, Bell instructed a group of nurses this way: "Cultivate absolute accuracy in observation, and truthfulness in report. . . . For example, children suffering from diarrhoea of a wasting type sometimes take a strong fancy for old green-moulded cheese, and devour it with best effect. Is it possible that the germs in the cheese are able to devour in their turn the *bacilli tuberculosis*[?]"

For Bell, traces on a patient's body that might go unnoticed by others stood as silent witnesses to a life. "Nearly every handicraft writes its sign-manual on the hands," he told an interviewer in 1892. "The scars of the miner differ from those of the quarryman. The carpenter's callosities are not those of the mason. The shoemaker and the tailor are quite different. The soldier and the sailor differ in gait—though last month I had to tell a man who was a soldier that he had been a sailor in his boyhood. . . . The tattoo marks on hand or arm will tell their own tale as to voyages; the ornaments on the watch chain of the successful settler will tell you where he made his money. A New Zealand squatter will not wear a gold mohur, nor an engineer on an Indian railway a Maori stone."

Once Bell's connection to Sherlock Holmes became known, the world press regularly sought him out to watch the original in action. In an 1893 interview, a reporter for the *Pall Mall Gazette* asked him, "Is there any system by which the habit of observation is to be cultivated among the police?"

"There is among doctors," Bell replied. "It is taught regularly to the students here. . . . It would be a great thing if the police generally could be trained to observe more closely. . . . The fatal mistake which the ordinary policeman makes is this, that he gets his theory first, and then makes the facts fit it, instead of getting his facts first of all and making all his little observations and deductions until he is driven irresistibly by them . . . in a direction he may never have originally contemplated."

Those words might have issued from the mouth of Sherlock Holmes. In hindsight, they would be an unimpeachable diagnosis of police behavior in the Slater case.

BELL ALSO WORKED AS a forensic expert for the British Crown, and here, too, he was a worthy father to his fictional heir. Though he did this work for decades, he was a man of such utter professional discretion that only a few of his cases are known. "For twenty years or more I have been engaged in the practice of medical jurisprudence on behalf of the Crown, but there is little I can tell you about it," he said in 1893. "It would not be fair to mention that which is the private knowledge of the Crown."

One case that is known—it concerned one of the most celebrated crimes in Victorian Britain—is that of the wife-murderer Eugène Chantrelle. A Frenchman, Chantrelle settled in Edinburgh in the 1860s, teaching languages at a private school there. In 1868, he married one of his pupils, sixteen-year-old Lizzie Dyer, whom he had seduced and impregnated. Their decade-long union was tempestuous and, increasingly, violent. "My dear Mama," Lizzie Chantrelle wrote in a letter home. "I might have been sleeping for an hour or more, when I was awakened by several severe blows. I got one on the side of the head which knocked me stupid. . . . My jaw bone is out of place, my mouth inside skinned and festering and my face all swollen."

In 1877, Chantrelle insured his wife's life for more than a thousand pounds. One day soon afterward, their maid heard moaning from Lizzie Chantrelle's bedroom. She found her unconscious; on the bedside table were orange segments, grapes, and a glass of lemonade, half drunk. The maid called to Chantrelle, then ran for a doctor. Returning, she saw the glass had been emptied and the fruit removed. She also saw Chantrelle exiting through the bedroom window.

Lizzie Chantrelle died a short time later; her doctor ruled the death a case of coal-gas poisoning. Thinking the case would interest Sir Henry Littlejohn, Scotland's most eminent forensic scientist, the doctor called him in. Littlejohn brought Bell along. Examining Mrs. Chantrelle's room, "Bell and Littlejohn found evidence of poison everywhere," Bell's biographer Ely

Liebow has written. "There were many brownish spots on [her] pillow, a few on her nightgown, and analysis revealed that these spots contained opium in a solid form, along with minute traces of grape-seed fragments. The same combination was found in her alimentary canal." Interviewing local chemists, Bell learned that Chantrelle had recently bought a large quantity of opium.

Besides this positive evidence, there was a spectacular piece of negative evidence: Though Lizzie was supposed to have been killed by a gas leak, the maid told investigators that she had smelled gas only when she *returned* from fetching the doctor—not when she first found her mistress unconscious. To Bell, it was the *absence* of gas that was the truly striking thing.

An investigation by the gas company found a broken gas pipe outside Lizzie's bedroom. "The maid, who had heard and seen the arguments and blows over the years, felt that Chantrelle himself had ripped the pipe loose," Liebow wrote. "Chantrelle objected that he didn't know the pipe existed." Unconvinced, Bell made further inquiries in the neighborhood and discovered a pipefitter who had repaired that pipe the year before. Eugène Chantrelle, he recalled, had taken an unusual interest in the pipe and its workings. Tried and convicted, Chantrelle was hanged in Edinburgh in 1878.

IN THE LATE 1880S, when the fledgling writer Conan Doyle was casting about for a detective, he did not have far to look. Though Bell, who appeared to grow weary of the press attention, often took pains to say that he was *not* the inspiration for Holmes, the affinity was plain to any reader who knew him.

One such reader was Robert Louis Stevenson, a writer Conan Doyle had long admired. A fellow Scot, Stevenson had studied engineering and law at the University of Edinburgh between 1867 and 1875, graduating the year before Conan Doyle entered. Though the two men apparently never met, Conan Doyle wrote a series of letters to Stevenson expressing his pleasure in works like *Treasure Island, Kidnapped,* and *The Strange Case of Dr. Jekyll and Mr. Hyde.* In 1893, Stevenson, who suffered from tuberculosis and had moved to Samoa for his health, sent Conan Doyle a reply that, as the Conan Doyle biographer Michael Sims notes, "blended the praise of a reader and the condescension of a rival."

"Dear Sir," Stevenson wrote. "You have taken many occasions to make yourself agreeable to me, for which I might in decency have thanked you earlier. It is now my turn; and I hope you will allow me to offer you my compliments on your very ingenious and very interesting adventures of Sherlock Holmes. That is the class of literature I like when I have the toothache. As a matter of fact, it was a pleurisy I was enjoying when I took the volume up; and it will interest you as a medical man to know that the cure was for the moment effectual."

To this paragraph, Stevenson appended a resonant last line. "Only one thing troubles me," he wrote. *"Can this be my old friend Joe Bell?"*

## Chapter 7

# THE ART OF REASONING BACKWARD

BY THE TIME OF THE GILCHRIST MURDER, THE HOLMESIAN method of rational inquiry, in which observed facts rather than reflexive prejudices dictate the solution, was well established, at least among fictional detectives. Holmes was so skilled at this way of working that Conan Doyle's stories anticipate the use of similar methods by actual police forces. "To-day criminal investigation is a science," the distinguished forensic pathologist Sir Sydney Smith wrote in 1959. "This was not always so and the change owes much to the influence of Sherlock Holmes."

As early as 1932, the true-crime writer Harry Ashton-Wolfe could declare:

> Many of the methods invented by Conan Doyle are today in use in the scientific laboratories. Sherlock Holmes made the study of tobacco-ashes his hobby. It was a new idea, but the police at once realised the importance of such specialised knowledge, and now every lab-

> oratory has a complete set of tables giving the appearance and composition of the various ashes, which every detective must be able to recognise. Mud and soil from various districts are also classified much after the matter that Holmes described. . . . Poisons, hand-writing, stains, dust, footprints, traces of wheels, the shape and position of wounds, and therefore the probable shape of the weapon which caused them; the theory of cryptograms, all these and many other excellent methods which germinated in Conan Doyle's fertile imagination are now part and parcel of every detective's scientific equipment.

In the Gilchrist investigation, alas, these techniques were either irrelevant or of little help, a circumstance that worked to Slater's cost. But even with scant scientific means at their disposal, the Glasgow police had access to one powerful forensic tool, though they rarely seem to have used it: logical reasoning. That, after the rigorous sifting of empirical evidence, is the next step in the Holmesian method and in many ways its soul. Though Holmes himself often describes this brand of reasoning as deductive, it actually entails no deduction.* It hinges, more properly, on a logical process known as *induction*—or, still more properly, *abduction*.

"Abduction" was first used in this sense by the American philosopher Charles Sanders Peirce. A polymath whose work had profound implications for philosophy, logic, semiotics, mathematics, psychology, anthropology, and other fields, Peirce (pronounced "purse") was born in Cambridge, Massachusetts,

* Conan Doyle, per common parlance, tended to use "deduction" as a general rubric denoting any type of logical inference.

in 1839; his father, Benjamin Peirce, a Harvard mathematics professor, had helped establish the Smithsonian Institution. After graduating in 1859 from Harvard, where he studied chemistry, Charles took a job as a surveyor with the United States Coast and Geodetic Survey, work that for the next thirty-two years would support his wide-ranging philosophical investigations: at his death in 1914, he left a written legacy of some twelve thousand published pages and eighty thousand manuscript pages.

Abduction, or "retroduction," as Peirce also called it, is much like Huxley's "retrospective prophecy." Presented with a set of *effects*—animal tracks, medical symptoms, crime-scene clues—the investigator uses abduction to pinpoint their most logically probable *cause*.

"A given object," Peirce wrote, "presents an extraordinary combination of characters of which we should like to have an explanation. That there is any explanation of them is a pure assumption; and if there be, it is some one hidden fact which explains them; while there are, perhaps, a million other possible ways of explaining them, if they were not all, unfortunately, false. A man is found in the streets of New York stabbed in the back. The chief of police might open a directory and put his finger on any name and guess that that is the name of the murderer. How much would such a guess be worth?" (The Glasgow police, of course, did essentially this in fingering Slater.)

The abductive method permits no such precipitate conclusions. "*Abduction* makes its start from the facts, without, at the outset, having any particular theory in view, though it is motivated by the feeling that a theory is needed to explain the surprising facts," Peirce writes. "*Induction* makes its start from a hypothesis which seems to recommend itself, without at the outset having any particular facts in view, though it feels the need of facts to support the theory. Abduction seeks a theory. Induction seeks for facts."

Abduction, as a group of British scholars explain in an article on medical diagnosis, takes the following form:

FACT C is observed.
IF A were true, C would be a matter of course.
*Therefore there is reason to suspect that A is true.*

That process is the mirror image of deduction: In deduction the investigator reasons forward, from *cause* to *effect*. When Holmes says, as he does in his debut appearance, "In solving a problem of this sort, the grand thing is to be able to reason backward," he is singing the praises of abduction. To illustrate the differences among deduction, induction, and abduction, Peirce invoked a trio of syllogisms like these:

Deduction

RULE: All serious knife wounds result in bleeding.
CASE: This was a serious knife wound.
THEREFORE [the deduced result]: There was bleeding.

Induction

CASE: This was a serious knife wound.
RESULT: There was bleeding.
THEREFORE [the induced rule]: All serious knife wounds result in bleeding.

Abduction

RULE: All serious knife wounds result in bleeding.
RESULT: There was bleeding.
THEREFORE [the abducted case]: This was (likely to have been) a serious knife wound.

In assembling their case against Slater, police and prosecutors were working *deductively*, to the detriment of justice. If their preposterous reasoning were schematized, it would look much like this:

RULE: All murders are committed by undesirables.
CASE: Oscar Slater is an undesirable.
THEREFORE, Oscar Slater committed the Gilchrist murder.

Abduction, like the reconstructive sciences of the Victorian age, generates *narrative*. Zadig used precisely this method in spinning an etiological thread that would account for the observed facts of a case. So, more than a century later, did Sherlock Holmes:

"We are coming now rather into the region of guesswork," Holmes's client Dr. Mortimer protests in *The Hound of the Baskervilles*.

"Say, rather," Holmes replies, "into the region where we balance probabilities and choose the most likely. It is *the scientific use of the imagination*, but we have always some material basis on which to start our speculation."

In case after case, Holmes uses abduction to solve mysteries, reasoning backward until, he said, "the whole thing is a chain of logical sequences without a break or flaw." In "The Adventure of the Six Napoleons," a 1904 story, London is plagued by a string of bewildering crimes: the theft and smashing, one by one, of a set of identical plaster busts of Napoleon. To the dependably dim Inspector Lestrade of Scotland Yard, the obvious explanation is that the thefts are the work of a madman, someone "who had such a hatred of Napoleon the First that he would break any image of him that he could see."

But to Holmes, Lestrade's theory accounts for the facts only trivially. If a madman were indeed moved to smash Napoleon's every image, then, why attack *those particular* busts, "considering," Holmes points out, "how many hundreds of statues of the great Emperor must exist in London"? And why, Holmes asks further, did the culprit, having made off with one of the busts, wait to smash it until he reached a particular spot in the street? "Holmes pointed to the street lamp above our heads," Conan Doyle writes. "'He could see what he was doing here, and he could not there. That was his reason.'"

These rational observations, combined with empirical legwork, allow Holmes to construct, as he tells Lestrade with no little ego, a *narrative* of the crime "by a connected chain of inductive reasoning." The real object of stealing and smashing the busts, he correctly concludes, was to find a priceless jewel concealed inside one of them.

"Holmes . . . operates like a semiotician," the critic Rosemary Jann has written. "He 'reads' crimes like literary texts, as if they were systems of signs. The true significance of each sign is determined by its relation to others *in a particular network of meaning*. . . . He is able eventually to recognize the one relationship capable of accounting for all the clues."

In contrast, the police of the period—in the Holmes canon and all too often in life—tended to think not in terms of a subtle web of contingencies but of a straight line, drawn in unambiguous black and white. Holmes acknowledges this danger in an 1891 story, "The Boscombe Valley Mystery," when he declares, "There is nothing more deceptive than an obvious fact."

"Many men have been hanged on far slighter evidence," Watson concurs.

"So they have," Holmes replies. "And many men have been wrongfully hanged."

## Chapter 8

# A CASE OF IDENTITY

ON FEBRUARY 11, 1909, THE U.S. STATE DEPARTMENT approved the Crown's extradition warrant. On the fourteenth, Detectives Pyper and Warnock escorted Slater, with his baggage, sealed by U.S. Customs, onto the steamer *Columbia*. Arriving in Scotland on the twenty-first, the ship sailed up the river Clyde. To avoid the throng, straining for a glimpse of the notorious suspect, that was anticipated at Glasgow, Slater was removed from the ship at Renfrew, some five miles away, to be taken the rest of the way by car. As he disembarked, in handcuffs, a member of the *Columbia*'s crew kicked him.

At Glasgow police headquarters, Slater's baggage was unsealed. There, among his neatly folded, carefully packed clothing, was the little hammer—not much more than a tack hammer. To the police, the hammer appeared to have been washed, as did a fawn-colored waterproof coat, which bore dark stains. There was an array of hats, including two cloth caps, though nothing resembling the Donegal cap Mary Barrowman had invoked. Nor did police find the checked trousers, fawn spats, or brown boots that some witnesses had described the "watcher" as wearing as he eyed Miss Gilchrist's house.

"In the fierce popular indignation which is excited by a sanguinary crime, there is a tendency, in which judges and juries share, to brush aside or treat as irrelevant those doubts the benefit of which is supposed to be one of the privileges of the accused," Conan Doyle wrote in *Strange Studies from Life,* his nonfiction survey of three murders in nineteenth-century England. "Far wiser is the contention that it is better that ninety-nine guilty should escape than that one innocent man should suffer."

The Glasgow police appeared to have no such scruples. The case against Slater was weak, and they knew it. The brooch clue—the spark that had ignited the manhunt—had long since fallen away. But they had settled on their man, and they would have him. As a result, the case would need to hinge almost entirely on witness identification. But even where there is no intent to deceive, eyewitness memory is a risky proposition. It is patchy, fungible, and highly susceptible to suggestion. Though the inherent unreliability of eyewitness testimony would not be demonstrated scientifically until the late twentieth century, it was already well known anecdotally in Edwardian Britain.

A decade before the Gilchrist murder, another wrongful conviction had driven the point very publicly home. In 1895, a London woman accused Adolf Beck, a down-at-the-heels Norwegian dandy, of having swindled her out of jewelry by posing as a nobleman. On arresting Beck, the police learned that a man playing just this confidence game had swindled almost two dozen women in recent years. Police convened a lineup, known in Britain as an identity parade. Many of the former victims identified Beck—the only man in the lineup with a mustache and distinguished gray hair—as the swindler.

Beck protested that he was a victim of mistaken identity: he had been in South America, he said, when the earlier crimes occurred. But damned by eyewitness testimony, he was convicted and sentenced to seven years' penal servitude. Paroled in 1901, he was rearrested, tried, and convicted on a similar charge soon afterward. Only in 1904 did police discover the real culprit: a gray-haired Viennese man named Wilhelm Meyer. Meyer, who was living in England under an alias, superficially resembled Beck. He confessed, Beck was pardoned, and the case endured as a seminal cautionary tale.

"It is notorious," Conan Doyle would write in 1912, "that nothing is more tricky than evidence of identification." Cognizant of this fact, police and prosecutors in the case against Oscar Slater made certain that it would not fail.

On February 21, 1909, at Glasgow's Central Police Station, Slater was displayed before witnesses in an identity parade. Standing alongside the dark-haired, olive-skinned suspect were eleven other men: nine pale pink Scottish plainclothes policemen and two pale pink Scottish railway officials. Not every witness could spot the man who had been the "watcher" outside Miss Gilchrist's home, but those who made an identification chose Slater immediately.

"To expect a row of Glasgow constables and railwaymen to offer 'cover' to the identification of a German Jew, of unmistakable foreign appearance, was very much . . . like attempting to conceal a bull-dog among ladies' poodles," the journalist William Park wrote acidly years later. It also did not hurt that several witnesses had been shown Slater's photograph before the lineup, common practice at the time.

On the twenty-second, Slater, accompanied by his solicitor, Ewing Speirs, was formally charged with Miss Gilchrist's murder. He was remanded to Glasgow's Duke Street Prison to await trial. "Slater impressed everyone with his coolness and courtesy," Peter Hunt wrote. "He asked Mr. Speirs to thank the police for their kind treatment." Soon afterward, Speirs told the newspapers: "The more I see of Slater the more convinced I am of his innocence. I do not say this, remember, as the agent of his defence. As man speaking to man as I have done with Slater, I cannot help feeling that some dreadful mistake has been made by someone. He is not at all the type of man who would associate with such a revolting crime."

Before long, the trial venue was changed to Edinburgh, the capital, and Slater was transferred to Edinburgh's Calton Jail. At the trial, scheduled to begin that spring, the Crown would be represented by James Hart, the procurator fiscal for Lanarkshire, the county that included Glasgow.* Hart, who pursued the Slater prosecution with uncommon zeal, would prove to be one of the great malign forces in the case. The defense team included Speirs and the barrister Alexander Logan McClure, who would handle the courtroom arguments.

On April 6, Slater was indicted; his hammer, his raincoat, and one of his hats were sent for testing to Dr. John Glaister of Glasgow University. Glaister, one of the leading forensic medical experts in Scotland, had led the autopsy of Miss Gilchrist's body. His testimony at trial—including a catalogue of Miss Gilchrist's devastating injuries and the assertion that Slater's little hammer could have caused them all—almost certainly helped bring about Slater's conviction.

* A uniquely Scottish post that endures to this day, the office of procurator fiscal combines investigative and prosecutorial functions: it is somewhat akin to that of district attorney in the United States.

—

THE QUESTION THAT VEXED Conan Doyle has persisted for a century: Why, when the police knew within a week that the brooch clue was false, did they pursue Slater anyway? There was a reason, and it resides in an unfortunate accident of history.

At the time of the Gilchrist murder, the identification of criminal suspects was at a crossroads. Standing at that pass, a detective on the trail of a criminal had two choices. There was the way forward, a nascent, rationalist twentieth-century science that would come to be called *criminalistics*. There was the way back, the murky nineteenth-century pseudoscience known as *criminology*, rooted in the work of Cesare Lombroso and his ilk. In taking the path of criminology, the Glasgow police doomed Slater. Then again, as was confirmed long afterward, framing him for the Gilchrist murder had been their objective from the very start.

The Victorian age has been called the Age of Identification, and the name is apt. The technology that had spawned the era's cities also fostered mobility: railways and faster steamships let ordinary people cross borders with ease. The trouble was, they let criminals do likewise. And the cities themselves, in their seething anonymity, offered criminals safe havens in which identity became fluid: one had only to adopt an alias and dissolve into the crowd. As a result, the anxieties of the era focused on the need to identify criminals at a distance. But individual identification—finding the uniquely correct needle in a dense cosmopolitan haystack—is no mean feat, and for the Victorians, an urgent question was how to go about it.

The identification of any criminal suspect involves the reading of signs: at the crime scene, on the victim, or on the criminal himself. Today, the best-known way of doing this is through forensic sciences like ballistics, fingerprinting, serology, and toxicology. These are the reconstructive sciences of the post-modern age, letting investigators reestablish past events after the fact, sometimes long after, as DNA fingerprinting has done since its introduction in the 1980s.

But in the Victorian era, forensic science was in embryo: the very concept of a "crime scene" did not exist until the end of the nineteenth century. And forensic investigation as we now understand it—involving rigorous professional protocols, up-to-date scientific procedures, and state-of-the-art police laboratories—did not begin to come into its own until the 1930s and '40s.

Yet the need for criminal identification is as old as mankind. Think of Cain, who committed the first recorded homicide and was marked ever after by God. How, then, did people identify criminals before the mid-twentieth century? The answer lies in the locus of the signifiers: if the signs used today are read mainly off the crime scene, those of the past were read directly off the criminal.

AN INVESTIGATOR IN PURSUIT of a suspect has three chances at identification. He can identify the suspect *after* the fact, through forensic analysis of the scene. He can identify him *during* the fact, via eyewitness testimony. Irrational as it sounds, he can also identify the suspect *before* the fact, in a preemptive strike meant to safeguard the community. Which technique an investigator employs depends partly on circumstance and partly on the technology available. It also depends—tellingly—on the era's prevailing attitudes toward crime, criminals, and punishment.

In antiquity and long afterward, Western culture viewed crime as sin. In the interest of public safety, criminals, once known, had to be marked: think of Hester Prynne, and of the vivid capital letter chalked onto the coat of the murderous Peter Lorre in *M,* Fritz Lang's 1931 thriller. During the Middle Ages, offenders were often given visible stigmata that signified the nature of the offense. "Branding and ear-boring, as a means of marking the deviant status of the criminal, had been statutory punishments in England from at least the late fourteenth century," one historian has written, adding:

> A labour statute of 1361 declared that fugitives were to be branded on the forehead with "F" for "falsity." The Vagabonds Act of 1547 . . . ordered that vagrants should be branded with a "V" on their breast. Ear-boring was introduced in 1572, when a statute was passed requiring all vagabonds to be "grievously whipped and burned through the gristle of the right ear with a hot iron." By an Act of 1604, incorrigible rogues were to be "branded in the left shoulder with a hot burning iron of the breadth of an English shilling with a great Roman 'R' upon the iron."

The marks offered threefold social control. Visible brands alerted members of the honest public. In principle, they also deterred people contemplating a life of crime. And in an era before widespread literacy and comprehensive penal records, they could be "read" by law officers as signs of prior conviction: criminal suspects were routinely strip-searched in pursuit of them.

In medieval England, an enfranchised system of street justice also dealt with undesirables. It was tied to the concept of the outlaw, a word denoting not a criminal per se but a person deemed to be outside the law's protection. In legal cases of the era, a criminal defendant (or the subject of a civil action) who repeatedly failed to appear in court—and whom the authorities could not locate—could be declared an outlaw. Once a man had been "outlawed," any citizen encountering him had the right to do with him as he pleased, including commit homicide.* "Outlawry was the capital punishment of a rude age," two twentieth-century historians have written. "To pursue the outlaw and knock him on the head as though he were a wild beast [was] the right and duty of every law-abiding man."

But by the Enlightenment, the perception of crime and criminals had changed. Crime was now seen as a misguided ethical choice, which allowed for the possibility, after removal from society and sufficient contemplation, of rehabilitation.† For citizens of the era, though, the essential question on encountering a stranger remained the same as ever: "Who are you, with whom I have to deal?," as the philosopher Jeremy Bentham put it in the early 1800s.

Because Enlightenment sensibilities deemed the mutilation and mob justice of a prior age inhumane, the state now began keeping meticulous dossiers on criminals. The main function of these records was to identify recidivists. A check of the files in a police department or prison could reveal whether a suspect had been convicted before, much as the brands had done in earlier times. But the system had a fundamental flaw: it was utterly useless if a suspect had changed his name, and this fact bedeviled law officers for decades.

* Because women of this era were already less than full citizens under the law, they technically could not be outlawed. But a court considering the case of a female suspect could achieve the same end by declaring her a "waived" woman—that is, a "waif"—in effect making her a piece of ownerless property.

† The word "penitentiary" as a synonym for "prison," used in this sense since the early nineteenth century, embodies the idea of a place of penance and reflection. So, too, in a more aggressive way, does "reformatory," which entered English in the mid-eighteenth century.

In the 1870s, Alphonse Bertillon, a civilian employee of the French police, sought a better way to identify repeat offenders. Exploiting the relatively new medium of photography, he created what we now call the mug shot: full-face and profile images of a convict, affixed to a card. To this card, he added copious data about the convict's bodily dimensions. At a police station or prison, a newly arrived convict would be rigorously measured and the results compared against the sets of measurements already on file. A match, Bertillon argued, would prove identity even if the convict was using an alias.

The system, known as bertillonage, was widely adopted by police departments in Britain and the United States. But while it did identify some recidivists, it was unwieldy, requiring intensive training to administer. By definition, it did not work with juvenile offenders, who were likely to have grown between measurements. And its very nature meant that it could be used only after the fact, when the suspect was already well in hand.

Lombroso's "scientific criminology" was designed to circumvent these problems. Anchored firmly in Victorian prejudice, it was a diagnostic approach that unapologetically trained the lens of the majority culture onto the Other. But even more than its underlying bias, the great hazard of Lombroso's method was this: under the system, criminal identity was no longer *read* but was instead *constructed.*

BEFORE VICTORIAN TIMES, preemptive identification was simpler. When stranger met stranger, a set of well-known class signifiers—accent, attire, bearing, coiffure—reliably broadcast to each whether the other could be trusted or should be given a wide berth. No matter that these signifiers could not actually identify criminals: they successfully identified the Other, and that, for bourgeois citizens, was more than good enough. In the view of the seventeenth- and eighteenth-century upper crust, it was far better to have a warning system that overgenerated rather than undergenerated, and simply to throw all the lower-class babies out with the criminal bathwater.

But with the coming of modernity, time-honored signifiers began to blur. As foreigners thronged their cities, Victorians, who could unerringly tell Cockney from the Queen's English, found their ear for dialect of little avail. Even more worrisome, almost anyone seeking upward mobility—or illicit gain—could manipulate the old signals, adopting particular accents or modes of dress to counterfeit class identity.

For the Victorian bourgeoisie, a modern identification system was needed, and if the old signifiers had broken down, they would simply invent new ones. It is here that Lombroso's "scientific criminology" enters the fray. If public order depends on social control, its guiding principle went, then it is vital to be able to recognize *whom* one needs to control. And so Lombroso set out to produce a field guide to the common criminal.

Where *criminalistics*, rooted in real science, would focus on the crime scene, *criminology* focused on the criminal. Like many intellectual enterprises of the period, it was inspired by Darwinian theory, which coursed through the age like an electric charge. But in the hands of Lombroso and his fellows, criminology proved to be Darwinism of the darkest kind.

To these criminal anthropologists, criminality was inborn—an innate predisposition that no amount of reform could undo. What was required, they argued, was a way to identify habitual criminals (along with those men and women, guilty of no crime, who possessed inherited criminal tendencies) through a set of anatomical signifiers. These signs were broad enough that they could be read from afar, like the topmost line of an eye chart.

In his magnum opus, *Criminal Man,* published in Italian in 1876, Lombroso wrote of having spied the link between physiognomy and criminal character in the 1860s, when he performed an autopsy on a known malefactor. "This was not merely an idea, but a revelation," he wrote. Whipping himself into a lather of gothic melodrama, he continued:

> At the sight of that skull, I seemed to see all of a sudden, lighted up as a vast plain under a flaming sky, the problem of the nature of the criminal—an atavistic being who reproduces in his person the ferocious instincts of primitive humanity and the inferior animals. Thus were explained anatomically the enormous jaws, high cheekbones, prominent superciliary arches, solitary lines in the palms, extreme size of the orbits, handle-shaped or sessile ears found in criminals, savages, and apes, insensibility to pain, extremely acute sight, tattooing, excessive idleness, love of orgies, and the irresistible craving for evil for its own sake, the desire not only to extinguish life in the victim, but to mutilate the corpse, tear its flesh, and drink its blood.

Lombroso's work did not appear in English until 1911, but Victorian Britons knew it from secondary sources. Among them were the writings of Havelock Ellis, the English physician and eugenicist, who had helped popularize the term "criminology" in the 1890s. Even more influential for British criminology of the day was the work of Francis Galton, an ardent eugenicist and a cousin of Charles Darwin. Seeking to ensure the purity of the British gene pool, Galton experimented with composite photography: he superimposed criminals' faces atop one another, producing what he hoped would be an image of the ur-criminal, with features common to the entire criminal class. Once identified, members of that class could be kept from breeding.

Galton's work, like Lombroso's, overtly married criminal anthropology to the eugenic program, a common coupling then. A fringe benefit of their systems was that once classifications of criminal features were drawn up, they could be extended to any unwanted group, be it Gypsies, Jews, or other immigrants. This—a social enterprise that the criminologist Paul Knepper would call "the racialization of crime"—the Victorians enthusiastically set out to enact.

Excluding immigrants was easy, as bans could be legislated. In the United States, the first major law restricting immigration, the Chinese Exclusion Act, was passed by Congress in 1882 and signed into law by President Chester A. Arthur. In Britain, Parliament passed the Aliens Act in 1905. The act denied entry to "undesirable immigrants," a conveniently elastic term understood as code for Eastern European Jews. It is striking to note the conflation of foreignness with criminality, a contrivance used to justify identifying, marginalizing, and punishing the convenient Other. Today we call it "profiling."

THE FIRST TRULY *CRIMINALISTIC* approach to identification began in the late 1800s with the work of Hans Gross. An Austrian jurist who was fascinated by the application of the new science to the solution of crime, he published his monumental work, *Handbuch für Untersuchungsrichter, Polizeibeamte, Gendarmen,* in 1893.

Gross's work represented a significant advance over the dark anthropology of Galton and Lombroso.* To their subjective, racialized approach, he brought the rigor of scientific method: instead of reading imagined signs off the criminal's body, investigators would read them from the locus of the crime. His handbook ranged over such subjects as "What to Do at the Scene of Offence," "Search for Hidden Objects," "Construction and Use of Weapons," "Reproduction of Footprints," and "How to Register and Describe Traces of Blood." But it did not see English translation for more than a decade, appearing only in 1906 under the title *Criminal Investigation: A Practical Handbook for Magistrates, Police Officers and Lawyers*.

In 1908, when detectives confronted the Gilchrist murder, the old criminological methods of Galton and Lombroso and the nascent criminalistic ones born of the scientific revolution existed side by side. This was their forensic watershed, and to their credit, they did try the new methods. But in the Gilchrist case these methods were still so primitive that they proved either immaterial or unworkable. As a result, Slater was consigned to the mercy of criminology, which neatly constructed guilt where none had existed before.

It is not clear whether Glasgow detectives knew Gross's work, which had appeared in English just two years earlier. They were familiar with fingerprinting, introduced in Britain at the turn of the twentieth century.† Dusting Miss Gilchrist's flat

* Even Gross, however, was not stainless in this regard. He displayed a particular animus toward what he called "Wandering Tribes," notably Gypsies, and his handbook recapitulates timeworn stereotypes of Gypsies as thieves, poisoners, and child-stealers.

† Fingerprinting was such an untried technology in Victorian and Edwardian times that the entire Holmes canon contains scarcely more than half a dozen references to its forensic use, a clear indication that Conan Doyle did not accord it much weight as a diagnostic method.

for prints, they found a suspicious one, on the workbox in the spare bedroom. But the best fingerprint technology in the world is only as good as the database against which a print can be compared, and the department's files, barely a decade old, yielded no matches.

With criminalistic techniques of little help in identifying Miss Gilchrist's killer *after* the fact, police were left to fall back on the two alternative means of criminal identification. One was identification *during* the fact, by means of eyewitness testimony. This is where the spate of neighbors' statements, methodically solicited, about the "watcher" outside the Gilchrist home came in. It is also where the testimony of Lambie and Barrowman, manipulated to damning effect, was allowed to do its work.

But more than anything, the police reverted to the most pernicious means of identification of all: criminology, or the fingering of the criminal *before* the fact. It was this method, so closely bound up with the racialization of crime, that ensured the identification, pursuit, and conviction of Oscar Slater. As it transpired, the Glasgow police had begun their identification of Slater well before Miss Gilchrist's murder.

CRIMINOLOGY'S CHIEF FAILING IS that it is the bluntest of blunt instruments. Because it can't work after the fact, it can't identify individual culprits. It can only tag a targeted person as belonging to a particular class—ethnic, social, religious, and so on. But given the anxious preoccupations of the Victorian age, the method's great failing was also its great strength. At a time when the salient question between strangers was no longer "Who are you?" but "To which group do you belong?" criminology worked brilliantly as a means of preemptive social control, training a spotlight on members of marginalized populations.

In a criminalistic investigation, detection *precedes* identification. By reading the "infinitely little" traces at the crime scene, the investigator homes in on the culprit's identity. That is the logical order of things.

Victorian criminology reversed the process. Criminology sees only the big taxonomic picture—the foreigner, the gambler, the pauper, the Jew. This approach, an unsavory exercise of the diagnostic imagination, is the time-honored refuge of the bigot. By criminology's hall-of-mirrors logic, detection now *follows* identification, a topsy-turvy arrangement that recalls the Queen's biting line from Lewis Carroll's 1865 classic, *Alice's Adventures in Wonderland:* "Sentence first—verdict afterwards."

With criminology as their primary tool, the Glasgow police knew that they could never use it to prove Slater's guilt. But they could use it, masterfully, to *construct* his guilt. And thus, by the bourgeois imperatives of the day, the apprehension of Slater was a grand success, whether he had killed Miss Gilchrist or not. For if Oscar Slater was no murderer, then he was at the very least a convenient Other writ large.

To the police, the brooch clue was a singular stroke of luck, for it netted a man of the kind Edwardian Glasgow wanted off its streets anyway—one who, to borrow the words of the American defense lawyer Eleanor Jackson Piel, was "available and disposable." That the clue foundered scarcely mattered, for Slater's capture and conviction remained a fourfold coup: in one blow, the city would be rid of a foreigner, a Jew, a gambler, and a member (at least intermittently) of the lower classes. Slater might as well be hanged for a sheep as for a lamb, the prevailing sentiment seemed to run, and of course he very nearly was.

That Slater's guilt had been rigged from the start was confirmed in 1927, when the Scottish journalist William Park interviewed him after his release from Peterhead. "For some time *before the murder* the police were watching his house to get him on a charge of immoral housekeeping," Park wrote to Conan Doyle that year. He continued:

> He saw Lieut. Douglas & other officers watching him and was quite well aware of it. Just close on his arrest he saw repeatedly his men in observation.
>
> I find . . . a statement by Gordon Henderson, club master at the Sloper Club,* that the police called there on Wednesday 23d Dec. asking for Oscar Slater. *This was two days before McLean reported the pawnticket. . . .*
>
> This gives us a new theory altogether. *Slater was being watched for another crime & was rolled into the Gilchrist case as a handy sort of fellow to convict. . . .* As far back as 1911 Slater disclosed this fact of the police watching & letting him [get] away from Glasgow so as to roll him into "flight from justice." . . . The police admitted they were at Slater's house two hours or so before he departed and did not arrest him. . . .
>
> The further we go into this terrible business we see nothing but pure manufacture of a case: deliberately operating beforehand to make a prosecution.

In the end, then, it all came down to this: Oscar Slater arrived in Glasgow in the autumn of 1908. He was almost certainly known to the police from his previous stays. This time he was targeted on arrival and his movements observed. Then

* A Glasgow gambling establishment.

came the Gilchrist murder and, for the police, the happy coincidence of the brooch. That was all the pretext they needed to identify, pursue, and arrest Slater. When their case proved weak, police and prosecutors shored it up with dubious eyewitness statements, suborned perjury, withheld exculpatory evidence, and all the inflammatory illogic that the criminological method allows. At trial, the judge told the jury that Slater "has not the presumption of innocence in his favour . . . of the ordinary man"—branding him an outlaw in all but name.

The case, a capstone to a century "virtually hypnotized by class," as the historian Peter Gay has written, turned out to be about class in both senses of the word: it centered not only on Slater's threadbare background but also on the set of damning, classifying labels that the majority culture had long affixed to him. It would fall to Conan Doyle to bring to the case the criminalistic approach it badly needed. It was this approach—scientific, rationalist, exquisitely abductive—that would ultimately redeem Slater, one of the most convenient "convenient Others" of his age.

# BOOK THREE

---

# GRANITE

## Chapter 9

# THE TRAP DOOR

AT 10:00 A.M. ON MAY 3, 1909, SLATER'S TRIAL OPENED in Edinburgh at the High Court of Justiciary, Scotland's highest criminal court. The presiding judge was the Hon. Lord Charles John Guthrie. On his right in the Georgian courtroom sat the jury of fifteen men, among them a warehouseman, a retired farmer, a clerk, a tinsmith, and a watchmaker. On Lord Guthrie's left was the witness box; in front of him were the tables for the Crown counsel and the defense.*

The Crown's chief prosecutor, known as the Lord Advocate, was Alexander Ure, assisted by two deputies. His table was laden with exhibits, known in Scottish law as "productions." The Crown planned to introduce sixty-nine of them, including Miss Gilchrist's workbox, Slater's pawn ticket, his raincoat, the hammer, and a set of his calling cards printed with the pseudonym "A. Anderson."

At the defense table were Slater's barrister, Alexander McClure; his assistant, John Mair; and the solicitor, Ewing

* We know the physical arrangement of the room because cameras were allowed in British courts until the 1920s.

Speirs. Behind the tables was the dock in which the defendant (who is known in Scottish courts as the "panel" or "pannell") would sit; behind the dock was the gallery, packed with journalists and the curious public. Over the coming four-day trial, Lord Guthrie, through reflexive Victorian censure, and Ure, through malign advertence, would do more than anyone except perhaps the procurator fiscal, James Hart, to ensure Slater's conviction. By virtue of his ineffectual representation, McClure, the defense counsel, would do almost as much.

Escorted from his basement cell by two policemen, Slater entered the courtroom—or rather he seemed to glide upward, "like a pantomime genie," as one writer has put it, through a trap door in the floor. It was an eerie harbinger in reverse of what might happen on the scaffold.

THE CASE AGAINST SLATER was deeply flawed. The brooch clue had long since broken down. So had the scenario of his supposed flight from justice. Nor could the Crown, even after tireless investigation, demonstrate a single link between Oscar Slater and Marion Gilchrist. But the crime was a newspaper sensation, and the police had the onus of solving it. By chance, fortune had delivered them a more than suitable suspect. To build an artificial case against Slater, then, witness identification would have to shoulder the burden, as it had at the extradition proceedings.

"Evidence of this kind might be of some value if supplementary to some strong ascertained fact," Conan Doyle would point out. "But to attempt to build upon such an identification alone is to construct the whole case upon shifting sand."

The prosecution's case would take up the first two and a half days. Unlike their English and American counterparts, Scottish trials have no opening statements by counsel, instead cutting straight to the examination of witnesses. The Crown planned to present ninety-eight of them, who besides Lambie, Barrowman, Arthur Adams, and various law officers included a spate of neighbors who claimed to have seen the "watcher"; Allan McLean, the bicycle dealer who had led the police to Slater; forensic experts; a Glasgow subway clerk; and Hart, the procurator fiscal. The defense had just thirteen names on its witness list.

Testifying for the Crown, Glasgow detectives glossed over their initial reason for suspecting Slater. "It is one of the new points against the police," a period article in the *Empire News* said, "that the Jury was entirely misled at the trial as to the nature of the originating cause of the arrest of Slater. . . . As little as possible, apparently, was said about the brooch clue. . . . The Lord Advocate told the Jury that the description furnished by [the] eye-witness, Barrowman, had been so accurate it had enabled the police to trace the prisoner."

The undisputed star of day one was Lambie, last to enter the box. "Helen Lambie's evidence had greatly stiffened during the three months between the New York and the Edinburgh proceedings," Conan Doyle would write. "In so aggressively positive a frame of mind was she on the later occasion, that, on being shown Slater's overcoat and asked if it resembled the murderer's, she answered twice over: 'That is the coat,' although it had not yet been unrolled."

Lambie's testimony had stiffened in other ways. On the night of the murder, she told the police that she hadn't seen the intruder's face. Later, in New York, she said she recognized Slater by his walk, as well as by his height and hair color. Now, cross-examined by Slater's lawyer McClure, she cemented her identification even more firmly:

Q. Was it only his walk and his height and dark hair?
A. Yes, and the side of his face . . .
Q. You have told us to-day that you recognised him by his face?
A. The side of his face.
Q. I will read the question again that was put in America, "Now, will you describe, please, this man that you saw on that night that passed you at that doorway, the height if you can tell, the clothes if you can tell, or such other description of him that would in any way identify him to anybody else?" and your answer is, "The clothes that he had on that night he has not got on to-day, but his face I could not tell"—did you say that?
A. Not the broad face, but the side.
Q. The Commissioner said, "What did you say about his face?" and your answer is, "I could not tell his face; I never saw his face." Now, when you said these things in America and stated on two different occasions that you never saw his face, why do you go back upon that now and say that you saw the man's face and recognised him?
A. I did see his face. . . .
Q. Why did you say "I could not tell his face; I never saw his face"?
A. I did not see the broad face. He held down his head, and it was only the side of his face. . . .
Q. What are you going on now?

A. I am going on his face now.

There was a reason for Lambie's newly acquired certainty about Slater's face, though it would not be widely known for years.

THE CROWN'S CASE CONTINUED the next day and was if anything even more damning. Testifying was Mary Barrowman, who, like Lambie, was more certain than ever of Slater's guilt. Shown a black felt hat taken from his luggage, she identified it as the Donegal cap that the intruder had worn on the night of the murder. (The hat presented to her was no Donegal cap.)

Cross-examined about her New York testimony, Barrowman disclosed the following:

Q. You were shown a photograph at Mr. Fox's office before you went to the Court?
A. Yes.
Q. How many photographs?
A. Three . . .
Q. Now, as soon as you saw the photographs, did you recognise the man?
A. Yes . . .
Q. You recognised the photographs at once?
A. One of them.
Q. Then when you went down to the Court were you looking for a man who was like the photograph?
A. Yes.

Barrowman's courtroom testimony differed markedly from her original statement to the police. This time, she took pains to say that the man running from the scene had bumped into her as he fled and had done so directly under a streetlamp—two points she hadn't mentioned initially. Those things, she now said, let her scrutinize him minutely as he tore down the street.

Also testifying on day two was Arthur Adams. Characteristically moderate, he said only that Slater was a man "closely resembling" the intruder. He added: "It is too serious a charge for me to say from a passing glance."

A third Crown witness was Annie Armour, a ticket clerk in the Glasgow subway.* She testified that on the night of the murder, she was on duty behind the window at the Kelvinbridge station, not far from Miss Gilchrist's home. At about 7:45—more than half an hour after the crime—she saw a dark-haired man come tearing into the station. The man, who wore a light overcoat, flung down a penny for his fare and, without stopping to collect the proffered ticket, dashed for the stairway leading to the platform. She did not notice any blood on his clothing. Two months later, at Glasgow's Central Police Station, Armour identified Slater as having been that man. It did not hurt that she, too, had been shown Slater's photograph.

To account for the unnatural length of time it had apparently taken Slater to walk from Miss Gilchrist's house to the Kelvinbridge station (normally a journey of about seven minutes), Ure, the prosecutor, asserted that he had spent the intervening half hour weaving up and down side streets, to put police off the scent, before entering the subway.

* Unlike in England, where "subway" refers to an underground pedestrian passage and "underground" to a subterranean metro line, the word "subway" in Scotland, as in the United States, denotes the metro. Glasgow's subway system, the world's third-oldest after the London Underground and the Budapest Metro, opened in 1896.

The last major Crown witness on day two was the forensic pathologist John Glaister. A Glasgow University faculty member, Glaister was professor of medical jurisprudence, the field at the nexus of medicine and the law that is today known as forensic medicine. At the Crown's request, he had examined the crime scene, led the autopsy of Miss Gilchrist's body, and conducted forensic examinations of Slater's hammer, raincoat, and other belongings.

Glaister, born in 1856, was something of a legend in Scottish criminal courts. "Over his 33 years as a medical jurist he developed his innate sense of theatre which both served the purpose of the prosecuting counsel and endeared Glaister to press and public," two historians have put it. "Smoking thick black cheroots incessantly, he gave an impression of immense energy. In old age his hawk-like features, shiny bald head, vigorous moustache and small 'imperial' beard, together with his idiosyncratic retention of the Victorian style of silk hat, frock coat and wide Gladstonian collar, made him an unmistakable figure. . . . Like other great medical detectives, Glaister believed himself completely impartial in his evidence, but his reputation and sharp repartee had an obvious power to diminish the defence's case."

Taking the witness box, Glaister read the autopsy report into the record. "The body was that of a well-nourished elderly woman," it said, continuing:

> The following marks of violence were seen externally: Generally speaking, the face and head were both badly smashed. . . . Several fractures of the lower jaw, upper jaw, and cheek bones were found, the bones being driven into the mouth. . . . On deeper examination it was found that the bones of the orbit, the nose, and the forehead were completely smashed in and broken into many pieces. . . .

> The entire hair of the scalp, which was grayish at the roots, was, with the scalp itself, saturated and covered with blood. . . .
>
> On removal of the brain it was found that the skull was fractured through its base, extending from the front right to the back. . . . On dissecting [the chest] cavity, it was found that the breast bone had been fractured completely through its entire thickness. . . . On the right side of the chest in front, fractures of the third, fourth, fifth, and sixth ribs were found, the third rib being broken in three different places. . . .
>
> From the foregoing examination we are of the opinion . . . that the said injuries were produced by forcible contact with a blunt weapon, and that the violence was applied with considerable force.

Glaister went on to state confidently that Slater's eight-ounce hammer could have caused those injuries. "I did not find in the dining-room," he said, "any implement which looked as if it had been used for the purpose of murdering Miss Gilchrist," a statement that conspicuously overlooked the heavy chair that seemed a more likely weapon.

On Slater's raincoat, Glaister identified twenty-five stains, most brownish red. Microscopic examination, he said, showed that some contained red corpuscles resembling those of mammalian blood. But in so small a sample, tests of the period could not distinguish between human blood and that of any other mammal. Though Glaister did not acknowledge the fact, the stains on Slater's coat could have been, in the words of Charles Dickens in *A Christmas Carol*, "more of gravy than of grave."

The defense would put on its own medical expert, but by then Glaister's testimony had almost certainly done its work.

"In the absence of more definite proof, the medical evidence should have counted for very little," the historians have written. "But in the hysterical atmosphere surrounding the trial, Glaister's air of certainty doubtless influenced the jury." They added: "The case later provided . . . substantial instruction to police cadets in Glasgow as an example of how not to conduct a murder inquiry."

DAY THREE SAW THE last Crown witnesses. Among them was McLean, the bicycle dealer, who recounted Slater's efforts to sell his pawn ticket. Midway through the day the Crown rested its case, though it would do worse to Slater before the trial was over.

Throughout the prosecution's case, Slater's lawyer, McClure, had seemed well intentioned but weak. On day two, cross-examining Superintendent John Ord, he did get him to admit that the brooch clue had proved worthless:

Q. Did you find out that the crescent brooch which Slater was endeavouring to sell . . . was one which had been in pawn originally in the month of November?
A. Yes . . .
Q. Was it the coincidence in the date, 21st December, of the last advance upon this brooch that made you think it might be Miss Gilchrist's brooch?
A. Most assuredly that had some bearing on the case.
Q. Did you discover immediately that this was not the brooch at all?
A. *We knew that morning.*

But for reasons known only to him, McClure failed to ask the essential follow-up question: Why, when the clue collapsed, did police pursue Slater anyway? His examination of other Crown witnesses was also lackluster. He did not probe the inconsistencies in Lambie's and Barrowman's testimony, nor press Glaister on the question of how a small hammer could have caused Miss Gilchrist's devastating injuries, nor ask the police to account for the fact that Slater's fingerprints were found nowhere in her flat.

"McClure would have scored heavily if he had merely tabulated some of the lunacies of which Slater was guilty, supposing that he was the murderer," Hunt has written. "This admittedly intelligent man is supposed to have got rid of the clothes in which he was watching the house, whilst retaining those in which he murdered the old lady, together with the murder weapon. Once inside the house he did not leave the door open anywhere for a quick escape, wasted time murdering its occupant when all he wanted was her jewels, . . . ran away from the house in a direction entirely opposite to his nearest point of safety, and then (without changing his clothes) walked out into the streets. . . . Then, when the hue-and-cry for the murderer was on, he walked all over Glasgow, just as usual, making no attempt to conceal his movements." But McClure invoked none of these things.

Nor could McClure protect his own witnesses from the Crown's suggestive cross-examination. Testifying for the defense, Slater's friend Hugh Cameron replied this way when cross-examined by Ure, the Lord Advocate:

Q. When you first knew him in 1901 what was the name he went by?
A. Oscar Slater . . .

Q. After you became acquainted with him did you become aware what he was?
A. He was a gambler.
Q. Anything more?
A. Yes, I had it that the man, like a great number of those who came to Glasgow, lived on the proceeds of women.
Q. Did you not know from the first that his mode of living was on the proceeds of women's prostitution?
A. I cannot say that I knew from the first.*

As in New York, Slater was advised by counsel not to testify on his own behalf. At issue were his uncertain English and heavy accent; of even greater concern were the profound ways in which he discomforted middle-class British society. "The treasured and conspicuous emblems of this civilized style were good manners at the table, a piano in the parlor, a well-thumbed library, concert tickets and museum visits, a program to help others help themselves, and the public subscription to a favorite charity," Peter Gay has written, describing the late Victorian bourgeoisie. "Naturally, temperance in all its meanings figured prominently in this idealized self-portrait."

To post-Victorian sensibilities, Slater's foreignness, his Jewishness, and his intemperate livelihood were disturbing enough. But what may have rattled the public even more was that in a period still highly dependent on social signifiers, Slater was unsettlingly beyond category. To outward appearances he was a

* At this point, as the historian Ben Braber has pointed out, the judge, Lord Guthrie, should have instructed the jury to disregard evidence about Slater's character, as it was irrelevant to the crime with which he had been charged. Not only did Lord Guthrie fail to do so, but in his own subsequent charge to the jury, he drove the point about Slater's alleged pimping home even further.

superlatively well-tailored man of leisure, yet he was no gentleman. For all his alleged debauchery, he had seemed, until the murder case against him, neither desperate nor depressed—he appeared, in fact, almost constitutionally cheerful. Slater's entire mien (one to which, by the prevailing mores of the time, he was not remotely entitled) confounded the protective ease with which social diagnoses were traditionally made.

Testifying for the defense, Schmalz and Antoine added to the discomfort. Taking the witness box, Schmalz stated that Slater was dining at home at the time of the murder. Cross-examined by Ure, however, she disclosed information that was bound to cause the jury immense disquiet:

Q. Who engaged you?
A. Madame Junio.
Q. Was she living then at 45 Newman Street, London?
A. Yes.
Q. She received gentlemen there?
A. Yes.
Q. And among the gentlemen was Oscar Slater one?
A. Yes.
Q. Did he come oftener than the other gentlemen did?
A. Yes.
Q. Did he sometimes live there?
A. He stayed sometimes there. . . .
Q. Stayed there as the husband of Madame Junio?
A. Yes . . .
Q. When you came to Glasgow, to 69 St. George's Road . . . did anybody come to the house at all except Madame and Slater himself?
A. Yes, friends of Madame came.
Q. Gentlemen in the evening?

A. Yes.
Q. And did Madame go to the Empire and Palace Music Halls?
A. Yes . . .
Q. What did Slater do during the day?
A. He went out sometimes in the morning and in the afternoon—I do not know what he did.
Q. So far as you know, he did no business?
A. Not so far as I know.

Antoine's turn in the box only made things worse. The Victorian ideal of the woman as the "angel in the house"—articulated in Coventry Patmore's effusive 1854 poem of that name—was still held dear in the early twentieth century. This domestic angel came in two varieties: virginal (the virtuous daughter) and maternal (the doting, asexual wife and mother). Antoine was conspicuously neither. Even her avowed profession, music-hall singer, was shameful enough. "The public careers of actresses, singers, and dancers were considered almost by definition to connote sexual promiscuity," the scholar Rosemary Jann has written. "The expression 'a young person of the theater' . . . was a euphemism for a prostitute."*

Antoine, too, alibied Slater as having been home at the time of the murder. But by the time she took the witness box, Schmalz had told the court about her stream of gentleman callers. Between them, the two women managed to trigger the full spectrum of late Victorian unease: over class, over sex, over foreignness, and perhaps above all over knowing—or rather *not*

* When Holmes, in the 1891 tale "A Scandal in Bohemia," describes the actress Irene Adler—the only woman who ever truly bewitched him—as "this young person," Conan Doyle could be assured that his readers knew precisely what those words telegraphed.

knowing—one's place in the rigorous social order of the day. Offered the chance to cross-examine Antoine, the Lord Advocate replied simply, "I have no questions to ask," a clear indication that as far as the prosecution was concerned, she had already been remarkably effective.

Besides Slater, conspicuously absent from the box were several people whose testimony could have helped him. They included Dr. John Adams, the first medical man at the crime scene, who was not on the witness list for either side. As a result, the jury never heard his conclusion that Miss Gilchrist had been bludgeoned to death by the chair. Writing to Conan Doyle in 1927, William Park said that Slater's most recent legal team had "never heard of a case where the Doctor first on the scene was rejected by the Crown."

Also not on anyone's list was a Glasgow man named Duncan MacBrayne. A greengrocer in Slater's neighborhood, he knew Slater well by sight. In February 1909, MacBrayne told the police that at eight-fifteen on the night of the murder he had seen Slater calmly standing on his own doorstep. At that hour, as the Crown's case had it, Slater—after killing Miss Gilchrist, weaving frenziedly through the streets, plunging into the subway, riding to an outlying part of town, and hiding there for a time—was working his way stealthily home on foot, arriving there at about nine-thirty. The defense was never informed of MacBrayne's statement.

But the most striking omission of all was the absence of testimony from Miss Gilchrist's niece Margaret Birrell. For in an interview with the police shortly after her aunt's death—material that was never shared with the defense—she said that on the night of the murder Helen Lambie had come running to her house to say that she had seen the killer and knew exactly who he was.

## Chapter 10

## "UNTIL HE BE DEAD"

On day four, May 6, 1909, Slater's lawyer, Alexander McClure, called the last defense witnesses. There remained only the closing statements from both sides, followed by the judge's charge to the jury. As things played out, any one of these alone would have been enough to sink Slater.

Ure, the Lord Advocate, spoke first, "crushing the while his handkerchief in his clenched right hand, as though it were a symbol of the prisoner's fate," the Scottish criminologist William Roughead wrote. Speaking for nearly two hours, without notes, Ure addressed the jury with an amalgam of whichever facts best suited the drama, a cocktail of preposterous logic (anyone immoral enough to be a pimp, he implied, was immoral enough to be a murderer), plus more than a few outright untruths:

> Up to yesterday afternoon I should have thought that there was one serious difficulty which confronted you—the difficulty of conceiving that there was in existence a human being capable of doing such a dastardly deed.

> Gentlemen, that difficulty, I think, was removed yesterday afternoon [during Cameron's testimony] when we heard from the lips of one who seemingly knew the prisoner better than any one else . . . that he had followed a life which descends to the very lowest depths of human degradation, for, by the universal judgment of mankind, the man who lives upon the proceeds of prostitution has sunk to the lowest depths, and all moral sense in him has been destroyed and has ceased to exist. That difficulty removed, I say without hesitation that the man in the dock is capable of having committed this dastardly outrage.

The motive for Miss Gilchrist's murder, Ure continued, in "a house situated in a respectable and very quiet . . . street," was robbery. (The assertion glossed over the fact that apart from the brooch, nothing was taken.) "We shall see," he told the jury, "how it was that the prisoner came to know that she was possessed of these jewels." Ure never made good on that promise.

"I come now," Ure continued, "to his flight from justice":

> I say, deliberately, "His flight from justice," because I am going to demonstrate that there was one reason, and one reason only, for his leaving Glasgow at that time, and that was to escape the hands of justice. . . . It is said that a fortnight, or three weeks, or a month before he spoke of going to America. I dare say he did; I am certain he did. There is no doubt whatever he had made up his mind, as soon as the deed was accomplished, that he would not stay in this country one moment longer than was absolutely necessary. . . . I say that his flight was precipitated, and the moment fixed by the publication of his

description in the newspapers at two o'clock on the afternoon of 25th December.*

In conclusion, Ure told the jury:

> Gentlemen, I have done. . . . I do not for a moment deny that you have to-day to discharge the most serious and the most responsible duty which you will probably have to discharge during the whole course of your natural lives. On your verdict undoubtedly depends a man's life. . . . He may be, and probably is, the worst of men; but he is entitled to as fair a trial as if he was the best of men. He may be one of the most degraded of mortals, he may be a cheat, he may be a robber, a burglar, or the worst of characters, but that does not infer that he committed murder. . . . Gentlemen, he is entitled to justice, to no less than justice, but to no more than justice. My submission to you is that his guilt has been brought fairly home to him, that no shadow of doubts exists, that there is no reasonable doubt that he was the perpetrator of this foul murder.

After Ure's speech came the defense summation. Addressing the jury, McClure invoked the breakdown of the brooch clue, the conflicting descriptions of the "watcher," Lambie's mercurial evidence, and the allegations that Slater was a pimp. ("That, however," he said delicately, "is a subject we are not to go into.")

* Slater's name did not actually appear in the papers until December 26, the day he set sail on the *Lusitania*.

"Can you lay your hands on your hearts now and say that you are convinced that this is the man who committed that murder?" he asked the jurors. "If you are, then the responsibility is yours, and not mine."

McClure's address was commendable in many ways. But he failed to do two critical things: point out the inaccuracies in Ure's speech and dispel the innuendo with which Slater had been tarred. "Clarence Darrow could have done it standing on his head," Hunt wrote. "McClure was not quite the man for such a test."

The judge's charge to the jury, which came next, reached new heights of manipulative excess. Lord Guthrie was by all accounts a fair-minded jurist, but he inevitably carried the prejudices of his time, place, and class. He was from a distinguished, righteous background. His father, the Rev. Thomas Guthrie, had been a leader of the Free Church of Scotland; in the 1840s the elder Mr. Guthrie had helped found a Ragged School, devoted to educating slum children, in Edinburgh.

Lord Guthrie himself, a temperance crusader, became president of the Boys' Brigade in 1909; the organization had been founded in Victorian Glasgow to save street children from lives of crime. It is likely that he saw Slater as embodying the very evils of which he and his father had sought to rid Scotland's cities. Addressing the jury at the close of the trial, he said:*

* The excerpts from Lord Guthrie's charge to the jury quoted here are taken from the court stenographer's official transcript, long thought to have been lost. What was not known until years after Slater's trial was that in supplying a copy of his charge to William Roughead for inclusion in his *Trial of Oscar Slater,* first published in 1910 and widely understood to be an official record of the case, Lord Guthrie had significantly revised its content. (The judge's revised version made his charge, if anything, rhetorically stronger in its condemnation of Slater than the charge he actually gave.) Roughead was later able to obtain a copy of the official transcript, and the fourth edition of his book, published in 1950, reproduces both versions of Lord Guthrie's charge. The actual charge is given here.

> You have heard a good deal about [a] class of evidence—the evidence, first, of character. . . . About his character . . . there is no doubt at all. He has maintained himself by the ruin of men and on the ruin of women, and he has lived in a way that many blackguards would scorn to live. . . .
>
> I use the name "Oscar Slater." We do not know who that man is. His name is not Slater. . . . He is a mystery. . . . We do not know where he was born, where he was brought up, what he was brought up to, whether he was trained to anything.* The man remains a mystery as much as he was when this trial began. . . . A man of that kind has not the presumption of innocence in his favour which is . . . a reality in the case of the ordinary man. . . .
>
> Mr. McClure spoke of his witnesses being a credible body of witnesses. You have seen them. You know their occupation, you know how Antoine's fate is bound up with the prisoner's in the past and will be in the future, you know what kind of person the servant is, and in what employment she has been, and it is for you to say whether it is a credible body of evidence or not. . . .
>
> Gentlemen, the case is entirely in your hands. . . . If you think there is no reasonable doubt about it, then you will do your duty and convict him; if you think there is, then you will acquit him.

THE JURY RETIRED AT 4:55 p.m. Scottish criminal cases may be decided by majority verdict, and jurors have three verdicts from which to choose: "guilty," "not guilty," and "not proven," a

* By the time of Slater's trial, all of these facts had been reported in the Scottish press.

verdict that in the sardonic parlance of Scottish lawyers is said to mean "not guilty, and don't do it again." The three-verdict system, the permissibility of a majority vote, and the odd number of jurors—fifteen—were mechanisms instituted centuries ago to preempt hung juries.

At 6:05, the jury reentered the courtroom. It returned a verdict of nine guilty votes, one not guilty, and five not proven—enough to condemn Slater.* After the verdict was read aloud, there came an outburst that William Roughead, who was present, described as the most painful utterance he had ever heard:

"My lord," Slater cried, "may I say one word? Will you allow me to speak?"

"Sit down just now," Lord Guthrie admonished him.

"My lord," Slater persisted, "my father and mother are poor old people. I came on my own account to this country. I came over to defend my right. I know nothing about the affair. You are convicting an innocent man."

Addressing McClure, the judge said: "I think you ought to advise the prisoner to reserve anything he has got to say for the Crown authorities. If he insists on it, I shall not prevent him now—will you see what he says?"

"My lord," Slater continued, "what shall I say? I came over from America, knowing nothing of the affair, to Scotland to get a fair judgment. I know nothing about the affair, absolutely nothing. I never heard the name. I know nothing about the affair. I do not know how I could be connected with the affair. I know nothing about it. I came from America on my own account. I can say no more."

Slater fell silent, and Lord Guthrie donned the traditional

* Had the case been heard in England, the divided jury would have guaranteed Slater a new trial.

black cap to pronounce sentence: "The said Oscar Slater to be carried from the Prison of Edinburgh, thence to be forthwith transmitted to the Prison of Glasgow, therein to be detained till the twenty-seventh day of May, nineteen hundred and nine, and upon that day between the hours of eight and ten o'clock forenoon, within the walls of the said Prison of Glasgow, by the hands of the common executioner, to be hanged by the neck upon a gibbet until he be dead, and his body thereafter to be buried within the walls of the said Prison of Glasgow."

The trap door opened, and Slater descended. As a result of his outburst, William Park wrote, an act was passed not long afterward "whereby a prisoner, once the verdict is announced, may be hustled downstairs to the cells without the interval of waiting for it to be recorded and signed."

Slater was consigned to Duke Street Prison to wait out the twenty-one days he had left to be alive. With no criminal appeals court in Scotland, his sentence seemed incontestable. But as the execution drew near, public hostility toward him was replaced by a growing disquiet. "During the trial Glasgow had been living through an atmosphere like that of Salem," Conan Doyle's biographer Pierre Nordon has written. "With the verdict, the fever subsided; a vague shame felt by some, and a conviction that Slater was innocent on the part of fewer still, combined to create a wave not exactly of sympathy but of tolerance towards the prisoner."

On May 17, Slater's solicitor, Ewing Speirs, drew up a formal entreaty to John Sinclair, the Secretary for Scotland, requesting the commutation of Slater's death sentence.* His entreaty, a document known in Scottish law as a memorial, was a model of

* The Secretary for Scotland (known from 1926 on as the Secretary of State for Scotland) was the senior British government minister in charge of Scottish affairs.

legal argument, reprising the case against Slater in all its flaws. It included a cogent explanation of why Slater himself did not testify:

> The Memorialist thinks it is only fair to [the] prisoner to point out that he was all along anxious to give evidence on his own behalf. He was advised by his Counsel not to do so, but not from any knowledge of guilt. He had undergone the strain of four days' trial. He speaks rather broken English—although quite intelligibly—with a foreign accent. . . . Your Memorialist, who has all along acted as Slater's Solicitor since he was brought back from America . . . begs respectfully to state his absolute belief in Slater's innocence. . . .
>
> May it therefore please the Right Honourable the Secretary . . . to take this Memorial into his most favourable consideration, and thereafter to advise His Most Gracious Majesty to exercise his royal prerogative to the effect of commuting the sentence passed upon the prisoner.

The memorial was accompanied by a public petition on Slater's behalf, signed by more than twenty thousand people.

Crown authorities, meanwhile, resolute in the belief that they had convicted the right man, parceled out the £200 reward offered for information leading to the arrest and conviction of Miss Gilchrist's killer. Mary Barrowman received half, very likely a year's income for her family, with the balance divided among several other witnesses.

The Crown was also busy arranging Slater's execution. The gallows, which had been on loan to Inverness for a hanging there, arrived at Duke Street and were erected near his cell. An inveterate tinkerer, Slater, "somewhat to the astonishment of his warders," Hunt wrote, "took a technical interest in the intricacies of 'the drop.'"

On May 25, 1909, forty-eight hours before Slater was to be hanged—he had just arranged to be buried with a photograph of his parents—Secretary Sinclair, on authorization from King Edward VII, commuted his sentence to life at hard labor. "It was a curious compromise," a British journalist later wrote. "Slater was held to be too guilty to be released, yet not guilty enough to be hanged."

Slater was told of the reprieve by a prison guard, who, in a memorable act of kindness, slipped him some candy. "Should you visit Duke Street Prison again," Slater would write from Peterhead to Reverend Phillips of Glasgow, "please inform this good old man Gov that the officer who gave me 3 pieces of sweets in the condemned cell after I was reprieved, shall have 3 pieces of gold for it, when I am free."

That day would not come for almost twenty years.

## Chapter 11

## THE COLD CRUEL SEA

*Through my small window I can see the north-sea. We call it here German Sea, and all day I dream of olden times.*

—Oscar Slater, in a letter to his parents, 1914

PETERHEAD PRISON WAS BORN OF THE VIOLENT NORTH Sea outside its doors. By the late nineteenth century, the port of Peterhead had become a major center for whaling, a lucrative enterprise that sent oil, meat, and bone round the world. But the storm-tossed sea posed a perennial danger to the whalers and their crews, and to Peterhead's fleet of small fishing vessels. Conan Doyle himself described the lashing he and his shipmates took in 1880 aboard the Arctic whaler *Hope:*

> It was, I find by my log, on February 28th at 2 p.m. that we sailed from Peterhead, amid a great crowd and uproar. . . . We ran straight into bad weather and the glass went down at one time to 28.375, which is the lowest reading I can remember in all my ocean wanderings. We just got in

> to Lerwick Harbour* before the full force of the hurricane broke, which was so great that lying at anchor . . . we were blown over to an acute angle. If it had taken us a few hours earlier we should certainly have lost our boats—and the boats are the life of a whaler. It was March 11 before the weather moderated enough to let us get on, and by that time there were twenty whalers in the bay.

What was needed, Peterhead's town fathers had concluded by the mid-1880s, was a vast breakwater, built from native granite, to tame the savage sea. The brutal work of hewing the stone and erecting the breakwater could be given to convicts. That there was no prison in the area was no impediment: the town would simply build one, ensuring a perennial supply of captive labor.

A looming fortification known during the reign of Queen Victoria as Her Majesty's Prison Peterhead, the penitentiary opened in 1888. "We are always being told that the treatment in the Scottish prisons is very just, so that no further evil can happen to you," Slater's mother would write to him hopefully in 1910. She was only partly correct.

If the turn of the twentieth century was a pivotal time in British criminology, it was also an era of transition in penology. The nineteenth century had viewed criminals as incorrigibles, and as a result incarceration was a thoroughly punitive affair, with isolation, hard labor, and meager rations the wide standard. The new century saw the rise of a more progressive approach, with the nation's most enlightened prison governors, as the chief wardens are known, treating prison as a place of rehabilitation. To a degree, Peterhead embodied this divide: it had a library and at least a few social activities, including the debating

* The main port of Scotland's Shetland Islands, about 180 miles north of Peterhead.

society at which Slater would pass his covert message to William Gordon. But it remained overwhelmingly a place of spartan brutality, home to some of Scotland's most notorious convicts. "I would rather be immediately put to death than condemned to a life sentence in Peterhead," the Scottish revolutionary socialist John MacLean, who was incarcerated there more than once, said in 1918.

The original prison building housed some two hundred men, one to a cell. Each cell measured roughly four feet by eight feet, with the ceiling less than seven feet high—"just a little box," MacLean wrote. The only furniture in each cell was a sleeping hammock, secured to two walls, and a narrow, wood-topped iron table that folded down from one wall. In each cell was a single window, eighteen inches square and heavily barred.

"Each cell is heated by warmed air from the hall," MacLean, who had been imprisoned at Peterhead for sedition, wrote:

> The air in the hall is heated by American stoves burning coal, and enters the cell by two slits or openings at the foot of the door. Most cells are very cold in winter as the method of heating is of no use, and to wrap oneself round with blankets is a crime the governor can punish by sending a man to the "separate" cells, each more miserable than the others. Of course, anything can be made a crime, and by nagging and threatening to bring men before the governor the warders are able to make their charges' lives unbearable. The purpose is to break up the men's nervous system, and veritable wrecks are made of many.

An essay by Gerald Newman, another convict of the period, further describes Peterhead life: "The endless dreary days spent in the Quarries, the harsh treatment, the coarse & badly served food, the punishment of dark cells & bread & water. . . . The freezing winter nights in a cell in which not one particle of heat can enter, the blazing summer sun striking down upon your head in the dry & dusty quarry, where the very chisel & mallet you are working with seem to burn your very hands & the glare of the sun scorches your very eyes."

In MacLean's time, a prisoner's uniform consisted of a pair of stout boots, moleskin knickers, woolen stockings, shirt, waistcoat, and vest. For outdoor work in winter, there was a jacket of dense brown wool and a pair of mittens. Convicts' hair, cut twice a month, was kept closely cropped by the prison barber; a tam of thick brown wool, like that of the jacket, kept the head warm. Each man's underclothing, MacLean wrote, with no apparent irony, was "kept clean and sanitary by being washed once a fortnight."

Prison warders were also specially accoutered. Because many inmates had to leave Peterhead to perform their labor, the guards who supervised them were heavily armed. From the prison's earliest days through the late 1930s, each guard was issued a cutlass; until the late 1950s, some also carried rifles. "The blades were no ornamental comic opera pieces of weaponry," the Scottish journalist Robert Jeffrey has written. "To an unarmed man a crack across the chest with a sword blade was a considerable disincentive to misbehaviour, and the warders knew it."

It was into this setting, 180 miles northeast of Glasgow, that Oscar Slater was transported on July 8, 1909. He would be known for the next eighteen and a half years as Prisoner 1992.

SLATER'S PRISON INTAKE SHEET, filled out for Peterhead officials by Detective Superintendent Ord, encapsulates much of the cultural bias that had caused him to be where he was in the first place:

> NAME AND ALIASES: Oscar Slater, alias Otto Sands [*sic*], alias Oscar Leschziner . . .
>
> CHARACTER AS REGARDS HONESTY: Is a Gambler and a resetter of stolen property.
>
> CHARACTER AS REGARDS INDUSTRY: Follows no lawful occupation.
>
> CHARACTER AS REGARDS SOBRIETY: Is temperate in his habits.
>
> MEANS OF LIVELIHOOD: Gambling and living on the immoral earnings of prostitutes. He is also a reputed thief and resetter.
>
> CLASS OF LIFE: Low. A thorough blackguard. Cannot be said to have a single good quality.
>
> OCCUPATION: No lawful occupation . . .
>
> CHARACTER OF FRIENDS AND ASSOCIATES: Thieves, Resetters, Gamblers, Prostitutes, Blackmailers. (With the exception of his parents who are comparatively respectable.)
>
> NAMES AND ADDRESSES OF ANY *RESPECTABLE* PERSONS WHO CAN GIVE *TRUSTWORTHY INFORMATION ON THE FOREGOING POINTS:* . . . Detective Superintendent John Ord and Detective Inspector Pyper, Criminal Investigation Department, Glasgow.

At five each morning, inmates awoke to the clang of the prison bell. At five-thirty, each man got porridge and skim milk in his cell. At seven, they were herded outside to the prison yard, where each was searched before joining his work party. Slater was assigned to the quarry, "to break great granite blocks

Helen Lambie in 1909.
"This woman," one of Slater's supporters declared, "holds the secret."

GLASGOW CITY COUNCIL: ARCHIVES; TD1560/6/23

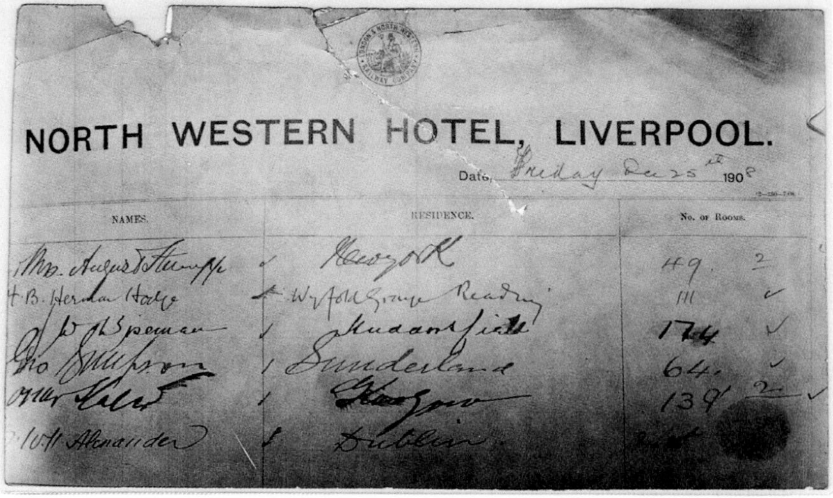


TOP: This torn paper wrapper, addressed "Oscar Slater, Esq., c/o A. Anderson," first put the police on Slater's trail.

NATIONAL RECORDS OF SCOTLAND, JC34/1/32/12

BOTTOM: Hotel register signed on the penultimate line "Oscar Slater, Glasgow"

NATIONAL RECORDS OF SCOTLAND, JC34/1/32/43

New York.
Centre Street
Tombs
2/2. 1909

No 53.

Dear friend Cameron!

To day it is nearly 5 Weeks- I am kept here in Prison for the Glasgow murder.
I am very down hearted my dear Cameron to know that my friends in Glasgow like Gordon Henderson can tell such liars about me to the Glasgow Police. I have seen here his Statement he made in Glasgow, telling the police that a German came up to him and has told him Oscar Slater has comitted the murder, also that I have been on the night of the murder in his place asking him for mony I was very excited and in hurry.
I dont think it was very clever from him, because he like to make himselfs a good Name by the Police to tell such liars-
I dont deny I have been in his place asking him for mony because I went broke in the Sloper Club. Only I will

Slater's 1909 letter from the Tombs in New York to a Glasgow friend, Hugh Cameron. Cameron immediately showed this letter to the police.

NATIONAL RECORDS OF SCOTLAND JC34/1/32/16

TOP: Mary Barrowman, with her parents, arrives to testify at Slater's trial.

© CSG CIC GLASGOW MUSEUMS AND LIBRARIES COLLECTION: THE MITCHELL LIBRARY, SPECIAL COLLECTIONS

BOTTOM: The trial of Oscar Slater. Slater is visible seated in the dock, just left of center, between two policemen.

WILLIAM ROUGHEAD, *TRIAL OF OSCAR SLATER* (1910)

In case of Oscar Slater – Sentenced to Death at High
Ct Edin 6/5/09 for murder of Miss Gilchrist W. Princes St / 5

H.M. Duke Street Prison Glasgow

7th May 1909

May 7th 4.10 pm — I took charge of prisoner No 942 Oscar Slater under sentence
of death at 4.10. He appeared to be very upset and he made the
remark wishing he was dead. J. Marshall

I relieved Wr. Marshall at 5.0 P.M. & found prisoner
sitting in a chair crying. prisoner afterwards sat &
talked about his case & seemed to be more composed
at 5.30 supper, which consisted of tea. 3 slice of
toast & 1 egg, was served. prisoner seemed to enjoy
his supper leaving only a portion of the bread
Visited by the Governor at 6.50. who gave pris
a telegram & some cigarettes prisoner who
was now in very good spirits sat smoking
& talking about his experience in Edinburgh
At 7.40 prisoner made down his bed & went
to bed at 7.55. I was relieved by Wrs. J. Geekie
& J. Stevenson

Thos. McCrorie

We relieved Wr. T. McCrorie at 8 P.M. and found
prisoner in bed but not asleep, he fell asleep at
8th — 8.20. Visited by Governor at 9.50. Prisoner awoke
at 1.30 A.M. and asked what time it was, and also
passed the remark that he had slept better and felt
much better than he did the previous night, he then
lay and talked about his case, and then went
to sleep again. At 2.45, Prisoner sat up in bed
and asked where Prisoners, that got Sentences of
Penal Servitude went to, and how far it was from
Glasgow. At 3.15, Prisoner sat up in bed, crying for
his Father & Mother, he afterwards got more composed, and
asked for a drink of water, and then lay down again
At 5 A.M. Prisoner asked if he would still be allowed

Warders' log, Duke Street Prison, Glasgow, 1909, shortly after Slater had been sentenced to death. "He appeared to be very upset and he made the remark wishing he was dead," an entry from May 7 reads.

NATIONAL RECORDS OF SCOTLAND, HH12/11

TOP: Under guard, a work party leaves Peterhead Prison, mid-1930s.

BOTTOM: The prison train hauled granite, hewn by convicts, from a nearby quarry.

BOTH: PETERHEAD PRISON MUSEUM

Before and after: Oscar Slater (top) on his admission to Peterhead Prison in 1909 and (bottom) on his release in 1927

BOTH: NATIONAL RECORDS OF SCOTLAND, HH15/20/1/6

Arthur Conan Doyle with his father,
Charles Altamont Doyle, 1860s

ARTHUR CONAN DOYLE COLLECTION—LANCELYN GREEN BEQUEST,
PORTSMOUTH CITY COUNCIL

(hard like iron) with a tremendous heavy hammer," as he would write. They were destined for a new prison building.

A stark narrative of his life at hard labor can be found in a newspaper article written by William Gordon after his release in 1925. In it, Gordon, who early that year had carried Slater's plea to Conan Doyle in his mouth, described working beside him in the quarry. His prose was doubtless polished by editors, but the account is evocative nonetheless.

"He was a quiet, well-spoken man, and I took an instinctive liking to him," Gordon wrote. "Each man working in the quarries—in that particular party—had to drill 30 holes in a day: 30 holes over a foot deep in solid blocks of granite. It is a hard day's work when you are accustomed to it. . . . Slater and I worked side by side in the quarries day after day for months on end."

At eleven-thirty, the convicts reassembled in the yard, where each was searched before being returned to his cell for lunch, which consisted, MacLean wrote, of "a pint of broth, seven oz. of beef, six oz. of bread with variations as to potatoes, cheese, etc." At one in the afternoon, they went back to work, returning at five, when "14 oz of dry bread and a pint of coffee was served out (less since 1917)." The men could read in their cells until lights-out at eight-thirty. The sleeping hammock could be used only between 8:30 p.m. and 5:00 a.m. without medical dispensation.

This regimen was broken only by mail from home, for Slater a tangible lifeline across the sea. "My innocent Oscar," his mother, Pauline, wrote in one of her earliest letters to him, "I can send you the joyful assurance that we are not sitting idle with our hands in our laps. . . . God keep you in health, don't lose courage, innocent of my heart. The sun will yet bring all to the light of day. The warmest kisses from your Mother who loves you with her last breath."

Some time afterward, Slater wrote: "In your last letter you ask me, dearest mother, if I can retain your letters. Yes, I can do this; still this does not assist me to remember what answer I have sent to your letters, not being allowed to keep a copy [of the replies], however we will not worry over this, and if I should sometimes repeat myself I am sure you will excuse me. . . . Your letters, dear mother, I have pasted together like a prayer book, and when my thoughts, as they often do, wander across to my dear home, I read your letters over again and find great consolation. . . . I also, dear father, endeavor with all my might to keep bright, and the humourous way of my dear mother helps me greatly."

The letters from the Leschziners, most written by Pauline in the early years, are filled with homey evocations of the family circle ("You need not get anxious my child if you do not see father's handwriting; he is still fond of his dominoes, but he has asked me specially to leave him some space as he intends to add his greeting") and portraits of village life: "You would hardly know Beuthen, so many changes have taken place during the last few years," Pauline wrote. "There are only a few houses left that do not have electric light now." (From Slater: "Electric light is very convenient, especially for elderly people. You must consider this.")

There was also quotidian gossip ("Yes! It is quite correct Mrs. Lechtenstein has a big wart with long hair on her face") and, above all, deep, spiritual affirmations of support. "You were always a good child, and why should you not extend the same affection towards us in your days of misfortune, which, after all, is all that we can exchange," his mother wrote. She continued:

> *With you my dear child I begin the day, and you are never out of my thoughts. I count the days when I again may look*

*for a letter from you. I often dream about you and picture you as a free being possessed with plenty of the good things of this world.*

*Would to God it were true. . . . Yes, dearest Oscar, one gets accustomed to everything.*

*We have reconciled ourselves to your misfortune and are happy when we know that you are well. . . . My only wish is that that Almighty might bring us together if only for a quarter of an hour before our days in this life are to come to an end. . . .*

*All the other friends and relations make constant enquiries about you. . . . Aunt Eva sends special regards. . . . I do my best to make ends meet by letting some of our rooms.*

Alas, such letters were not something on which Slater could depend. Convicts' mail in both directions was rigorously monitored, and inmates could send and receive mail only at specified intervals, depending on their conduct and time served. On arriving at Peterhead, and for at least several years afterward, Slater was allowed to write home only once every six months. Problems of translation increased the delays: prison censors required correspondence in both directions to be in English. Whenever Slater's parents wrote to him, they had to cast about Beuthen for someone who knew the language; otherwise, their German letters, on reaching Peterhead, were sent to Edinburgh for translation before Slater could see them. His letters to them, which he was obliged to write in English, had to be translated on the receiving end.

"We were very much rejoiced over your letter which I have had properly translated into German," Slater's mother wrote him in September 1909, when he was newly arrived at the prison. "We are all eager to hope that it may be possible to discover the real murderer or to bring proof of your innocence to light, my dearest child, and you may recover your freedom as soon as possible. . . . May courage be given to you to bear your sad lot, and may your trust in the Almighty to do justice be strengthened. . . . How we all look forward yearningly to the moment when we can embrace you."

As his parents' correspondence makes clear, finding a translator in Beuthen was an uncertain proposition. "My beloved and good son," Pauline wrote him the next year:

> *We were dying to get a sign of life from you. . . . The lady who wrote the letters for me in English was a teacher and has left Beuthen, and I have not been able to come across any gentleman who could undertake English correspondence. . . . The anxiety about you, my beloved and innocent child, has shaken all my nerves. I will now do everything in my power to gather strength again, so that I may still be preserved for the sake of my dear Oskar; the moment that you, my dear child, obtain your just freedom then there will be no more worry about our existence, even if you were to earn your bread as a common labourer for yourself and us. . . . Now, my darling child, may God give you courage and health and protect you further. Be kissed by your ever loving Mother.*

For a man reported not to possess "a single good quality," Slater penned a stream of letters home that pulsate with tenderness.

"I should like to give you some news, but, alas, I know nothing of what goes on the outer world," he wrote on New Year's Day 1912. "The knowledge that you my dearest mother are living as the only one of all the many sisters makes me happier, and gives me hope that there is a possibility of your attaining the age of 100; of course you must keep dear father well in hand that he also may reach that great age. . . . May God keep you in our midst for a long time to come, this, and this alone, is my earnest desire. Your photograph, which I have in my cell, will of course take the place of honour over my bed on your birthday."

Even Peterhead could not completely extinguish Slater's roguish humor, as some letters attest. "When I was sitting at my supper the photographs were handed to me and so, with joy, leisure, and a full stomach, I have been pondering over them for a long time," he wrote his parents in 1913. "You should not worry, dear father if your legs (at your age) are not so willing to do their duty as you would wish them. . . . I am healthy and pray God that you may yet live a long time and look no worse than you do in your photograph. . . . God protect you my dear parents and I remain—Your son, considered guilty, Oscar."

But these loving exchanges could not buoy Slater's spirits for long, as his other correspondence makes plain. Grim, melancholic, sometimes bitter, it is anguishing to read. In May 1910, in a letter to a Dr. Mandowsky, a lawyer in Beuthen known to his family, he wrote: "This is a very deep business. . . . From the beginning, I was sought out to serve as a scape-goat and . . . all levers were operated to prevent the injustice which was done me being brought to light. . . . My affair is a second Dreyfus affair. . . . I am a broken and a ruined man and will—so long as I live—make every endeavor—so far as possible—to free my family from this awful shame."

Prisoners were allowed scant correspondence with their lawyers and few visits from them, or from anyone else apart from immediate family. At the start of Slater's incarceration, Antoine wrote several times to Peterhead officials, asking to see him. Her requests were always denied, and she soon fades from view.

Though the Leschziners remained steadfast in their support, their precarious finances kept them from traveling to Scotland. "The question of visiting you . . . would cost as much as 1000 marks," Pauline wrote in 1910. "As we are, as you know, not in a position to face the smallest outlay . . . we would need to give up on the idea of the journey. . . . The whole business, also, involves heavy expenses, without any expectation of the least result.* . . . They are great at taking money but they can effect very little at home, how much less abroad." In his nearly two decades in Peterhead, Slater was not able to see a single member of his family, even once.

And so it went, month by month and year by year. In October 1912, when Slater had been at Peterhead for just over three years, he sent his parents an especially heartrending dispatch. "Unfortunately I have to confess that in my case, it doesn't look very promising with hope," he wrote. "The police is my chief enemy, it is the police who has fabricated the whole affair. They have . . . done everything possible to see me hanged. . . . My only hope which I still have is, that the murderer, before closing his eyes for ever and forced by remorses, will make a confession before witnesses."

That wish would never come to pass. But although Slater almost certainly did not know it, his great champion, Arthur Conan Doyle, had already joined his case.

* She is referring to the family's efforts to retain a lawyer on Slater's behalf, which were ultimately of no avail.

# Chapter 12

## ARTHUR CONAN DOYLE, CONSULTING DETECTIVE

SLATER'S SOLICITOR EWING SPEIRS, WHOSE MEMORIAL had helped avert his client's judicial murder, died in December 1909, at thirty-seven, after an apoplectic fit. He was succeeded on the case by a colleague, Alexander Shaughnessy, and it was almost certainly Shaughnessy who persuaded Conan Doyle to take up Slater's cause.

Shaughnessy could not have enlisted a better advocate. By 1912, when he began looking deeply into Slater's conviction, Sir Arthur Conan Doyle was one of the most famous men in Britain. He had built steadily, and increasingly publicly, on his earlier exploits, in 1896 covering the war between the British and the Dervishes in Egypt for the *Westminster Gazette,* and in 1900 volunteering as a military doctor in a pestilence-ridden South African field hospital amid the Boer War. ("For them the bullets, for us the microbes, and both for the honour of the flag," he would write, with characteristic patriotic grandeur.) He published an account of the conflict, *The War in South Africa: Its Cause and Conduct,* in 1902, and that year was knighted for his services in connection with the war. He lectured throughout Europe and America on a variety of subjects.

He also continued publishing Sherlock Holmes tales, which had already made him one of the highest-paid writers of the day. "At a time in history when a middle-class British professional might make £150 a year, Conan Doyle earned £100 per *thousand words*," the American mystery writer Steven Womack has observed. "The American magazine *Collier's Weekly* would eventually offer $25,000 for six Sherlock Holmes short stories, roughly a decade's income or more for most Americans of the time. To describe it in today's terms, Conan Doyle was the Stephen King of his time."

Though Conan Doyle personified late Victorian sensibilities as much as any other public figure, he seemed refreshingly, if not entirely, free of the period's endemic anti-Semitism. His account of touring World War I battlefronts, for instance, reveals an attitude of commendable liberalism, though for present-day readers it is marred by more than a dash of stereotype:

> I lunched that day at the Head-quarters of Sir John Monash, an excellent soldier who had done really splendid work, especially since the advance began. . . . He showed that the long line of fighting Jews which began with Joshua still carries on. One of the Australian Divisional Generals, Rosenthal, was also a Jew, and the Head-quarters Staff was full of eagle-nosed, black-haired warriors. It spoke well for them and well also for the perfect equality of the Australian system, which would have the best man at the top, be he who he might.

To the extent that he embodied the ethos of his age, Conan Doyle sought to impose that ethos wherever he could: in his ceaseless flow of letters to newspapers on issues he held dear; in his public campaign to make British divorce laws more favorable to women who sought to escape, he wrote, "from the embraces of drunkards, from bondage to cruel men, from the iron which fetter locks them to the felon or the hopeless maniac"; and in his role as a parent.

In a letter to Conan Doyle's biographer Pierre Nordon in 1959, nearly thirty years after his father's death, Adrian Conan Doyle recounted a telling anecdote:

> When I shot a crocodile in East Africa—an actual man-eater which had taken a negro the night before—a lad plunged into the water to see if he could reach with a pole the body which had submerged. We did not know if the monster was dead or not or whether it had a mate. The lad went in against my father's shouted orders, but once in, I had to go in too: Terrified, of course, but I knew that my father would take it as a natural necessity that I should *disobey* his orders rather than permit someone of lower status than his son to take a hideous risk from which I shrank. It was a code as clear as a flame before an altar and just about as comfortable as the periodic application of that flame to one's living flesh.

For Conan Doyle, the Victorian code of personal deportment was ironclad. "Two white lies are permitted to a gentleman," he wrote in 1924: "to screen a woman, or to get into a fight when the fight is a rightful one." As to what defined a gentleman, Nordon wrote, "Mr. Adrian Conan Doyle and Miss Mary Conan Doyle both recall hearing their father declare: 'There are three tests, and three tests only, of a gentleman and they have nothing to do with wealth, position or show. What alone counts is: Firstly, a man's chivalry towards women; Secondly: his rectitude in matters of finance; Thirdly, his courtesy towards those born in a lower social position, and therefore dependent.'"

At once benevolent progressive and paternalistic traditionalist, Conan Doyle fully encapsulated the dual sensibility of his age. In *The True Conan Doyle,* his monograph about his father, Adrian recalled the contrast:

> There was a breadth of mind in the man who could convey to a son's consciousness that in the case of sexual illness he could rely absolutely upon the parental comprehension and assistance. *Au contraire,* there was narrow-mindedness in the man who revolted violently to the mildest of *risqué* observations. . . . The same may be said about his reaction to the most harmless liberty taken by any well-meaning stranger. Indeed, there were few things that could stir Conan Doyle more swiftly to a roar of Celtic rage than a clap on the back, the uninvited use of his Christian name, or the presumptuous observation. . . . We meet him in the hands that violently broke his son's pipe into matchwood in a public place because the writer of this article insisted on smoking it despite the presence of women. . . . With this hard and sometimes threatening figure before us, the reader will not find it difficult to believe that even at the age of 70, my father sallied out in a capital city of the Empire with the express purpose of thrashing with his favourite umbrella the rascal who had publicly stated that he was making psychic propaganda from the death of his eldest son.

At the same time, Adrian continued: "This is the very individual who would drive thirty miles out of his route in order that he might have the honour to be of assistance to some old gypsy woman; the man who . . . would sit all night by the bedside of a sick servant to read aloud to him or soothe his pain. One can understand why, when Conan Doyle went to the Boer War, his butler went with him as a devoted squire."

Conan Doyle's sense of honor extended to matters of the heart. In 1893, his first wife, Louise, fell ill with tuberculosis. There was evidently little grand passion between them, but Conan Doyle was fond of her and did everything in his power to restore her to health. Though doctors had given Louise only months to live, he managed, by seeking the finest medical care and traveling with her to the clear air of Switzerland, to prolong her life for thirteen years. Yet for the last nine of those years he was deeply in love with another woman.

In 1897, Conan Doyle had met Jean Leckie, a wealthy, golden-haired Englishwoman of Scottish ancestry some fifteen years his junior. In the years that followed, until Louise's death in 1906, Conan Doyle and Jean maintained an ardent, but by all accounts chaste, courtship. Ever the Victorian man of honor, he told Jean that he would not leave his wife; nor would he divorce her or be unfaithful. "Even among writers who were English gentlemen, this was astonishing behavior," Womack has written. "H. G. Wells and Charles Dickens, two other acclaimed English gentlemen of letters, had both mistresses and illegitimate children." In 1907, the year after Louise's death, Conan Doyle married Jean.

But there was something else—something even more than Conan Doyle's wealth, probity, and acclaim—that made his recruitment to Slater's cause especially valuable: when it came to solving real-life mysteries, Sir Arthur Conan Doyle had done this sort of thing before.

LONG AN AVID READER of detective fiction, Conan Doyle was also deeply interested in true crime. He amassed a library of nonfiction crime books and clippings that, while doubtless not as sprawlingly untidy as the one Holmes maintained at Baker Street, was probably almost as comprehensive. Among the titles in his collection were *The Tryal of Mary Blandy, Spinster, for the Murder of Her Father Francis Blandy, Gent.; Murder at Smutty Nose and Other Murders; The Great Forgeries of William Roupell, Late M.P. for Lambeth;* and Alexandre Dumas's eight-volume *Celebrated Crimes*. Though Conan Doyle acquired most of this library between 1911 and 1929, after two-thirds of the Holmes tales had already appeared in print, it doubtless provided grist for later stories in the canon and, more generally, for his diagnostic imagination.*

In the early twentieth century, Conan Doyle wrote several magazine articles recounting actual murder cases; three were published posthumously in book form as *Strange Studies from Life*. In 1904, he became an inaugural member of the Crimes Club, a secret London dining society devoted to the discussion of contemporary and historical cases. Other members included the mystery novelist Max Pemberton; Harry Irving, son of the celebrated stage actor Sir Henry Irving; and the journalist Fletcher Robinson, who in regaling Conan Doyle with a ghost story from the brooding Dartmoor countryside had inspired *The Hound of the Baskervilles*. The cases they analyzed are not

* In 1911, Conan Doyle purchased fifty-one true-crime volumes from the estate of the lyricist W. S. Gilbert, the "Gilbert" of Gilbert and Sullivan.

known with certainty, but are believed to include that of Thomas Neill Cream, the Victorian physician and serial poisoner; the Adolf Beck mistaken-identity debacle of 1895; and the theft in 1907 of the Irish crown jewels.

As his renown grew, Conan Doyle was inundated with letters from ordinary men and women, beseeching him to look into disappearances and other unexplained events. "We have the epitome of Holmes at work," Adrian Conan Doyle recalled:

> My memories as a youth are mottled with sudden, silent periods when, following upon some agitated stranger or missive, my father would disappear into his study for two or three days on end. It was not a question of affectation but complete mental absorption that checked and counter-checked, pondered, dissected and sought the clue to some mystery that had been hurried to him as the last court of appeal. The hushed footfalls of the whole household, the tray of untasted food standing on the threshold, the subconscious feeling of tension that would settle on family and staff alike, were no less than the reflected essence of the brain, the lamp, and the letter that wrought their unpublicized drama on the inner side of that curtained door.

Of these cases, Conan Doyle solved more than his share. Once, with a single question, he unraveled a mystery that had vexed the police for years. The case concerned a woman, Camille Cecile Holland, who in 1899 had disappeared from Moat House Farm, the isolated home in the English countryside she had shared with her common-law husband, Samuel Herbert Dougal. Nothing was heard from Holland for years, though Dougal continued to cash a stream of checks in her name. She was rumored to have been murdered, but a police search of the farm, where Dougal was living with his new lover, turned up nothing.

In 1904, when Holland had been missing nearly five years, a group of London journalists solicited Conan Doyle's opinion of the case. Yes, he agreed, she had almost certainly been murdered, but the question remained: Where was the body?

No one knew, the journalists told him. Even Scotland Yard, brought in to assist the local police, had scoured every room of the house, along with the outbuildings and grounds of Moat House Farm, but had found nothing.

"What about the moat?" Conan Doyle said simply.

And there, in a former drainage trench, cut into the moat but later filled in with earth, police found the body of Camille Cecile Holland, dead from a gunshot wound. Dougal was arrested, tried, and convicted. He confessed his guilt on the scaffold, moments before he dropped to eternity.

Another case Conan Doyle tackled involved a man who had vanished from the Langham Hotel in London. His solution is a model of abductive logic worthy of Holmes. "A few of the problems which have come my way have been very similar to some which I had invented for the exhibition of the reasoning of Mr. Holmes," he wrote in 1924. "I might perhaps quote one in which that gentleman's method of thought was copied with complete success." The case was this:

> A gentleman had disappeared. He had drawn a bank balance of £40 which was known to be on him. It was feared that he had been murdered for the sake of the money. He had last been heard of stopping at a large hotel in London, having come from the country that day. In the evening he went to a music-hall performance, came out of it

about ten o'clock, returned to his hotel, changed his evening clothes, which were found in his room next day, and disappeared utterly. No one saw him leave the hotel, but a man occupying a neighbouring room declared that he had heard him moving during the night. A week had elapsed at the time that I was consulted, but the police had discovered nothing. Where was the man?

These were the whole of the facts as communicated to me by his relatives in the country. Endeavouring to see the matter through the eyes of Mr. Holmes, I answered by return mail that he was evidently either in Glasgow or Edinburgh. It proved later that he had, as a fact, gone to Edinburgh, though in the week that had passed he had moved to another part of Scotland.

There I should leave the matter, for, as Dr. Watson has often shown, a solution explained is a mystery spoiled. At this stage the reader can lay down the book and show how simple it all is by working out the problem for himself. He has all the data which were ever given to me. For the sake of those, however, who have no turn for such conundrums, I will try to indicate the links which make the chain. The one advantage which I possessed was that I was familiar with the routine of London hotels—though I fancy it differs little from that of hotels elsewhere.

The first thing was to look at the facts and separate what was certain from what was conjecture. It was all certain except the statement of the person who heard the missing man in the night. How could he tell such a sound from any other sound in a large hotel? That point could be disregarded, if it traversed the general conclusions.

The first clear deduction was that the man had meant

to disappear. Why else should he draw all his money? He had got out of the hotel during the night. But there is a night porter in all hotels, and it is impossible to get out without his knowledge when the door is once shut. The door is shut after the theatre-goers return—say at twelve o'clock. Therefore, the man left the hotel before twelve o'clock. He had come from the music-hall at ten, had changed his clothes, and had departed with his bag. No one had seen him do so. The inference is that he had done it at the moment when the hall was full of the returning guests, which is from eleven to eleven-thirty. After that hour, even if the door were still open, there are few people coming and going so that he with his bag would certainly have been seen.

Having got so far upon firm ground, we now ask ourselves why a man who desires to hide himself should go out at such an hour. If he intended to conceal himself in London he need never have gone to the hotel at all. Clearly then he was going to catch a train which would carry him away. But a man who is deposited by a train in any provincial station during the night is likely to be noticed, and he might be sure that when the alarm was raised and his description given, some guard or porter would remember him. Therefore, his destination would be some large town which he would reach as a terminus where all his fellow passengers would disembark and where he would lose himself in the crowd. When one turns up the time table and sees that the great Scotch expresses bound for Edinburgh and Glasgow start about midnight, the goal is reached. As for his dress-suit, the fact that he abandoned it proved that he intended to adopt a line of life where there were no social amenities. This deduction also proved to be correct.

I quote such a case in order to show that the general lines of reasoning advocated by Holmes have a real practical application to life.

Conan Doyle would take up his first major real-life case, the wrongful conviction of George Edalji, in 1906. It was a saga that in its miscarriage of justice, high public drama, undiluted xenophobia, and vindication brought about chiefly through Conan Doyle's efforts acutely prefigured the Slater case.

## Chapter 13

# THE STRANGE CASE OF GEORGE EDALJI

THE ELDEST OF THREE CHILDREN OF AN INDIAN FATHER and an English mother, George Ernest Thompson Edalji was born in England in 1876. His father, Shapurji Edalji, a Parsi from Bombay, had converted to Christianity in the 1850s and after settling in England was ordained as an Anglican minister. In 1874, he married Charlotte Elizabeth Stuart Stoneham; two years later, he was appointed vicar of St. Mark's Church in the parish of Great Wyrley, a mining and farming community in Staffordshire. A second son, Horace, followed George in 1879; a daughter, Maud, was born in 1882.

Reverend Edalji was one of the first South Asians to serve as a parish vicar in England, and his background, along with his mixed marriage, doubtless raised Victorian eyebrows. But the family's life in Great Wyrley seemed untroubled at first. "Placed in the exceedingly difficult position of a coloured clergyman in an English parish, he seems to have conducted himself with dignity and discretion," Conan Doyle would later write. "The only time that I can ever find that any local feeling was raised against him was during elections, for he was a strong Liberal in politics."

In 1888, when George was twelve, the Edaljis began to receive anonymous threatening letters; after a police investigation, a maidservant at the vicarage was arrested. She was tried, though not convicted, and the letters stopped—for a time. Then, in 1892, a new series of hateful letters began arriving in Great Wyrley, many sent to the vicarage but others directed to the Edaljis' neighbors. "Before the end of this year your kid will be either in the graveyard or disgraced for life," an 1893 letter to Reverend Edalji ran. During this period, an unknown hoaxer also carried out a series of practical jokes at the Edaljis' expense, with objects stolen from around the village left conspicuously outside the vicarage and bogus advertisements, couched as George Edalji's apologies for having written the hate mail, appearing in local newspapers.

By all accounts a brilliant student, George attended law school and in 1899 became a solicitor. He continued to live in the vicarage, commuting each day by train to his office in Birmingham, some twenty miles away. In 1895, the second round of letters ceased, though there would be far worse to come.

In early 1903, when George was in his late twenties, the countryside around Great Wyrley was beset with a series of fatal animal maimings, with horses and cattle eviscerated alive in the fields. The savagery, which became known as the Wyrley Outrages, continued for months, with no trace of a culprit. At the same time, the Edaljis became the targets of a third series of letters, sent to neighbors and the local police. Some of the letters identified George Edalji as a member of a gang that had attacked the animals. He was arrested in August 1903 and charged with mutilating a pony.

The police searched the vicarage and seized several items, including a set of Reverend Edalji's razors, which bore dark stains, and a damp coat of George's, also stained. The stains on the razors were found to be rust, but at trial, an expert witness identified those on the coat as mammalian blood.

Covering the trial, the press did little to stanch the race hatred that flowed freely among the public. One article, from the Birmingham *Daily Gazette,* described Edalji in language that could have come straight from Lombroso's anthropomorphic index: "He is 28 years of age but looks younger.... There was little of the typical solicitor in his swarthy face, with its full, dark eyes, prominent mouth, and small round chin. His appearance is essentially Oriental in its stolidity, no sign of emotion escaping him beyond a faint smile as the extraordinary story of the prosecution unfolded."

In another, from the Wolverhampton *Express and Star,* the writer reported, "Many and wonderful were the theories I heard propounded in the local ale-houses as to why Edalji had gone forth in the night to slay cattle, and a widely accepted idea was that he made nocturnal sacrifices to strange gods."

Tried in October 1903, Edalji was convicted and sentenced to seven years' penal servitude. That the mutilations continued while he was in prison was not remotely exculpatory in the eyes of the police: they maintained that the work was being carried out by members of Edalji's gang. England had no criminal appeals court then, and it seemed a foregone conclusion that Edalji would serve his entire sentence. But over time, as it would in Slater's case, a measure of public unease arose; a petition drawn up by Edalji's supporters garnered ten thousand signatures. In October 1906, after he had served three years, Edalji was released, without pardon or explanation.

As a convicted felon, he could no longer practice law. Attempting to clear his name, Edalji wrote a number of articles about his plight. He had read the Sherlock Holmes stories in prison, and after his release he sent a packet of his articles to Conan Doyle.

"As I read, the unmistakable accent of truth forced itself upon my attention and I realized that I was in the presence of an appalling tragedy, and that I was called upon to do what I could to set it right," Conan Doyle later wrote. "What aroused my indignation and gave me the driving force to carry the thing through was the utter helplessness of this forlorn little group of people, the coloured clergyman in his strange position, the brave blue-eyed, grey-haired wife, the young daughter, baited by brutal boors and having the police, who should have been their natural protectors, adopting from the beginning a harsh tone towards them and accusing them, beyond all sense and reason, of being the cause of their own troubles."

Conan Doyle's modus operandi, which he would repeat on a grand scale in Slater's case, took three forms: investigation, publication, and agitation. After reviewing newspaper accounts and other documents relating to the case, he arranged to meet Edalji at a London hotel. A single glance, he reported in his 1907 pamphlet, *The Case of Mr. George Edalji,* told him that the young man could not possibly have been the culprit:

> The first sight which I ever had of Mr. George Edalji was enough in itself to convince me both of the extreme improbability of his being guilty of the crime for which he was condemned, and to suggest some at least of the reasons which had led to his being suspected. He had come to my hotel by appointment, but I had been delayed, and he was passing the time by reading the paper. I recognised my man by his dark face, so I stood and observed

> him. He held the paper close to his eyes and rather sideways, proving not only a high degree of myopia, but marked astigmatism. The idea of such a man scouring fields at night and assaulting cattle while avoiding the watching police was ludicrous to anyone who can imagine what the world looks like to eyes with myopia of eight dioptres. . . . But such a condition, so hopelessly bad that no glasses availed in the open air, gave the sufferer a vacant, bulge-eyed, staring appearance, which, when taken with his dark skin, must assuredly have made him seem a very queer man to the eyes of an English village, and therefore to be naturally associated with any queer event. *There, in a single physical defect, lay the moral certainty of his innocence, and the reason why he should become the scapegoat.*

What astounded Conan Doyle, who had trained as an ophthalmologist, was that Edalji's lawyers had not brought this defect to light. "So bad was this defence that in the whole trial no mention, so far as I could ascertain, was ever made of the fact that the man was practically blind, save in a good light, while between his house and the place where the mutilation was committed lay the full breadth of the London and North-Western Railway, an expanse of rails, wires and other obstacles, with hedges to be forced on either side, so that I, a strong and active man, in broad daylight found it a hard matter to pass."

To drive home the point empirically, Conan Doyle had a pair of glasses made up that would replicate Edalji's eyesight in a wearer with unimpaired vision. "My own sight is normal," he wrote, "and I can answer for the feeling of helplessness which such a glass produces. I tried it upon a Press man, and defied him to reach the lawn-tennis ground in front of the house. He failed. . . . To my mind it was as physically impossible for Mr. Edalji to have committed the crime as it would have been if his legs, instead of his eyes, were crippled."

Combing the trial transcript, Conan Doyle pinpointed the ambiguous nature of the stains that the police found on Edalji's coat:

> Now the police try to make two points here: that the coat was damp, and that there were stains which might have been traces of the crime upon it. Each point is good in itself; but, unfortunately, they are incompatible and mutually destructive. If the coat were damp, and if those marks were blood-stains contracted during the night, then those stains were damp also, and the inspector had only to touch them and then to raise his crimson finger in the air to silence all criticism. But since he could not do so it is clear that the stains were not fresh. . . . How these small stains came there it is difficult to trace—as difficult as to trace a stain which I see now upon the sleeve of my own house-jacket as I look down. A splash from the gravy of underdone meat might well produce it. At any rate, it may most safely be said that the most adept operator who ever lived would not rip up a horse with a razor upon a dark night and have only two threepenny-bit spots of blood to show for it. The idea is beyond argument.

In January 1907, Conan Doyle set forth his conclusions in a series of articles in the *Daily Telegraph,* later published as *The Case of Mr. George Edalji*. Afterward, he wrote, "England soon rang with the wrongs of George Edalji." Once his involvement in the case became public, Conan Doyle, too, began receiving letters threatening his life, written in the same hand as those the Edaljis received—"a fact," he wrote, "which did not appear to shake in the least the Home Office conviction that George Edalji had written them all."*

From his work on the case, Conan Doyle formed a private theory about the identity of the culprit, a disreputable local youth named Royden Sharp. Among the points that told against Sharp logically, Conan Doyle came to believe, were the fact that he had worked as a butcher's apprentice, which gave him both a knowledge of animal anatomy and skill with a knife, and the fact that he was away at sea during the periods when the menacing letters came to a halt. Mindful of the danger of accusing someone who hadn't been charged, Conan Doyle suppressed this information; his pamphlet outlining his argument, *The Case Against Royden Sharp,* was published fully only in 1985.

As a result of Conan Doyle's investigation, the Home Secretary, Herbert Gladstone, convened a government commission to review Edalji's conviction. In May 1907, the commission published its findings. "The conclusions it came to were very strange," Conan Doyle's biographer Pierre Nordon observed. "On one hand it disagreed with the jury which had condemned George Edalji in 1903 for disembowelling a pony, and declared the verdict unfounded; on the other hand it stated that Edalji was the writer of the anonymous letters incriminating himself. . . . There was no question of granting him damages for his three years in prison nor an official vindication."

Though the result was a partial victory, Conan Doyle viewed it with bitterness. "It was a wretched decision," he wrote. "This unfortunate man, whose humble family has paid many hun-

* The Home Office is the British ministerial department in charge of domestic affairs; its purview includes judicial matters in England and Wales.

dreds of pounds in expenses, has never been able to get one shilling of compensation for the wrong done. It is a blot upon the record of English Justice."

For Conan Doyle, however, there were three bright spots in the rest of 1907. The first was that Edalji was reinstated to the bar and could practice law again. The second, in September, was that he married his longtime love, Jean Leckie. Edalji was a guest at the wedding reception, and "Conan Doyle claimed," his biographer Daniel Stashower has written, "that there was no guest he felt prouder to see." The third was that his efforts on Edalji's behalf helped spur the establishment of England's first criminal appeals court. As a result of his highly public work on the case, Conan Doyle would be drafted into the even more formidable battle to exonerate Oscar Slater.

## Chapter 14

# PRISONER 1992

IN THE ARCHIVES OF THE NATIONAL RECORDS OF SCOTland lies a remarkable artifact. A tall, hardbound ledger, it contains a handwritten log by Peterhead warders, recording their observations of Slater over the course of a single week in 1911. From his eighteen-year incarceration there, this fragmentary account appears to be the only record of its kind that has survived. Its entries include these:

> Feb. 5: Prisoner was very quiet.... Conduct very bad, had to be removed to separate cells....
>
> Feb. 5: At 7.20 the prisoner was very excited and talked a lot of nonsense to the Warder. At 2 pm the Prisoner was crying, and asked a mattress to lie on as his head was so sore he could not keep it up....
>
> Feb. 8: The prisoner has been singing at times also talking to himself now and again. When his cell door is opened he usually has a lot to say, mostly nonsense.... During exercise he persisted in talking in a loud excited manner to the Officer in charge....

> Feb. 11: Nothing unusual except he won't work but walks about his cell singing. The prisoner remarked that . . . he could feel the smell of his clothing. . . .

Slater's erratic behavior appears to have begun almost as soon as he arrived at Peterhead, as a sheaf of disciplinary reports from the prison governor attests. Accumulated steadily during Slater's eighteen and a half years, these reports form a thick stack of loose pages distinct from the bound warders' log.

"The convict is somewhat excited and seems to imagine that Prison Officials and the Police are working hand in hand against him," reads one report, from April 1910, when Slater had been at Peterhead for nine months. From later that year: "Conduct somewhat indifferent. Is going to be a troublesome man." Over time, Slater did garner the occasional "Conduct fair" and even "Conduct good," but for the most part, the best he could hope for was "Conduct very indifferent," a citation that shows up many times.

Slater was often in trouble for failing to perform his quarry work satisfactorily, and, as his voluminous disciplinary record indicates, for a spate of other infractions. Entries during his first years include:

> July 19, 1909: Refusing to work . . .
>
> May 22, 1909: Disobedience of orders—refused to go to bed, saying drugs were placed among the blankets . . .
>
> Nov. 29, 1909: Destroying prison property (clinical thermometer) . . .
>
> Dec. 31, 1909: Disobedience, creating a disturbance, and attempting to assault an officer.

The one stabilizing force was the stream of letters from home. From his mother's steadfast pen came family news ("As regards Georg,* it is a pity to waste many words over him, he is a man without heart, and now that he is rich he has become more miserly than ever. His wife is no better, and the same may be said about his daughter") as well as comic small talk ("Fanny's girls are both unmarried—without effort it would be difficult, as you quite well know"). Through it all ran the inexorable passage of time:

> *My beloved innocent Oscar . . . When I see your handwriting then I thank God, that you are feeling well. . . . Now there is nothing but solitude round us. . . . I am now the only one of all my . . . brothers and sisters who is still living. As you know, Uncle Salo and Aunt Minna died in the same year. . . . We had to remove, as our landlord had intolerably increased the rent. . . .*
>
> *If only God's will would be, that your terrible affair will be cleared up, then we certainly . . . can enjoy the remainder of our life . . . even you had to work for us in the pit, my beloved child. . . . Father's illness is always the same. . . . Of course he prays daily for his beloved Oscar and is blessing you every time, when he uses your name.*

Slater's replies can display his characteristic tenderness. "I am most unhappy dearest to know that you are worrying about me," he wrote to his mother on one occasion. "I have been here so long now that I am allowed to receive a letter from you every two months. . . . It would be a happy thought for me if one of the younger generation could visit me during the summer, it is not so very expensive as you may imagine. There is a direct ship

* Slater's brother, a prosperous landowner.

from Hamburg to here. . . . The letter paper is not large enough to contain all my feelings for you."

Other letters home betray a darker tone. "I have appealed for reprieve at least seven to eight times, and always receive the same answer, 'there is no ground for interfering,'" Slater wrote. "I wish a volcano would open and swallow up the unjust gentlemen with all their skin, bones and hair. You have no conception, dearest parents, without wishing to complain to you, how unhappy I often feel, and often wish I was out of this world if it were not for the thought of still possessing you in the outer world."

Still others are suffused with resignation, as Slater tries to assuage his family's sense of loss—and his own. "Dear parents, do not grieve, this makes me still far unhappier than I am already," he wrote. "To keep up my senses I try now always to think, It must be so. . . ."

SLATER'S PRISON FILE IS also thick with letters of complaint, written by him and directed to the board of commissioners that oversaw the prison. In many of them, he insists, in his impeachable English, that he knows he will soon be released; in others, he professes to have discovered who really killed Miss Gilchrist. In one, from 1912, he begs to be relieved of his quarry work:

"I don't likely satisfy the officials with my stone-dressing work, or the work, to break, great granite blocks . . . with a tremendous heavy hammer," Slater wrote. "I would make myself very useful as a baker or cook. . . . My Father is also a baker, and I am especially good in preparing pies & puddings, in fact pastery of all kinds." (In a memorandum written in response, an unnamed Peterhead official said, "I did not consider him suitable as at times he becomes very excited.")

In March 1911, Slater wrote to Reverend Phillips, the Glasgow Jewish leader who would remain his advocate throughout his incarceration. This letter, with its desperate fantasies of release, was suppressed by Peterhead officials and never sent:

> *I hope to get my liberty before long. . . . I never can forget till my dying day, when you have just your arms around me and you said: Slater, I believe in your innocence, only trust in God, not everything is lost. . . . This was in the court-house cellar in Edinburgh, after I was brought down and been found guilty to be a brutish murderer; lonely* [Slater has underlined this word three times] *I was standing between all my enemies and you appeared like a Saint in my misery to me. . . .*
>
> *When I am out I am determined to show for humanity sake to the public, how my case in reality stands, and I assure you I will make some people sweat. . . . When I am out, I will unmask dodgery to the world.*

Over time, Slater's accusations grew even more concrete. In 1911 and afterward he wrote a stream of anguished letters to the chairman of the prison commission, who held the title Master of Polworth and who periodically visited Peterhead. One, from March 1911, reads:

> *Master of Polworth, it is against humanity what was done against me, kindly listen: On the 21 of March . . . I was put in S.C. Cells* on 4 false charges and bread and water. . . .*

* Prison nomenclature for the "separate cells"—i.e., solitary confinement.

> *It was also this time that drugs* [this word is underlined three times] *between my cough mixture have been given to me, to drink and for 36 hours I was madly raving in my cell and still it is not out of my bones and brain altogether. Please listen doctor and Governor, who are implicated in the affair I have to complain of, work hand in hand. It was intended to bring me before you . . . in a drugged condition. . . . Master of Polworth this is more than murder and I must respectfully ask for your aid. . . . How can on earth, such bad man as the doctor allow himself to play with my health like this, my nerves are total out of order through this drug.*

Writing again the next day, Slater outlined an even more extreme scenario:

> *On Saturday last this unchristian game was again used against me. Over my bed, blankets and especially pillows powder was spread the same I had in my milk and cough mixture before. . . . My spiritual adviser visited me on the 15 this month, and after he left on a Saturday night the drug has been in my cell. . . . The symptoms have been the same as when drinking my cough mix. . . . As sure as I write this letter, Sir, I am going to lay down shortly with brain fever, if this don't get stopped. I know my constitution is strong, I stood a lot only never I felt so nervous as at present time. . . . Master of Polworth I ask for nothing more only fairness. . . . Only let me come out as an innocent man before the world, especially for my dear old parents sake. . . . I have only you in here and Mr. Phillips outside whom I fully trust. . . . I am your most humble and obedient servant, Oscar Slater.*
>
> *P.S. I pray Sir, have this drugging game stopped.*

What Slater describes sounds like little more than paranoid delusion. Strikingly, though, the socialist leader John MacLean recounted something similar taking place at Peterhead—"an intractable hell through the drugging of the food"—when he was imprisoned there during the First World War. Addressing the jury from the dock at his 1918 trial for sedition, MacLean, describing an earlier incarceration, said:

> When I was in Peterhead it was plain sailing until the middle of December, and then the trouble began. I was fevered up, and being able to combat that, I was then chilled down. . . . I protested that my food was being drugged. . . . I know that potassium bromide is given to people in order to lower their temperature. It may have been potassium bromide that was used. . . . I was aware of what was taking place in Peterhead from hints and statements by other prisoners there; that from January to March, the so-called winter period, the doctor is busy getting the people into the hospital, there breaking up their organs and their systems.
>
> I call that period the eye-squinting period, because the treatment then given puts the eyes out of view. Through numerous experiments I was able to hold my own. I saw these men round about me in a horrible plight. . . . Attacks were made upon the organs of these men and also upon their nervous system, and we know from the conscientious objectors that the Government have taken their percentage of these men—some have died, some have committed suicide, others have been knocked off their heads, and in this way got into asylums. . . . I experienced part of the process, and I wish to

emphasize the fact that this callous and cold system of destroying people is going on inside the prisons now.

It is as hard to evaluate MacLean's claims as it is to evaluate Slater's. But "what is not in question," one Scottish historian has written, "is that MacLean's experience in prison, both in 1916–17, and after the 1918 trial, enormously damaged his health." MacLean died in 1923, at forty-four.

PETERHEAD OFFICIALS WERE WELL aware of Slater's state of mind. "With respect to prisoner's mental condition," a June 1911 report from the prison medical officer reads, "Slater is obsessed with the idea that liberation is imminent, the obsession being the direct outcome of certain letters & communications* of which he has been the recipient. These have thrown his mind into such a chaotic condition that he has lost his entire sense of proportion." The report concluded, ominously: "I do not meanwhile regard him as insane, but there is no doubt that unless his correspondents observe more care he will become so."

By chance Conan Doyle joined the case soon afterward. His mandate, as he was well aware, was not to figure out whodunit, but to prove who had not. "Since I was generally given credit for having got Edalji out of his troubles, it was hoped by those who believed that Slater's condemnation was a miscarriage of justice that I might be able to do the same for him," he later wrote. "I went into the matter most reluctantly, but when I glanced at the facts, I saw that it was an even worse case than

* The report does not specify from whom, or the precise nature of their contents.

the Edalji one, and that this unhappy man had in all probability no more to do with the murder for which he had been condemned than I had."

As he began sifting the data, what he found only strengthened this resolve. "It is impossible to read and weigh the facts in connection with the conviction of Oscar Slater . . . without feeling deeply dissatisfied with the proceedings, and morally certain that justice was not done," he wrote in 1912. "It will, in my opinion, be a serious scandal if the man be allowed upon such evidence to spend his life in a convict prison. . . . How far the verdict was a just one, the reader may judge for himself when he has perused a connected story of the case." It was just this kind of story—a narrative chain forged from diagnostic traces—that Conan Doyle now began to construct.

# BOOK FOUR

---

# PAPER

## Chapter 15

# "YOU KNOW MY METHOD"

THE MORE CONAN DOYLE STUDIED THE SLATER CASE, the more disturbed he became. "It is an atrocious story," he wrote, "and as I read it and realized the wickedness of it all, I was moved to do all I could for the man." Though he could scarcely have imagined that he would be involved with the case until the late 1920s (his work for Edalji had spanned less than a year), his decision to commit himself to Slater's cause was not made lightly. "I have been in touch with several of his fellow convicts who have come out," Conan Doyle would later write, "and . . . they are agreed that his innocence is recognised by his criminal companions, and there could be no more knowing jury than that."

Though the Edalji case formed a template for Conan Doyle's work on Slater's behalf, there were crucial differences. Where Edalji had involved Conan Doyle the man of action, Slater was about Conan Doyle the cogitator. In his work for Edalji, Conan Doyle literally trod the same ground the assailant had covered, picking his way across muddy fields and tangled railway lines. He met his subject, and his subject's family, and was in contact with them throughout. For Slater, by contrast, he chose to work chiefly from documents. Conan Doyle met Slater only once, after his release; Peterhead's correspondence log, which records every letter Slater sent and received over eighteen and a half years, lists not a single communication between them.

There were several reasons for these differences. Conan Doyle had entered the Edalji affair shortly after the death of his first wife, Louise, and it offered a welcome distraction. By the time he took up Slater's case, he was happily remarried to Jean and, it is fair to assume, disinclined to range from home. Still more significant, although Conan Doyle's personal feelings toward Slater did not affect his commitment to the case ("Some of us still retain an old-fashioned prejudice in favour of a man being punished for the crime that he is tried for, and not for the morals of his private life," he wrote), good Victorian that he was, he clearly deplored him. Throughout the years he would spend on the case, Conan Doyle made a point of holding Slater at arm's length.

But if his work on Slater's behalf seemed closer to armchair ratiocination, it was no less vital a method of detection. Poe's great detective, Dupin, once solved a murder without leaving his rooms. Holmes himself resolved many a case from the untidy confines of 221B Baker Street. "Insurance companies are reluctant to reimburse anyone but the psychiatrist for talking with the patient," the physician Pasquale Accardo has written. "Yet the Holmesian ideal involves just that—to solve the case without ever leaving his sitting room—à la Nero Wolfe." In the Edalji case, Conan Doyle's work as a tracker was literal. In Slater's it was metaphorical, but no less powerful.

—

"DATA! DATA! DATA!" HOLMES famously cries in "The Adventure of the Copper Beeches," an 1892 story. "I can't make bricks without clay." And so in the Slater case, Conan Doyle began to amass his clay. The Gilchrist crime scene was long gone, of course; the crude forensics of the day had yielded nothing useful anyway. So he turned to the medium he knew best: the printed word. He began with a rigorous study of the trial transcript, first published and annotated by William Roughead in 1910.

A distinguished Scottish lawyer and criminologist, Roughead had attended every day of Slater's trial and had come away utterly persuaded of his innocence. "That his opinion was manifest in the magnificent introduction to his book on the trial," Peter Hunt has written, "is suggested by the fact that when Slater received his copy [in prison] the Introduction had been removed."

Delighted to have gained so formidable an ally, Roughead became his leg man, playing energetic Archie Goodwin to Conan Doyle's Wolfe, sending him additional documents, along with accounts of his interviews with various principals in the case. Conan Doyle also trained his diagnostic eye on the blizzard of news coverage of the crime and its aftermath, and on the stenographer's transcript of the New York extradition hearing. He was, in essence, taking a rigorously detailed case history. The data he amassed were the symptoms, or *effects,* of the case laid before him. His job was to rule out Slater as having been their cause.

The method by which Conan Doyle did this was admirably set out in his account of the Langham Hotel mystery: to separate the relevant details from the welter of narrative chaff, and to finger, among what remains, the telling clues. In so doing, aided by his deep understanding of human behavior, he would make the first truly seminal public discovery about Slater's case. It supplied a plausible motive for the seemingly motiveless murder of Marion Gilchrist.

WHILE CONAN DOYLE EMBARKED on fact-finding, Slater's arduous life continued, with time marked by the cherished correspondence with his parents. "The Iserbach has been filled up for years so that there is no more frog-concert, but instead of this the electric cars pass every ten minutes," Pauline wrote.

"On working with my granite-stones, I knock very often with my hammer my left hand, and I wish you for every stroke I have already and will still receive a very happy new year," Slater wrote one December. The next April, he wrote: "No doubt you would realise in Beuthen that the [Passover] holidays began yesterday, the Jews here are sending me food, oftentimes also fish, and when I get these extra dishes I always feel that I am eating real Jewish food."

As before, Slater's somber lines could show flashes of puckish humor. "Your letter has been handed over to me during my supper and I was very happy to know you [are] well and cheerful," he wrote. "When I saw your photo and contemplated father's growth of hair, I put unconsciously my hand on my head (there is no mirror here) and I felt very discouraged, however got consoled again, thinking that I was born already quite bald."

Pauline's letters remain unswerving in their faith and support. "My most beloved good son: A letter from you, my dear child, is for us a recreation, if even it comes from there, where, God knows, you do not belong to. It seems like a tale when I tell you, not a moment I have given up hope, that over short or long you will get your freedom again, which you well deserve. Do not lose courage, beloved child. The Almighty will hear the daily ardent prayers of your old good parents. . . . Surely the day will come when all will be discovered and we see us again and you will after think, my mother has prophesied correctly."

IN 1912, CONAN DOYLE published the fruits of his investigation as *The Case of Oscar Slater.* Spanning eighty pages, the book is a model of economy. But in it, with Holmesian acumen and Watsonian lucidity, he dismantles the case against Slater plank by plank. The volume is an object lesson in abductive reasoning, drawing on observed facts—and only the facts—to construct a logical, reverse-engineered narrative.

"You know my method," Holmes often remarks to Watson, and in *The Case of Oscar Slater,* Conan Doyle's approach followed precisely that of Holmes. Confronting the case, he sought to answer a set of questions: What is fact and what conjecture? Which data are so trifling as to have escaped earlier investigators' notice? When all the data are amassed, sifted, and codified, what patterns emerge? As Holmes, admonishing Watson, described the process, "Never trust to general impressions, my boy, but concentrate yourself upon details."

A pervasive theme in Conan Doyle's book is the utter illogic of the pursuit and prosecution. He pulls apart the tangle of narrative inconsistencies, punctures hyperbolic claims, and unravels the web of circular reasoning that pervaded the case from start to finish. Underlying his exposition of the crime and its aftermath is a central, urgent concern: By *what* can the seemingly anomalous aspects of the case be explained?

Conan Doyle sets the stage, describing Miss Gilchrist, her

jewels, and her fortified flat; reprising the night of the murder; and placing a worried Arthur Adams—and a curiously unruffled Helen Lambie—on the doormat. Then the diagnostic demolition begins.

One of the book's first, and most damning, indictments concerns Lambie's actions as she watched the intruder leave Miss Gilchrist's flat. The scene contains a clue of a very particular kind: negative evidence. In all of English letters, the single most famous example of the diagnostic use of negative evidence comes from Conan Doyle. It takes place in "Silver Blaze," a Holmes story from 1892. Investigating the disappearance of a prize racehorse, Holmes talks to a local police inspector about the behavior of other actors at the farm where it was stabled.

"Is there any point to which you would wish to draw my attention?" the inspector asks.

"To the curious incident of the dog in the night-time," Holmes replies.

"The dog did nothing in the night-time," the inspector protests.

"That," Holmes says, "was the curious incident."

For Holmes, the solution to the mystery lay precisely in that non-incident. Something similar might well be divined, Conan Doyle knew, from Lambie's odd behavior at the door. Consider the following scenario: If, on arriving home, you find a stranger sallying past you from inside your house, you are certain to say something—"Hey!" "Stop!" "Who are you?" But Lambie said nothing. Her curious silence was noted in passing by Roughead in 1910. Now, in *The Case of Oscar Slater,* Conan Doyle brought her behavior into stark relief. After describing the scene on Miss Gilchrist's doormat, he continued:

> The actions of Helen Lambie ... can only be explained by supposing that from the time she saw Adams waiting outside her door, her whole reasoning faculty had deserted her. First, she explained the great noise heard below: "The ceiling was like to crack," said Adams, by the fall of a clothes-line and its pulleys of attachment, which could not possibly, one would imagine, have produced any such effect.... On the appearance of the stranger she did not gasp out: "Who are you?" or any other sign of amazement, *but allowed Adams to suppose by her silence that the man might be someone who had a right to be there.* Finally, instead of rushing at once to see if her mistress was safe, she went into the kitchen, still apparently under the obsession of the pulleys. She informed Adams that they were all right, as if it mattered to any human being; thence she went into the spare bedroom, *where she must have seen that robbery had been committed,* since an open box lay in the middle of the floor. *She gave no alarm however,* and it was only when Adams called out: "Where is your mistress?" that she finally went into the room of the murder. It must be admitted that this seems strange conduct, and only* explicable, if it can be said to be explicable, by great want of intelligence and grasp of the situation.

*The Case of Oscar Slater* went on to chronicle the police investigation, the breakdown of the brooch clue, the transatlantic

* Conan Doyle doesn't mean "only," of course. The other explanation for Lambie's strange behavior, as he well understood, was that she was involved in the crime, or at the very least knew the killer. Though he had to exercise suitable restraint in print, it is clear from his private correspondence that he believed the latter hypothesis to be well within the realm of possibility.

pursuit of Slater, the extradition hearing, the preposterous identity parade in Glasgow, and the trial in Edinburgh. With polite acidity, Conan Doyle pointed out the unlikelihood of Lambie's account and Barrowman's having coalesced on their own into a unified description of the killer—something they began to do in New York, and did further at trial. "In Edinburgh Barrowman, like Lambie, was very much more certain than in New York," he wrote. "The further they got from the event, the easier apparently did recognition become. . . . It is remarkable that both these females, Lambie and Barrowman, swore that though they were thrown together in this journey out to New York, and actually shared the same cabin, they never once talked of the object of their mission or compared notes as to the man they were about to identify. For girls of the respective ages of fifteen and twenty-one this certainly furnishes a unique example of self-restraint."

Conan Doyle also demolished the idea, crucial to the prosecution, that a guilty Slater had fled Glasgow on Christmas night 1908. That theory, as he would later point out in more detail, rested on a fallacious premise:

> The Lord Advocate made a great point in his speech of this flight—how Slater, on leaving Glasgow, had taken all pains to cover up his tracks. *Yet all the time the Glasgow police held the following telegram from the Chief Detective of Liverpool:* "Only two people came off the Glasgow train. . . . They engaged a bedroom in the North-Western Hotel. The man gave the name of Oscar Slater, Glasgow. . . . The chambermaid had a conversation with the woman, who told her that they were about to sail by the S.S. Lusitania for America."
>
> There was, therefore, no concealment of tracks. . . . It

> is, of course, true that Slater aboard the ship took the name of Otto Sando. He wished to make a fresh start in America under that name.... The clear proof that the change of name was for America, and not to throw off any pursuit from Glasgow, lies in the fact that he signed the Liverpool hotel register with his true name and address, at the moment when, according to the police theories, he should have been most carefully concealing his identity. *Could you conceive a murderer flying red-handed with the knowledge that there was pursuit behind him and announcing at the first hotel his name and whence he came?*

The hunting of Slater, Conan Doyle wrote in 1912, had defied logic from its inception: "Consider the monstrous coincidence which is involved in his guilt, the coincidence that the police owing to their mistake over the brooch, by pure chance started out in pursuit of the right man. Which is A Priori the more probable: That such an unheard-of million-to-one coincidence should have occurred, Or, that the police, having committed themselves to the theory that he was the murderer, refused to admit that they were wrong when the bottom fell out of the original case and persevered in the hope that vague identifications of a queer-looking foreigner would justify their original action?"

Those "vague identifications," Conan Doyle stressed, were the foundation on which the prosecution had erected its entire case: "What the police never could produce," he wrote, "was the essential thing, and that was the least connecting link between Slater and Miss Gilchrist, or any explanation of how a foreigner in Glasgow could even know of the existence, to say nothing of the wealth, of a retired old lady, who had few acquaintances and seldom left her flat." Of the Lord Advocate's promise to tell jurors how Slater came to know of Miss Gilchrist's jewels, Conan Doyle reminded his readers, "No further reference appears to have been made to the matter."

Then there was the question of how the assailant got into Miss Gilchrist's flat in the first place. Reasoning abductively, Conan Doyle supplied a likely answer:

> How did the murderer get in if Lambie is correct in thinking that she shut the doors? *I cannot get away from the conclusion that he had duplicate keys.* In that case all becomes comprehensible, for the old lady—whose faculties were quite normal—would hear the lock go and would not be alarmed, thinking that Lambie had returned before her time. . . . That is intelligible. *But if he had not the keys, consider the difficulties.* . . . If the old lady had opened the flat door her body would have been found in the passage. Therefore, the police were driven to the hypothesis that the old lady heard the ring, opened the lower stair door from above (as can be done in all Scotch flats), opened the flat door, never looked over the lighted stair to see who was coming up, but returned to her chair and her magazine, leaving the door open, and a free entrance to the murderer. This is *possible,* but is it not in the highest degree *improbable*? Miss Gilchrist was nervous of robbery and would not neglect obvious precautions. . . . That a nervous old lady should throw open both doors, never look to see who her visitor was, and return to her dining-room is very hard to believe.

The absurdity of the police argument, Conan Doyle pointed out, became clear when the crime was envisioned from the killer's point of view—a technique that Holmes often used to good effect:

> He has planned out his proceedings. It is notorious that it is the easiest thing in the world to open the lower door of a Scotch flat. The blade of any penknife will do that. If he was to depend upon ringing to get at his victim, it was evidently better for him to ring at the upper door, as otherwise the chance would seem very great that she would look down, see him coming up the stair, and shut herself in. On the other hand, *if he were at the upper door and she answered it, he had only to push his way in*. . . . And yet the police theory is that . . . he rang from below. *It is not what he would do*. . . . If one weighs all these reasons, one can hardly fail, I think, to come to the conclusion that the murderer had keys.

To support the hypothesis that the murderer was no stranger, Conan Doyle conjured his behavior upon entering the flat: A stranger, he reasoned, would assume that Miss Gilchrist kept her jewels in her own bedroom. Here, too, Conan Doyle was able to induce narrative from negative action, for the intruder, he pointed out, clearly knew *not* to bother with Miss Gilchrist's room: "Presuming that the assassin was indeed after the jewels, it is very instructive to note his knowledge of their location," he wrote. "Why did he go straight into the spare bedroom where the jewels were actually kept? . . . Any knowledge gathered from outside (by a watcher in the back-yard for example) would go to the length of ascertaining which was the old lady's room. One would expect a robber who had gained his information thus, to go straight to that chamber. *But this man did not do so.*

*He went straight to the unlikely room.* . . . Is not this remarkably suggestive? *Does it not pre-suppose a previous acquaintance with the inside of the flat and the ways of its owner?*"

Taking a further page from the Holmesian playbook, Conan Doyle imagined what would have happened if Slater *had* been the murderer—and described the complications that would arise:

> It will be observed that save for the identifications, the value of which can be estimated, there is really no single point of connection between the crime and the alleged criminal. It may be argued that the existence of the hammer is such a point; but what household in the land is devoid of a hammer? It is to be remembered that if Slater committed the murder with this hammer, he must have taken it with him in order to commit the crime. . . . *But what man in his senses, planning a deliberate murder, would take with him a weapon which was light, frail, and so long that it must project from any pocket?* The nearest lump of stone on the road would serve his purpose better than that. Again, it must in its blood-soaked condition have been in his pocket when he came away from the crime. The Crown never attempted to prove either blood-stains in a pocket, or the fact that any clothes had been burned. *If Slater destroyed clothes, he would naturally have destroyed the hammer, too.*

Even before Slater's trial began, Conan Doyle pointed out, "the three important points of the pawned jewel, the supposed flight, and the evidence from clothing and weapon, had each either broken down completely, or become exceedingly attenuated." What that meant—he is too gentlemanly to say it outright, but it pulsates between every line of his book—was that the prosecution had used any means necessary to drive home its preposterous case.

TURNING TO THE TRIAL ITSELF, Conan Doyle dissected the courtroom arguments with the finesse of a forensic debater. "The Lord-Advocate spoke, as I understand, without notes, a procedure which may well add to eloquence while subtracting from accuracy," he wrote drily. "If the minds of the jury were at all befogged as to the dates, the definite assertion of the Lord-Advocate, twice repeated, that Slater's name had been published before his flight, was bound to have a most grave and prejudiced effect."

He continued: "Some of the Lord-Advocate's other statements are certainly surprising. . . . The murder was committed about seven. The murderer may have regained the street about ten minutes or quarter past seven. . . . Yet Schmalz says he was in at seven, and so does Antoine."

One of the most damnable logical errors in the Lord Advocate's speech, Conan Doyle pointed out, concerned the location of Miss Gilchrist's jewels. Because the killer was ignorant of their *precise* location (he knew which room to search but not that the jewels were secreted in the wardrobe there), then, the Lord Advocate declared at trial, "that answers to the prisoner." If the prosecutor's assertion were rendered as a logical argument, as Conan Doyle knew, it would take this form:

> The murderer was unfamiliar with Miss Gilchrist's spare room.
> Slater was unfamiliar with Miss Gilchrist's spare room.
> Therefore, Slater was the murderer.

"'That answers to the prisoner,'" Conan Doyle parroted, adding, with barely veiled contempt: "It also, of course, answers to practically every man in Scotland."

Examining the Crown's other arguments, Conan Doyle took pains to deflate hyperbole. "The Lord-Advocate said that [Slater's] change of name 'could not be explained consistently with innocence,'" he wrote. "That may be true enough, but the change can surely be explained on some cause less grave than murder."

Nor did the defense counsel escape Conan Doyle's criticism. Though he was diplomatic in his treatment of Slater's barrister, Alexander McClure, he did not ignore the deficiencies in his conduct of the case:

> Where so many points were involved, it is natural that some few may have been overlooked. One does not, for example, find the counsel as insistent as one might expect upon such points as, the failure of the Crown to show how Slater could have known anything at all about the existence of Miss Gilchrist and her jewels, how he got into the flat, and what became of the brooch which, according to their theory, he had carried off. . . .
>
> Only on one point must Mr. M'Clure's judgment be questioned, and that is on the most difficult one, which a criminal counsel has ever to decide. He did not place his man in the box. . . . It certainly told against his client.

Conan Doyle did not limit his scrutiny to the human actors in the case. One of his finest forensic achievements came in his "interrogation" of *objects* connected with the crime: the half sovereign, the wooden workbox, the missing brooch, the jewelry on the dressing table. For it was in persuading those objects to speak that he furnished the first truly credible motive for Miss Gilchrist's murder.

SOME OF THE MOST vital witnesses to a crime are not people but things. As a doctor can cajole a limb or organ into yielding its story, or an archaeologist coax a pot shard into divulging a slice of history, so, too, can a detective persuade a mute object to testify to a past otherwise out of reach. Among fictional detectives, there is no one more skilled at the diagnostic reading of objects than Sherlock Holmes.

One of the most delightful diagnostic set pieces in the Holmes canon is found in an 1892 story, "The Adventure of the Blue Carbuncle." Holmes has come into possession of a goose and a hat, both belonging to a man he has never seen. The hat in particular sets off a chain of abductive reasoning in the finest tradition of Zadig.

"What clue could you have to his identity?" Watson, now married and visiting Baker Street, asks.

> "Only as much as we can deduce."
>
> "From his hat?"
>
> "Precisely."
>
> "But you are joking. What can you gather from this old battered felt?" . . .
>
> He picked it up and gazed at it in the peculiar introspective fashion which was characteristic of him. "It is perhaps less suggestive than it might have been," he remarked, "and yet there are a few inferences which are very distinct, and a few others which represent at least a strong balance of probability. That the man was highly intellectual is of course obvious upon the face of it, and

also that he was fairly well-to-do within the last three years, although he has now fallen upon evil days. He had foresight, but has less now than formerly, pointing to a moral retrogression, which, when taken with the decline of his fortunes, seems to indicate some evil influence, probably drink, at work upon him. This may account also for the obvious fact that his wife has ceased to love him."

"My dear Holmes!"

"He has, however, retained some degree of self-respect," he continued. . . . "He is a man who leads a sedentary life, goes out little, is out of training entirely, is middle-aged, has grizzled hair which he has had cut within the last few days, and which he anoints with lime-cream. Also, by the way, that it is extremely improbable that he has gas laid on in his house."

Watson, dumbfounded, presses Holmes to explain.

For answer Holmes clapped the hat upon his head. It came right over the forehead and settled upon the bridge of his nose. "It is a question of cubic capacity," said he; "a man with so large a brain must have something in it."

"The decline of his fortunes, then?"

"This hat is three years old. These flat brims curled at the edge came in then. It is a hat of the very best quality. Look at the band of ribbed silk and the excellent lining. If this man could afford to buy so expensive a hat three years ago, and has had no hat since, then he has assuredly gone down in the world."

And so Holmes's abductions continue, through the foresight (shown by the presence of a hat-securer), the moral regression (failure to repair the hat-securer), and the lime-cream (cut hair-ends in the lining).

> "But his wife—you said that she had ceased to love him."
>
> "This hat has not been brushed for weeks. When I see you, my dear Watson, with a week's accumulation of dust upon your hat, and when your wife allows you to go out in such a state, I shall fear that you also have been unfortunate enough to lose your wife's affection." . . .
>
> "You have an answer to everything. But how on earth do you deduce that the gas is not laid on in his house?"
>
> "One tallow stain, or even two, might come by chance; but when I see no less than five, I think that there can be little doubt that the individual must be brought into frequent contact with burning tallow—walks upstairs at night probably with his hat in one hand and a guttering candle in the other. Anyhow, he never got tallow-stains from a gas-jet. Are you satisfied?"

Though he could not see them firsthand, Conan Doyle subjected the artifacts at the Gilchrist crime scene to similar interrogation. Where the police had seen only discrete objects, he saw a constellation: the half sovereign on the carpet beside Miss Gilchrist's body, the jewelry in the dish on her dressing table, and, in particular, the workbox on the floor. What was significant about these things, he was the first to realize, *was that they were where they were at all.*

"What so often leads the police astray in the Holmes stories," two American scholars have written, "is that early in the investigation of a crime, they tend to adopt the hypothesis which is most likely to account for a few outstanding facts, ignoring 'trifles' and thereafter refusing to consider data that do not support their position." That, Conan Doyle now realized, was exactly what the Glasgow police had done in positing robbery as the motive for Miss Gilchrist's murder. He wrote:

> One question which has to be asked was *whether the assassin was after the jewels at all. . . .* When he reached the bedroom and lit the gas, he did not at once seize the watch and rings which were lying openly exposed upon the dressing-table. He did not pick up the half-sovereign. . . . His attention was given to a wooden box, the lid of which he wrenched open. (This, I think, was "the breaking of sticks" heard by Adams.) The papers in it were strewn on the ground. *Were the papers his object, and the final abstraction of one diamond brooch a mere blind?* . . . Presuming that the assassin was indeed after the jewels, it is very instructive to note his knowledge of their location, and also its limitations. . . . If it were the jewels he was after, he knew what room they were in, but not in what part of the room. A fuller knowledge would have told him they were kept in the wardrobe. *And yet he searched a box. If he was after papers, his information was complete.*

As a craftsman of mysteries, Conan Doyle immediately recognized the missing diamond brooch as a red herring. The intruder, on hearing Adams ring the doorbell, very likely slipped it into his pocket before sailing coolly out of the flat. Diamonds were objects of widespread Victorian obsession, as the literature of the period amply reflects. Consciously or not, the killer seized upon precisely the right piece of jewelry—one that would become the focus both of the police investigation and of the public's fascination with the case. The brooch for which Oscar

Slater was almost hanged was, the diagnostician Conan Doyle realized, no more than a worthless symptom.

By focusing instead on the workbox and its rifled contents, Conan Doyle gave the case its first genuine motive. Why, he asked himself rhetorically, would an intruder disdain jewelry to go after papers? "It might be said," he wrote, "that *save a will* it would be difficult to imagine any paper which would account for such an enterprise."

His conjecture would prove correct. Though the fact would not be well known until 1914, members of Miss Gilchrist's family had begun wrangling over her estate even before she died. Afterward, they began quietly accusing one another of her murder.

*THE CASE OF OSCAR SLATER* was published on August 21, 1912, and went on sale for sixpence: Conan Doyle deliberately kept the price low to ensure as wide a readership as possible. "Since the publication . . . I have received numerous letters from correspondents all over the country urging me to use any influence I have in getting the authorities to reconsider the trial," he wrote the next month. "I trust, therefore, that by pointing out to the British public the possibility and probability of a miscarriage of justice having been perpetrated . . . I have awakened a more general interest in the case, and, if the British public agree with my views, it is for them to see that the case is reopened."

In publishing his book, Conan Doyle was attuned to the charge that he was acting as a murderer's apologist. "I may seem to have stated the case entirely from the point of view of the defence," he wrote. "In reply, I would only ask the reader to take the trouble to read the extended evidence. . . . If he will do so, he will realise that *without a conscious mental effort towards special pleading, there is no other way in which the story can be told.* The facts are on one side. The conjectures, the unsatisfactory identifications, the damaging flaws, and the very strong prejudices are upon the other." Or, as Holmes famously said, "When you have eliminated the impossible, whatever remains, *however improbable,* must be the truth."

In short, Conan Doyle concluded, "I do not see how any reasonable man can carefully weigh the evidence and not admit that when the unfortunate prisoner cried, 'I know nothing about it,' he was possibly, and even probably, speaking the literal truth."

But for all the Holmesian acumen of *The Case of Oscar Slater,* for all its cool lucidity and quiet outrage, it may simply have come too soon: Miss Gilchrist's murder was still fresh in public memory, and many still considered Slater guilty. Despite the fact that "each clue against Slater crumbles to pieces when examined," as Conan Doyle later wrote, his book had little immediate effect, and Slater remained where he was.

BY THE TIME THE BOOK appeared, Slater's paranoid desperation, so evident in 1911, seemed to have been replaced by a measure of acceptance. "As to my case, I have long ago resigned myself to the inevitable and as nobody else but the Almighty can help me, I have put all under His protection," he wrote to his parents in August 1912. "A force of will is the best medicine against grief. I have finally made up my mind, not to brood too much over my miserable situation." The next year, he wrote them: "I am happy to say that I am feeling strong and healthy, both bodily and mentally, and I am submitting to my fate with fortitude."

Slater's newfound resolve was just as well, for there would be no significant developments in the case for two years. Then, in 1914, a secret document in the files of the Glasgow police would cast suspicion on someone Miss Gilchrist had known for a very long time.

# Chapter 16

## THE RUIN OF JOHN THOMSON TRENCH

IN NOVEMBER 1912, NEARLY FOUR YEARS AFTER MISS Gilchrist's death, Jean Milne, a sixty-five-year-old Scotswoman, was found murdered in the town of Broughty Ferry, north of Edinburgh, near Dundee. By coincidence, many aspects of the case echoed the Gilchrist killing. The victim was reclusive and rich. Her body was found inside the elegant home in which she lived alone, bludgeoned to death with a poker. The house was full of money and jewelry, yet nothing seemed to be missing. There was no sign of forced entry: the killer appeared to have been admitted by the victim.

A bevy of witnesses spoke of having seen a man near Milne's house; based on their statements, the Dundee police circulated the suspect's description throughout Britain. Police in the English town of Maidstone, southeast of London, identified him at once: Charles Warner, a Canadian vagrant then serving two weeks in the Maidstone jail for evading his bill at a local hotel. Five of the Broughty Ferry witnesses were brought to Maidstone, and all five identified Warner as the man they had seen near Milne's home. As Peter Hunt recounted, "One of them wept as she said, 'I know I am putting the rope round his neck, but that's the man!'"

The Dundee police had requested help from the Glasgow force, a larger department. Detective Lieutenant John Thomson Trench of Glasgow's Central Division was dispatched to Maidstone, where he arrested Warner and escorted him back him to Dundee. There, twelve more witnesses identified him, and the local procurator fiscal began building a watertight case.

But something bothered Trench. Though Milne's body wasn't discovered until November, police determined that she had been killed several weeks earlier, on October 16. Warner had told Trench that he'd come to Europe from Toronto and spent the past several months traveling around Britain and the Continent. On the actual murder date, he said, he was in Antwerp. Trench asked whether he could confirm the fact through hotel registers. No, Warner replied: he had slept on park benches.

Then Warner remembered something. On October 16, 1912, he had pawned a waistcoat in Antwerp and had the ticket to prove it. As the case against him gathered momentum, Hunt wrote, "Warner found that his best friend was the man who had arrested him." Trench went to Antwerp, found the pawnshop, confirmed the date, and redeemed Warner's waistcoat. On the strength of this alibi, Warner was released. A spate of eyewitnesses had been mistaken.

BY THIS TIME, JOHN THOMSON TRENCH was one of the most respected police officers in Glasgow. The son of a Scottish plowman, he had joined the force as a constable in 1893 and was named a detective lieutenant in 1912. Multiply decorated, he would be awarded the King's Police Medal in 1914 for having been "conspicuous for gallantry in arresting dangerous criminals on several occasions, and [having] a distinguished record in the detective service."

Trench was by all accounts well liked. "His manners were easy, his disposition jovial, if a little quixotic at times," Hunt wrote. "In the opinion of a major whom he served under during the Great War, 'he was loved by his comrades, scorned to do a mean action, desiring justice for everyone.'" He was married and the father of six.

After playing a peripheral role in the Gilchrist investigation in the winter of 1908–9, Trench had harbored deep doubts about the case. Over time, he covertly copied from police files documents that had been altered or suppressed, including an explosive report that would come to be known as the Secret Document. In 1914, after what seem to have been five years of private agonizing, Trench came forward. His decision would prompt a judicial review of Slater's case that would play out as bitter farce. It would also cost Trench his career.

It is unclear what prompted Trench to wait so long to voice his concerns, or what finally moved him to do so. Perhaps the Broughty Ferry case, in which one witness after another had sworn that an innocent man was a murderer, had solidified his doubts about the Slater testimony. Perhaps he thought the King's Medal, bestowed on him by George V on New Year's Day 1914, would protect him from official retribution.

In early 1914, Trench confided his misgivings to his friend David Cook, a Glasgow lawyer. He told Cook that on December 23, 1908, two days after Miss Gilchrist's murder, his superiors had sent him to the home of her niece Margaret Birrell. Birrell told him that Helen Lambie had not only recognized the murderer but had also named him—a prominent member of Miss Gilchrist's extended family. On January 3, Lambie told Trench the same thing.

Cook wrote to Thomas McKinnon Wood, the Secretary for Scotland, requesting an official inquiry into Slater's conviction. He cautiously set forth Trench's willingness to testify. "If the constable mentioned in your letter will send me a written statement of the evidence in his possession," McKinnon Wood replied, "I will give this matter my best consideration." Trench appeared to interpret this as a guarantee of immunity and sent McKinnon Wood his evidence.

In March 1914, Cook contacted Conan Doyle. "You will be good enough to treat this letter meantime as confidential," he wrote. He continued:

> *Detective Lieutenant Trench of the Central Division is an officer of ability and integrity. From the time that Slater's name was mentioned in connection with the murder of Miss Gilchrist until this day, Trench has been of [the] opinion that Slater was an innocent man. I have never had any other view.*
>
> *Trench is my intimate friend, and I have frequently spoken to him regarding the case. He has time and again told me that he was not satisfied with the action of the police in the matter. . . .*
>
> *I may tell you that* the original statement of the girl Barrowman as copied from the Police Books bears no relation to the evidence which she gave at the trial. *I venture to say that had the original statement been produced at the trial, Slater would not have been convicted. . . .*
>
> *Frankly I am of opinion that Mary Barrowman was not in West Princes Street at or near 7 o'clock. Very probably*

> *she was in West Princes Street some hours afterwards, when the public had obtained information that a murder had taken place, and were standing wide mouthed and open eyed gazing at the locus. Barrowman may have been one of the crowd. Being a little late in getting home she took the edge off the greeting which she expected to receive by a little sensationalism. . . .*
>
> *With regard to Lambie, Trench is prepared to swear at the enquiry that he received from her on the 3rd of January, 1909, an emphatic statement that* another person whose name I need not mention here was the man whom she saw leave the house. *This statement persisted in on the 3rd of January was made by Lambie within fifteen minutes of the murderer leaving the house.* The police were in possession of the facts, and purposely concealed the information from the defence and from the Court. . . .
>
> *Miss Birrell (niece of Miss Gilchrist) is prepared to swear that Nellie Lambie called at her house at 7-15 pm on the night of the murder, entered the house, declared that her mistress had been murdered and that she saw the murderer—naming him. The information was given to the Police by Miss Birrell on the night of the murder.*

From Windlesham, his elegant home in Sussex, Conan Doyle took up Slater's case for the second time, joining Cook in pressing high-ranking officials for a review. Before the end of March 1914, Secretary McKinnon Wood indicated that a formal inquiry into the conviction would be held later that spring. The inquiry would review the following five points:

> (1) Did any witness to the identification on the night of the murder name a person other than Oscar Slater?

(2) Were the police aware that such was the case? If so, why was the evidence not forthcoming at the trial?

(3) Did Slater fly from justice?

(4) Were the police in possession of information that Slater had disclosed his name at the North-Western Hotel, Liverpool, stating where he came from, and that he was travelling by the S.S. *Lusitania*?

(5) Did one of the witnesses make a mistake as to the date on which she stated she was in West Princes Street?

Trench, encouraged, prepared to tell all; a finding for Slater on one or more points, he knew, could reverse the conviction. But though Trench would testify forthrightly, both he and Cook would be victimized beyond imagining.

BY ALL ACCOUNTS SLATER knew nothing of the efforts to reopen his case. His steadfast resolve to accept his lot, so movingly evident in his letters of 1912–13, had long since given way; his renewed stream of letters to prison officials, begun in 1914 and redolent of paranoia, attests as much. A chilling memorandum from Peterhead's medical officer, written in February 1914, suggests that Slater's mental state had been evident for some time:

> The convict named in the margin is, in my opinion, insane. On various occasions I have suspected that he was the subject of delusions of persecution and hallucinations of hearing and smell. At present he is highly excited and dangerous. He is extremely impulsive and not able to control his actions. He hears voices, he smells chloroform being administered to him; and he says I give

> him no treatment and am trying to kill him, which are delusions. He is not safe to be at work and I have requested the Governor to keep him under separate confinement and under strict observation.

THE INQUIRY INTO SLATER'S conviction would take place in Glasgow. Conducting the proceedings would be James Gardner Millar, a lawyer who was the sheriff of Lanarkshire. For Slater's supporters, the appointment raised concerns. "Sheriff Gardner Millar is an eminent lawyer and in a question of Civil Law, I know of no man whose opinion is entitled to more weight," Cook wrote to Conan Doyle in April 1914. "He however has no experience of Criminal matters. He is a babe in such matters, and *the guiding principle with him is the police can do no wrong.*"

Cook's concerns were quickly borne out. The proceedings, Millar announced, would be held behind closed doors, off-limits to press and public. They would be concerned only with issues of fact—not with the conduct of the trial. Witnesses would not be placed under oath, though they would be instructed to tell the truth. Those conditions, Cook wrote bitterly to Conan Doyle, "suggest to me that the Enquiry will be more or less a farce."

Of all the information Trench planned to bring to light, the most explosive was contained in the secret document he had copied from police files, detailing the statement made by Margaret Birrell shortly after the murder. In her statement, Birrell recounted Lambie's visit, and her naming of a man other than Slater as the intruder. To protect that man, who had not been charged, subsequent police copies of the document redacted his name, referring to him by the pseudonymous initials "A.B."

On December 23, 1908, two days after Miss Gilchrist's death,

The young doctor. Conan Doyle on his graduation from medical school, 1881

ARTHUR CONAN DOYLE COLLECTION—LANCELYN GREEN BEQUEST, PORTSMOUTH CITY COUNCIL

Conan Doyle's medical-school teacher Dr. Joseph Bell, whose diagnostic powers seemed to verge on sorcery. He was the real-life model for Sherlock Holmes.

ARTHUR CONAN DOYLE COLLECTION—LANCELYN GREEN BEQUEST, PORTSMOUTH CITY COUNCIL

The Anglo-Indian lawyer George Edalji. Investigating his wrongful conviction marked Conan Doyle's first extended involvement in a real-life case.

ARTHUR CONAN DOYLE COLLECTION—LANCELYN GREEN BEQUEST, PORTSMOUTH CITY COUNCIL

Gordon my boy, I wish you in every way the best of luck and if you feel inclined then please do what you can for me. Give to the English public your opinion regarding me personally and also in other respects. You have been for 5 years in close contact with me and so you are quite fit to do so.

Friend, if you get out of prison but especially out of this God-forsaken hole.

Farewell Gordon, we likely may never see us again, but let us live in hope, that it may be otherwise.

Your friend
Oscar Slater

P.S.
Please don't forget to write or see Conan D. also communicate with my cousin in Germany.

This secret message, carried to Conan Doyle in the mouth of a paroled convict in 1925, would bring about Slater's release.

GLASGOW CITY COUNCIL: ARCHIVES; TD1560/1/1.

The Glasgow police detective John Thomson Trench sacrificed his career after voicing doubts about the Slater case.

PETERHEAD PRISON MUSEUM

Conan Doyle and (part of) Windlesham, his vast home in southeast England

ARTHUR CONAN DOYLE COLLECTION—LANCELYN GREEN BEQUEST, PORTSMOUTH CITY COUNCIL

Conan Doyle with Craigie Aitchison, now regarded as the greatest Scottish criminal lawyer of all time, at the review of Slater's case in 1928

ARTHUR CONAN DOYLE COLLECTION—LANCELYN GREEN BEQUEST, PORTSMOUTH CITY COUNCIL

Mary Barrowman in the late 1920s, around the time of Slater's release. "She is in the streets & has been in prison," one Scottish journalist discovered.

PETERHEAD PRISON MUSEUM

Dapper again:
A post-release Oscar Slater, late 1920s

WILLIAM ROUGHEAD,
*TRIAL OF OSCAR SLATER* (1910)

Trench was assigned by Chief Superintendent Orr to interview Birrell at her home. As he later recounted: "I had particular instructions to question her with regard to [A.B.] and as to what Lambie said when she visited her house on the night of the murder. I visited Miss Birrell and from her received the statement word for word." Returning to the police station, he recounted what Birrell told him to two superiors, the similarly named Superintendent John Ord and Chief Superintendent John Orr. Orr seemed especially enthusiastic, saying, "This is the first real clue we have got." Birrell's statement, as taken down by Trench, reads:

> I am niece of the late Marion Gilchrist, who resided at 15 Queen's Terrace, West Princes Street. My mother was a sister of the deceased. Miss Gilchrist was not on good terms with her relations. Few if any visited her. . . .
>
> On her return [from a recent trip] she time and again declared her determination to alter her Will. It was believed by some of her relations that she had done so. She made no secret of her intention. She was positively nasty with any relative who might call. . . .
>
> I can never forget the night of the murder. Miss Gilchrist's servant Nellie Lambie came to my door about 7-15. She was excited. She pulled the bell violently. On the door being opened she rushed into the house and exclaimed "Oh, Miss Birrell, Miss Birrell, Miss Gilchrist has been murdered, she is lying dead in the Dining Room, and oh, Miss Birrell, I saw the man who did it."
>
> I replied "My God, Nellie, this is awful. Who was it, do you know him?"
>
> Nellie replied, "Oh, Miss Birrell, I think it was [A.B.]. I am sure that it was [A.B.]." I said to her, "My God,

> Nellie, don't say that, a murder in the family is bad enough, but a murderer is a thousand times worse. Unless you are very sure of it, Nellie, don't say that." She again repeated to me that she was sure that it was [A.B.].
>
> The same evening Detectives Pyper and Dornan visited me, and I learned from them that she had told them that it was [A.B.]. I told a number of my friends about it, including a member of the Glasgow Corporation,* who communicated with Chief Superintendent Orr. On Wednesday afternoon, 23rd Decr., 1908, Detective Trench visited me, and I told him exactly what Lambie had told me.

But before December 23 was out, efforts to quash the "first real clue" were under way: the man Lambie had named was a highly placed member of Glasgow society. While Trench was writing up Birrell's statement, Superintendent Ord was on the telephone to a colleague, Superintendent William Miller Douglas. Douglas ran the police department's Western Division, which had primary charge of the investigation. "I have been ringing up Douglas," Ord told Trench, "and he is convinced that [A.B.] had nothing to do with it." And that, as far as Birrell's statement went, was that: its existence was never disclosed to Slater's defense team.

On January 3, 1909, Trench, carrying a sketch of Slater, was dispatched to interview Lambie. She failed to identify the sketch. As Trench later testified:

> Although I had not spoken to Lambie, I was aware, having taken Miss Birrell's statement, that she had declared

* Then the name of the governing body that ran the city.

> that [A.B.] was the man. I touched on [A.B.], asking her if she really thought he was the man she saw. Her answer was, "It's gey* funny if it wasn't him I saw." . . . My conclusion after meeting Lambie was that if she had had any one to support her she would have sworn to [A.B.]. So much impressed was I that I mentioned the fact to Superintendent Ord next morning, asking if he thought that [A.B.] might not be the man. His only answer was, "Douglas has cleared up all that, what can we do?"

MARION GILCHRIST HAD A younger brother, James, who married a woman named Elizabeth Greer. James died in 1870, and three years later Elizabeth Greer Gilchrist married Professor Matthew Charteris, who taught medicine at Glasgow University. The couple had three sons: Archibald, born in 1874; Francis, born in 1875; and John, born in 1877.

The Charterises were a distinguished line—their forebears included eminent missionaries, theologians, and educators—and Elizabeth's sons bore out the family's expectations handsomely: Archibald became a prominent lawyer, Francis became a doctor who like his father taught at Glasgow University, and John became an army officer. By the turn of the twentieth century the family was among the prominent in Glasgow. Francis Charteris further cemented its position with his marriage in 1907 to Annie Fraser Kedie, the daughter of one of the city's wealthy manufacturers.

Though not related to Miss Gilchrist by blood, the Charteris brothers, as the sons of her former sister-in-law, became her de facto nephews. They visited her on occasion and by most

* A Scottish dialect term meaning "very" or "really."

accounts maintained as cordial relations with her as anyone ever did. Francis Charteris, whose wedding Miss Gilchrist attended, was especially attentive; it was from him that she had received her Irish terrier as a present. Despite these attentions, however, as Margaret Birrell told Trench, "Miss Gilchrist stated to me that none of the Charteris family would finger a penny of her money."

Francis Charteris was "A.B." Though Conan Doyle privately believed that he was the man in Miss Gilchrist's hall that night, he knew better than to accuse him. Cook, too, urged caution. "I intend to deal delicately with any allegations regarding the Doctor," he wrote to Conan Doyle in May 1914. "I have no right—no one has any right to say that Dr. Charteris is the man. We certainly have the right to say that if his name was mentioned by Lambie there ought to be an end of the Slater case."

But because the Charteris family appeared to have pulled strings at the highest level to have Lambie's disclosure suppressed, the hearing into Slater's case would turn out to be little more than a travesty.

THE CLOSED-DOOR INQUIRY INTO the case of Oscar Slater took place in Glasgow from April 23 to 25, 1914. Sheriff Millar heard testimony from some twenty witnesses, several of whom, including Mary Barrowman and the bicycle dealer Allan McLean, largely recapitulated what they had said at trial five years before.

The police officers who testified formed an implacable blue wall. Chief Superintendent Orr, who now held the rank of assistant chief constable, said that he recalled neither having sent

Trench to interview Margaret Birrell nor having said "This is the first real clue we have got." Inspector Pyper, now chief detective inspector, said that Lambie had never told him about A.B. on the night of the murder and had said she could not identify the intruder.

Millar also took testimony from Lambie and Birrell. Lambie, now married to a coal miner named Robert Gillon, denied having mentioned A.B.'s name. She further denied having been shown a sketch of Slater by Trench, having been questioned by Trench about A.B., and having told him, "It's gey funny if it wasn't him I saw." Birrell denied that Lambie had told her about A.B. and denied having recounted as much to Trench.

A few witnesses gave testimony that should have weighed in Slater's favor, including two not heard at the original trial: the greengrocer Duncan MacBrayne and Colin MacCallum, the bootmaker who was Barrowman's employer. MacBrayne testified to having seen Slater standing serenely in front of his own apartment-house door at eight-fifteen on the night of the murder—precisely the time he was alleged to have been weaving through the streets of suburban Glasgow after having killed Miss Gilchrist. MacCallum testified that Barrowman had no errand that would have taken her through West Princes Street that night.

Last to testify on day one was John Thomson Trench. The next day, David Cook wrote to Conan Doyle:

> *The Inquiry as you are aware opened yesterday. Trench was the last witness to be examined for the day. I saw him later on. He is a very shrewd man and absolutely upright. He told me that in his view the Inquiry was as big a farce as had been perpetrated for some considerable time in legal circles.*

> *In the first place the Sheriff went for him like a pick-pocket: told him that Miss Birrell and Lambie had denied the Charteris matter and would he dare to insist. He replied that he insisted, and produced his Diary which has been kept in first class order showing that he made the visits. . . .*
>
> *The hand of the police permeates the whole case. . . . To release Slater as a result of the present agitation practically means a censure on the Police, on the Fiscal, on the Lord Advocate and on the Judge. Rather than have the matter come to the light of day, every effort has been and will be made to burke honest investigation.*

When the hearing ended, Sheriff Millar sent a transcript to Secretary McKinnon Wood for review. "With regard to the manner of those making statements," he wrote in an accompanying note, "I think it is enough to say that Miss Birrell . . . seemed to be [a] very intelligent, careful and trustworthy witness. . . . Mrs. Gillon [Helen Lambie], Miss Mary Barrowman, and Mr. MacBrayne seemed to be honest and anxious to tell the truth." On June 17, 1914, McKinnon Wood announced his decision. "I am satisfied," he said, "that *no case is established that would justify me in advising any interference with the sentence*."

Incensed, Conan Doyle fired off a letter to the press that burned with rationalist rage. "This inquiry was held *in camera* before a single local sheriff, with no oath administered to witnesses," he wrote. "It savoured rather of Russian than of Scottish jurisprudence." He added: "The whole case will, in my opinion, remain immortal in the classics of crime as the supreme example of official incompetence and obstinacy."

Despite Conan Doyle's eminent anger, "we could do no more," he wrote, "and there the matter rested." For Trench and Cook, however, a dark new phase of the case was about to begin.

---

ON JULY 14, 1914, Detective Lieutenant John Thomson Trench was suspended from duty; on September 14, he was formally dismissed from the Glasgow police department. Disgraced and with few prospects, he joined the military, becoming a drill instructor, and later a provost sergeant, in the Royal Scots Fusiliers. In May 1915, as he was about to ship out with his battalion to the Dardanelles, two Glasgow police officers arrested him; Cook was arrested the same day. They were charged with having resold items stolen in the robbery of a Glasgow jeweler's shop in January 1914.

Trench had been a detective on that case. Authorized by his superiors, he had enlisted Cook to mediate between the shop's insurance company and the fence who had the jewels. Cook did, and, in exchange for £400 from the insurer, the jewels were returned. Now the procurator fiscal, James Hart, declared that he had never been told of the arrangement. The transaction by Cook and Trench, he charged, constituted an illegal sale of stolen goods.

The trial of Cook and Trench opened in August 1915. Mercifully, the judge nearly laughed the case out of court, instructing the jury to find them not guilty. The jury complied, with a unanimous verdict. Trench went on to serve with distinction in World War I and was discharged from the military in October 1918. Both he and Cook would die young, Trench in 1919, at fifty; Cook in 1921, at forty-nine.

IT WOULD BE MORE than a decade after the inquiry before Conan Doyle involved himself in Slater's affairs again. As he wrote:

> I got weary of this case for I spent months on it . . . but felt I was up against a ring of political lawyers who could not give away the police without also giving away themselves. There is no doubt that Mr. Ure went far too far in his speech for the prosecution, and that this must be admitted when justice is done. . . .
>
> We want a complete and impartial investigation. It will be a huge scandal when it comes—if it ever does come.
>
> Oscar Slater never knew that Miss Gilchrist existed, and there is no evidence worthy of the name against him. As to who did it that is dangerous ground. Anyhow Slater did not.

By 1924, when Conan Doyle published the first edition of his autobiography, which included a summary of the Slater case up to that time, most of the principals from the trial and secret inquiry were dead. "It is a curious circumstance that as I write . . . Judge Guthrie, Cook, Trench, . . . Millar and others have all passed on," Conan Doyle said. "But Slater still remains, eating out his heart at Peterhead."

## Chapter 17

## CANNIBALS INCLUDED

THE WAR YEARS WERE HELLISH FOR SLATER. ON ONE occasion, inflamed with the anti-German sentiment that pervaded Britain, Peterhead guards tied him to a post—as punishment either for talking or for failing to perform his quarry work—and left him outside in the sun for two hours. This incident, at least, which Slater recounted in a 1925 complaint to prison officials, seems not to have been paranoid fantasy: it is also described in William Gordon's newspaper article about Slater's life behind bars, published after Gordon's release in 1925. "It is a recognised thing for warders to turn a blind eye when they see a man talking or committing some other minor breach of prison rules," Gordon wrote. "But Slater was reported—and punished—more frequently than others."

War also put an end to the sustaining flow of letters from Beuthen. Slater's file of family correspondence, bursting with letters in both directions, is, from the summer of 1914 to the spring of 1919, utterly bare. "Dearest Parents," he would write in 1919. "Your last letter, my dears, I received on the 8/8/1914—five years ago." He continued:

*After the signing of peace, I hoped to hear from you first—my present feelings God only knows. . . . During the war I could get no letters. I have artificially kept up my courage, but now it is difficult. The war is finished, ways and means are open again for letters to be sent to me, and to be still without news from you, my dears, makes me quite unhappy. The uncertainty begins to tell on me. . . . You, my dearest parents are old, I am getting old and broken in health. We all go the same way, and I beg you with all my heart to write to me soon with all details—I am prepared for anything.*

In April 1919, Slater received his first piece of mail after the war: a letter from his sister Malchen. It was the first time a family member other than his parents had written. "I need not hide from you any longer, dear Oscar, that Mother was very ill, and it is a special grace from God that she has been spared to us," Malchen wrote. "We were all happy to get a sign of life from you again. I will write to you again as soon as I am permitted to do so. I visit our parents almost weekly or as often as possible."

Then, the following February, came the news for which Slater had long steeled himself. "I can imagine, dear Oskar, how the death of our dear ones would grieve you and I hope you have got over the first shock," Malchen wrote to him in a later communication. "I will now tell you something about the last days of our parents":

*Father had been frail for many years, so that his death was a relief. Mother took diabetes and suffered also from heart trouble, added to which she suffered on your account. . . . You cannot imagine how everything has changed, the terrible prices for everything in Germany and the scarcity of food. Georg took stomach trouble suddenly. It developed into cancer. . . . His wife died from a swollen throat, which could not be operated on, as she had a weak heart. . . . [Their] youngest boy Karl, a fine, intelligent fellow, fell in the war. Ernst the older one is in an institution for nervous troubles. . . . I do not come together with Phemie at all. She was very unkind to our departed mother. . . . After mother's death she behaved badly to me also, and the consequence is that I have lost the whole inheritance. I do not mind so much from a financial point of view, only her bad treatment worries me.*

Slater's reply has not survived, but in October 1920, Malchen wrote again:

*It is a pity that you have to write in English . . . as I am afraid I will not get your letters translated correctly, and some of their contents may, therefore, be lost to me. Now, I will answer your questions about the dying day of our dear parents. Our dear father died first, on the 11th of June, 1916; Georg on the 18th April, 1917; and a few days later on the 1st May, our dear mother. She was unaware of the death of Georg. . . .*

*My dear husband still travels in the cloth line and so does my eldest boy, Felix, who was established himself, but business is very bad now. The war has changed everything. Harry does not give me much joy, but Kätel and Felix make up for this. Now, dear Oscar, you know all the sad news. Keep your head high and remain in good health. With God's help we will see each other again, this is my daily prayer. Is there still no ray of light over your dark affair?*

To the end of his incarceration, Malchen would be Slater's primary link to the family. "Good Malchen . . . I shall write regularly every 6 weeks to you, & should I be bound to write to somebody else, then I will ask for special permission," Slater wrote her in an undated letter from the early 1920s. "I am very happy to hear that you are 44 years old, 25 years married. . . . I look like a old grey Tom-Cat."

In March 1922, Malchen, who lived in Breslau, a hundred miles northwest of Beuthen, replied:

> *Certainly I will write you promptly every six weeks if this is permitted and expect you in return to do the same. . . . With Phemie's children I am on good terms, but herself I will never meet in this life again. I promised this to our dear mother, and, besides, she has annoyed me a great deal. . . .*
>
> *Imagine, practically the whole of Upper Silesia including Beuthen has been assigned to Poland and a journey there now is connected with great difficulties and is very expensive.* Nevertheless, I intend going every year to visit the grave of our dear parents.*

Then, in August, a surprise: a letter from Phemie herself. "We often think of you, and our children have nothing but good to relate of Uncle Oscar," she wrote him. "All our dear ones have been called away too soon. My child Lilli died when 18 years of age. . . . Max and the children send heartfelt greetings."

In the envelope, Phemie enclosed a last letter from Slater's

* At the conclusion of World War I, after much of Silesia was awarded to Poland, Beuthen became known as Bytom and Breslau as Wrocław.

parents, written eight years before. Dated August 3, 1914, it had remained unsent throughout the war. "My beloved Oscar," Pauline wrote:

> *You may be sure, dearest child, I count every day to the time when your letters can reach us. . . . You must not give up hope till your last breath. Your innocence must be established sooner or later. A child such as you have been towards your parents can expect from God that his innocence will be established some day. . . . I often think of the Dreyfus affair where right conquered in the end. . . .*
>
> *Father is getting frail. His greatest amusement is to eat well and smoke a good cigar. Things are not so comfortable as they were two years ago. . . .*
>
> *The wife of the man with whom you served your apprenticeship has gone all wrong, as he only deserved. . . . Georg gives us every month 50 Marks and this even without having asked it of him. . . . I can earn nothing now myself, and father is able to do nothing whatever. . . . The arrival of your letter is always a pleasing event, and there is nothing suspicious about it. Even the postman has no suspicion of where the letter comes from. . . .*
>
> *Keep up your strength, and with hope of kisses from your loving Mother.*

IN JANUARY 1925, on his release from Peterhead, Prisoner 2988, William Gordon, underwent a rigorous search by prison guards, from the lining of his coat to the hollow handle of his suitcase. Despite their vigilance, he managed to pass out of prison with his false teeth, and Slater's note—whose glazed-paper wrapping had been lifted from the prison bookbinding shop—intact.

Gordon found his way to Windlesham, the home in southeast England that Conan Doyle shared with Jean; their sons, Adrian and Denis; and their daughter, also named Jean. (Years later, Adrian Conan Doyle recalled his father having shown him the rolled-up scrap containing Slater's urgent plea.) An expansive Victorian villa, Windlesham supported a staff that included, a biographer wrote, "a butler . . . a cook and five maids in the house, two gardeners and a chauffeur outside, plus a garden boy who cleaned the boots and shoes and doubled as a pageboy, with a green bellhop uniform and pillbox hat." As curious as it might seem to envision a freshly paroled convict turning up in such surroundings, given Conan Doyle's portfolio as a real-world detective, the sight was not altogether unknown.

Gordon's minuscule cargo seemed to embody the ethos of Joseph Bell, who had written, "The importance of the infinitely little is incalculable." For that message-in-miniature would set in motion a chain of events that in late 1927 would bring about Slater's release, including a new book about the case, edited and published by Conan Doyle; a widely read newspaper exposé; and dramatic recantations of their courtroom testimony by Helen Lambie and Mary Barrowman.

Though Conan Doyle had forsaken work on the case after the 1914 debacle, he had been far from idle. After making several visits to the front during World War I, where he came under fire, he began work on what would be a six-volume history of the war, *The British Campaign in France and Flanders.* Nor did he neglect crime fiction: by this time he had written fifty-four of the sixty Holmes tales.

"From time to time," Conan Doyle later wrote, "one hears some word of poor Slater from behind his prison walls like the wail of some wayfarer who has fallen into a pit and implores aid from passers-by." On receiving the smuggled note from Gordon, he was once again moved to lend his energies to Slater's cause.

Gordon's message was not Conan Doyle's first experience with secret communication. In 1915, he had sent a series of covert dispatches to British prisoners of war in Germany. "It was not very difficult to do," he explained, "but it had the effect of cheering them by a little authentic news, for at that time they were only permitted to see German newspapers. It came about in this way":

> A dear friend of my wife's, Miss Lily Loder Symonds, had a brother, Captain Willie Loder Symonds, of the Wiltshires, who had been wounded and taken in the stand of the 7th Brigade. . . . He was an ingenious fellow and had written home a letter which passed the German censor, because it seemed to consist in the description of a farm, but when read carefully it was clear that it was the conditions of himself and his comrades which he was discussing. It seemed to me that if a man used such an artifice he would be prepared for a similar one in a letter from home. I took one of my books . . . and beginning with the third chapter—I guessed the censor would examine the first—I put little needle-pricks under the various printed letters until I had spelled out all the news. I then sent the book and also a letter. In the letter I said that the book was, I feared, rather slow in the opening, but that from Chapter III onwards he might find it more interesting. That was as plain as I dared to make it. Loder Symonds missed the allusion altogether, but by good luck he showed the letter to Captain the Hon. Rupert Keppel, of the Guards, who had been taken at Landrecies. He smelled a rat, borrowed the book, and found my

> cipher. A message came back to his father, Lord Albemarle, to the effect that he hoped Conan Doyle would send some more books. This was sent on to me, and of course showed me that it was all right. From that time onwards every month or two I pricked off my bulletin.

For Conan Doyle, the Great War had been a time of consuming activity and consuming loss. After Britain entered the war, he tried, with characteristic patriotism, to enlist. The authorities declined: he was fifty-five. He busied himself instead in creating what became a nationwide network of two hundred thousand civilian reservists, who stood ready to defend the home front. "Our drill and discipline were excellent," Conan Doyle wrote, "nor were our marching powers contemptible when one remembers that many of the men were in the fifties and even in the sixties. It was quite usual for us to march from Crowborough to Frant, with our rifles and equipment, to drill for a long hour in a heavy marshy field, and then to march back, singing all the way. It would be a good 14 miles."

In 1914, after three British warships were sunk by German torpedoes in a single day, leaving more than a thousand sailors flailing in the water until they drowned, Conan Doyle wrote to the navy, proposing that every British sailor be issued an inflatable rubber collar that would keep him afloat in the sea. The navy adopted the measure soon afterward.

For Conan Doyle, as for many, the war brought the duality of the age into sharp relief: the wonders of science and technology, fields so bright with promise in the nineteenth century, seemed far less wondrous in the twentieth when realized as air warfare and nerve gas. The war had robbed him of two beloved family members: his eldest son, Kingsley, from his marriage to Louise, and his younger brother, Innes. Both had been in combat, and both, battle weary, had died soon afterward, in the influenza pandemic of 1918–19.

Now the foundational certainties of the Victorian age—class and honor; God, queen, and country—seemed to count for little. Amid the crush of modernity, many began seeking the kind of spiritual sustenance they felt the new century had expunged. Sir Arthur Conan Doyle, scientist, rationalist, and abductive logician par excellence, was one of the foremost among them.

Conan Doyle had long believed the gulf between science and the spirit to be bridgeable. First attracted to spiritualism in the 1890s, he had been exploring it with quiet, methodical skepticism ever since. Now the pull of the field, with its central belief in an afterlife and its promise of a vanished past that remained discernible in the present—allowing the living to converse with departed loved ones—became consuming. "Those who, in later years, professed astonishment that someone as down to earth as Conan Doyle should espouse spiritualism," his biographer Russell Miller has written, "failed to appreciate that the movement in the late Victorian era, far from being dominated by cranks and charlatans, attracted some of the country's leading scientific minds."

To his quest to determine whether life endured beyond death, Conan Doyle brought (or so he felt) the same brand of empirical investigation that he applied to the detection of crimes. His work involved attending séances by a spate of professed mediums, writing extensively on the subject, and releasing his findings through the Psychic Press, the publishing house he had founded. "How thorough and long were my studies," he wrote, "before I was at last beaten out of my material agnostic position and forced to admit the validity of the proofs. . . . When, on the other hand, it is found that the medium has introduced false drapery or accessories . . . we are in the presence of the most odious and blasphemous crime which a human being can commit."

On questions of spiritualism, it is clear that Conan Doyle's ardent personal longing eclipsed his scientific acumen. By the 1920s, he had come to believe almost unreservedly in ghosts, fairies, and the reality of life after death. In his books, articles, and lectures of the period, he espoused the conviction that Spiritualism embodied fundamental human truths more fully than Christianity did. Not surprisingly, Miller wrote, this stance did not sit well with many observers:

> At Windlesham, Conan Doyle became accustomed to receiving hate mail, most of which he disregarded, but there was one particularly vituperative letter, dated 16 December 1919, from Lord Alfred Douglas, Oscar Wilde's former lover and a relatively recent convert to the Roman Catholic church: "Sir, What a disgusting beast you are with your filthy caricatures of 'Christ.' The proper way to deal with such a man as you would be to give you a thrashing with a horse whip." . . . Douglas accused Conan Doyle of promoting spiritualism for the sake of money and notoriety, "in short for the same purposes and with the same flat-footed low persistence as you worked your idiot 'Sherlock Holmes' business." He went on to prophesy that Conan Doyle's "blasphemous ravings" would bring a "dreadful judgement" on him and signed himself "Yours with the utmost contempt." Conan Doyle replied the following day, with a masterful and succinct dismissal: "Sir, I was relieved to get your letter. It is only your approval which could in any way annoy me."

But even in the opinion of more moderate critics, Conan Doyle's involvement in spiritualism, and the public derision it aroused, may well have undercut his efforts on Slater's behalf.

AS THE 1920S UNSPOOLED, Slater's sisters continued their correspondence, with Malchen in particular assuming their mother's role as the keeper of the lamp in the window. "In vain I have waited so many months for a sign of life from you," she wrote in 1923. "As soon as you possibly can, dear Oscar, let us hear something from you. . . . Life is still very hard for Germany. . . . I pray daily to the dear God that your innocence will come to light and you will gain your freedom."

Some time later, Slater wrote: "You write me in your letters that there is no wonder if I have lost interest in you. . . . But you are very far wrong dear Malchen. I can only lose interest in you when I cease to exist. I think daily of you all."

Phemie, too, wrote regularly. "Max speaks often about you and the children do so as well," she wrote in March 1924. "Magda, Erna, Erich and Hans are married. Walter is still single and an eighteen year old daughter (Lilli) is most unfortunately lost by death during the war. My old Max (he is now 60 years old) is still quite robust and must still work skillfully and earn money. . . . If only there were a prospect of your being seen again! Our dear parents always prayed to God for that, but unfortunately they left this life so quickly. . . . From your loving sister, Phemie, Max and all 5 children."

The following September, she wrote: "I have just come from the grave of our dear blessed parents and send as a greeting a few leaves therefrom. . . . We would take you in gladly, myself as well as Malchen. You know well that Max had always plenty to spare for you and our brotherly love is not extinct. . . . Our dear mother would rejoice with all her heart, if she had seen how we are sticking to you and how willingly we would have you in our midst."

By the mid-1920s, Slater's lot at Peterhead had improved in one respect: after fifteen years, and many requests, he had been relieved of hard labor in the quarry and now worked in the prison carpentry shop. But though his letters from this period express relief at the new assignment, they remain shot through with despair.

"I don't know if there is a Being in this wide world (Cannibals included) who feel how I feel," he wrote expressively to a Glasgow friend, Samuel Reid, in 1924. "It [has been] 15½ years that I was thrown into prison for a crime, of which I feel myself guiltless. . . . At the present time I feel like bursting. . . . Will not a little allowance be made for the great doubt in my case?" Slater's smuggled message of 1925 would bring about that allowance at last.

## Chapter 18

# THE PURLOINED BROOCH

IN EARLY 1925, ON RECEIVING GORDON'S MESSAGE, CONAN Doyle wrote to Sir John Gilmour, the Secretary for Scotland. "After a careful analysis of the case I am personally convinced that Slater never knew that such a woman as the deceased ever existed until he was accused of her murder," he said. "Apart, however, from the original question of guilt or innocence, the man has now served 15 years, which is, as I understand, the usual limit of a life sentence in Scotland when the prisoner behaves well. I would earnestly entreat your kind personal attention to this case, which is likely to live in the annals of criminology."

Conan Doyle clearly expected a reply: he was accustomed to having his views heard and, on subjects other than spiritualism, taken seriously by Britain's leading lights. "The big atmosphere of Conan Doyle ran as an undiminished force throughout my twenty-one years under his roof," his son Adrian recalled. "As a little boy, I would be lifted to the window by a goggle-eyed nurse to watch my father and the then Prime Minister of England pacing slowly up and down the lawn in earnest discussion."

This time Conan Doyle got no answer. But he did receive a letter from the Glasgow journalist William Park, with whom he had been corresponding about the case since 1914, when Park became an impassioned supporter of Trench and Cook. Now Park, who had continued investigating the case on his own, contacted Conan Doyle again. "You may take it there will be no move for Liberation," he wrote. "Slater will never get out. It is my own intention, however, to publish at some later date a new book on the case. I shall go into the system of faking witnesses, suppressing those favourable to the prisoner and getting those not so favourable to cook their statements. It can be proved that the authorities put into the box at least one known *perjurer*."

Moved by Park's letter, Conan Doyle wrote to Gilmour again. On February 28, 1925, one of Gilmour's underlings sent a terse reply: "I am directed by the Secretary for Scotland to say that he . . . does not feel justified in advising any interference with Slater's sentence."

"I need not say that I am disappointed," Conan Doyle shot back. "I have done my best to set this injustice right. The responsibility must now lie with you."

SLATER HAD NOW BEEN imprisoned for so long that a third generation of his family had begun writing. "You will be astonished to hear from me, whom you will scarcely remember at all," read one letter, from September 1925, written just before Rosh Hashanah, the Jewish New Year:

*I am the old-time little Erna, the daughter of your sister Phemie. . . . We have had hard luck too. There were the war years which brought to us . . . heavy sorrow so that life was a burden, and financially we were thoroughly ruined. Then came the illness of our youngest (Lilli) and her death. After that it was just one blow after another. Poor Uncle Georg, his wife Anna, our dear grandparents—all these passed over in about two years. There were bitter hours and many tears. . . . Mother lets rooms and wears herself out with them. Papa is very much aged. Life is indeed very hard. It goes best with Aunt Malchen. Her husband remains an employee and has neither worry nor care.*

*A happy, healthy New Year to you with hearty greetings and kisses from us all, especially your niece Erna, now Mrs. Meyer.*

In reply, Slater wrote warmly:

*I was astonished to get a letter from you after seventeen years, still I say "Better late than never." I, at any rate, have forgotten none of you and daily think of you all; time and distance can <u>not</u> make me colder. . . . I still remember vividly the good times I had at Telegraph Street,* and I remember the English breakfast. At any rate I am now forced to exclaim, "Frau Meyer, for the last seventeen years I have not breakfasted on ham and eggs."*

*I can imagine very well that the various deaths in your family have caused you all much grief and sorry—especially to your dear mother. I have also felt these fateful blows both physically and mentally. . . . When I take into consideration*

* An apparent reference to Telegraph Street in London. Slater had lived in London during the first years of the twentieth century.

*all the circumstances and also my age I also cannot complain of my health. You must understand, my dear Erna, that after I have been for so long shut off from the world I have not much to write about. . . . Do not grieve over my lot and please do not forget my motto—"Learn to suffer without complaint."*

Soon afterward, Malchen's daughter, Käthe, known by the fond diminutive Kätel, began corresponding. "We have received your loving letter and are delighted that you want to know us children better," she wrote. "We truly believed we might only make your lot harder if we were always writing to you. . . . I hope to be married this year. You know the man very well indeed; he is Sam Tau, his first wife was Martha Jungmann from Beuthen. He is about eighteen years older than I, but that is nothing where there is love."

By the time Slater replied several months later, the wedding had taken place. "Among other things your dear mother also says in regard to your marriage—'Katie has not even a penny of money—not even a chair has she,'" he wrote, adding:

*The first thing, quite clearly is not necessary always for a marriage, for a good wife is worth far more than money; but I am worried about the second item, and I wish that I could help you. . . . Thirteen or fourteen years back my dear late mother sent me your photograph and since that time it has had an honoured place between the photos of my dead parents. Daily I contemplate the deceased and you. . . . I am very sorry indeed to hear that your father is not quite well, perhaps he will have recovered again. I also learn that the times in Germany are very bad but in this country where 1½ millions people have no work one does not dance on roses.*

---

AFTER THE DISMISSIVE REPLY from Gilmour's office, Conan Doyle knew that the Secretary would do nothing. The Crown clearly wanted to avoid the public inquiry, and public scandal, that would arise were the conduct of the police and the procurator fiscal made widely known. But there was another reason for keeping Slater in prison, one of which Conan Doyle may not have been aware: As a series of government memorandums shows, officials did not know what to do with Slater if he were paroled—"released on license," in British parlance. The subject had been under high-level private discussion as early as 1924, when Slater was approaching the fifteen-year mark at Peterhead, the standard length of time before parole could be considered. As the memorandums make clear, the Crown did not want him to stay in Britain after his release but was uncertain whether it could deport him back to Germany.

As British officials eventually learned, a German who had lived outside Germany for more than a decade automatically lost his citizenship. A memo on the subject from July 1924 appeared to seal Slater's continued incarceration. "Apparently we cannot get rid of Slater," it read. "In these circumstances I think that he should be allowed to remain where he is meantime. Case will come up for reconsideration when 20 years have been served."

Slater might not have been able to hold out that long. As his time at Peterhead wore on, he was increasingly volatile, as his disciplinary records attest:

> Aug. 14, 1914: Destroying prison property—Chamber (crockery) & a pane of glass.
>
> May 13, 1916: Talking. Idleness. Using filthy & abusive

> language, also threatening to assault an officer with a hammer.
>
> Sept. 25, 1917: Quarrelling with & assaulting a fellow prisoner on the works.
>
> July 14, 1921: Willfully destroying prison property (2 new library books).
>
> Dec. 20, 1924: Breaking a food dish.
>
> Nov. 16, 1925: Attempting to assault an officer.
>
> April 3, 1926: Offending against good order and discipline ie handing a packet to another Convict.

He vowed he would not pass the two-decade mark alive. "Poor Slater told us . . . that he intended to endure Peterhead till the end of 20 years," the journalist William Park later informed Conan Doyle. "If then no help came he intended to take his life. 'I will show them that Oscar Slater can die bravely,' was his sworn resolve to find an exit to his woes."

PARK WAS A DEDICATED journalist but something of a loose cannon. As his long exchange of letters with Conan Doyle makes clear, his personal life was a shambles: he drank to excess, had made an unhappy marriage, and was often desperate for money—a *New Grub Street* for the twentieth century. Professionally, he was tenacious, a fine attribute in a journalist but a liability when tenacity starts to shade into monomania. "This strange, self-tortured fanatic, whose avowed intent it was to disembowel the Glasgow police," Peter Hunt has called him, adding:

> Park was a remarkable man. Tall, broad-shouldered, rather delicate in appearance, well educated with a fine

ear for music and a photographic memory, he had known nothing of the case until Trench made it clear to him.

An exceptionally clear thinker, impatient of slower minds, overfond of whisky, he had one fault, a tendency to accept as proven facts which had not been thoroughly checked. Though he did much for Slater, he could never quite rid himself of the popular journalist's approach to facts for their "story" value. His correspondence with Conan Doyle shows an impassioned nature, slightly fanatic, seizing proof here and there without proper regard for all the circumstances.

He had got it into his head (and it must be admitted that events seemed to justify him) that the police were wrong from start to finish, corrupt through and through, perjured, vindictive, irresponsible, callous. He approached the Slater case, not merely as an individual mistake but as characteristic of what he considered an entirely corrupt system.

Fortunately, Park had Conan Doyle to sustain him editorially and financially: he sent Park money more than once. Under Conan Doyle's close supervision, Park began work on a book, *The Truth About Oscar Slater,* based on documents and his own reporting, including an extensive interview with Trench's widow. It is clear from their correspondence about the emerging manuscript that Conan Doyle vetted every page of it and made copious suggestions. Conan Doyle went on to release the book himself, through his publishing house, the Psychic Press.

Dedicated to John Thomson Trench, *The Truth About Oscar Slater* appeared in July 1927. As Conan Doyle had before him, Park laid out, with great cumulative impact, the chain of illogic and inconsistencies in the case. His reporting uncovered things that even Conan Doyle had not found, including two instances of fabrication by police and prosecutors.

In the first instance, Park discovered that the Crown had obtained the search warrant for Slater's flat under false pretenses. The application for the warrant, made by the procurator fiscal, James Hart, was dated January 2, 1909—the day Slater arrived in New York on the *Lusitania*. In it, Hart argued that searching the flat was essential because Slater had *already* been charged with Miss Gilchrist's murder and had "absconded" from Scotland. As Park pointed out, Glasgow officials knew that neither of those assertions was true. On the basis of Hart's application, however, the warrant was granted.

The second fabrication involved the failure of the brooch clue, a fact of which police were also aware by the time Slater reached New York. "Now that the whole world was looking on," Park wrote, "to have released their arrested man would have been to confess their blunders.... But, if to proceed was the order, what were they to proceed on?"

The answer, he explained, could be found in a document that Trench had copied from Glasgow police files. Before he died, he gave the copy to Park. In that document, written early in the investigation, Glasgow police weigh the value of the brooch clue relative to evidence against other potential suspects. As originally worded, the text described the brooch clue as *"very much less strong"* than evidence against others. But in the document's official version, those words had been replaced with a penciled substitution. The altered text described the brooch clue as merely *"not stronger"* than the other evidence.

Conan Doyle crowned Park's book with a long, forceful introduction. "It is certain that the case of the alien German Jew, who bore the pseudonym of Oscar Slater, will live in the history of criminology as a miscarriage of justice of a character very unusual in the records of our Courts," he wrote. "There is not one point of the evidence which does not crumble to pieces when it is touched." He continued: "Who is to blame for this great and persistent miscarriage of justice?" There follows a *J'accuse*-style list, which includes the judge, Lord Guthrie; the Lord Advocate, Alexander Ure; a series of Secretaries for Scotland; and Sheriff Millar, "but above all, the Procurator Fiscal and the police."

In conclusion, Conan Doyle wrote: "Finally, we may ask, what can now be done? I fear very little can be done for Slater. Who can restore the vanished years? But his name may be cleared, and possibly some small provision be made for his declining years. . . . Above all, for the credit of British justice, for the discipline of the police force, and for the teaching of officials that their duty to the public has to be done, *a thorough public enquiry should be made into the matter. But let it be a real enquiry,* with impartial men who are resolute for truth and justice upon the Bench. Only when this has been done will the public mind be at ease. . . . It is indeed a lamentable story of official blundering from start to finish. But eighteen years have passed and an innocent man still wears the convict's dress."

## Chapter 19

# THE GATES OF PETERHEAD

PARK'S BOOK SPARKED GREAT INTEREST ON THE PART of the press: the time at last seemed to be right. In the years after World War I, the perceived threat to the genteel classes was shifting. By the 1920s, bourgeois anxieties, once focused on foreigners, had begun to attach themselves to first-wave feminism and the woman suffrage movement, socialism, and the dehumanizing use of technology. Amid these concerns, it seems likely that a lone, aging Jewish rogue did not cut the menacing figure he once did. What was more, most of the actors who might have been tarred by the public investigation of his case—including Lord Guthrie, the judge; Hart, the procurator fiscal; and Sheriff Millar—were now dead.

While the press interest was welcome, Conan Doyle knew that news coverage alone would not suffice. In September 1927, resolving to catch the attention of the British government at the highest level, he sent a copy of Park's book to Ramsay MacDonald, who in 1924 had become Britain's first Labour prime minister. Though the Labour government had been swept out of office by the Conservatives late that year, MacDonald, now the leader of the Labour Party, remained one of the most powerful men in Britain.*

In MacDonald, Conan Doyle found an influential ally. "I have been going further into the case and am quite convinced that this man has received a most horrible injustice and that the matter must be wound up, not only by releasing him, but by clearing him," he wrote to Conan Doyle on September 26. "Everybody must be exceedingly grateful to you for the magnificent way you have stuck to the case, in [the] face of so much discouragement and apparent failure."

Park's book also moved the English journalist Ernest Clephan Palmer to action. Writing under the pseudonym The Pilgrim, Palmer produced a multipart investigative series on the Slater affair that ran in the *Daily News* of London from mid-September to mid-October 1927. "Each day Palmer attacked some fresh aspect of the case, the inaccuracies in the Lord Advocate's speech, Mary Barrowman's acrobatics, the almost lunatic behaviour of the murderer supposing that he was Slater," Peter Hunt has written. "He tested Mary Barrowman's story in West Princes Street and declared that her detailed description of the man running past her was impossible."

On October 23, the *Empire News,* based in Manchester, published its own explosive story—touted in its pages, with noteworthy immodesty, as "one of the most dramatic developments in a criminal case ever recorded." The article was a first-person account by Helen Lambie, who had disappeared from Scotland and was widely presumed dead. The *Empire News* had found her, living with her husband in America, near Pitts-

* MacDonald would serve as prime minister again between 1929 and 1935.

burgh. Her story, stemming from an interview with her there, appeared under the headline "Why I Believe I Blundered over Slater." It read in part:

> It has been said and denied that when first questioned by the police as to whether I had any idea of the identity of the man leaving the house of my mistress on the evening of the murder, I mentioned the name of a man who was in the habit of visiting here.
>
> It is quite true that I did so, because when I returned from buying the evening paper and encountered the strange man coming from the house he did not seem strange to me.
>
> Otherwise, I should have wanted to know more about his presence there. . . .
>
> When I told the police the name of the man I thought I recognised they replied "Nonsense! You don't think he could have murdered and robbed your mistress!" They scoffed so much at the notion of this man being the one I had seen that I allowed myself to be persuaded that I had been mistaken. . . .
>
> I had my reasons for not looking too closely. The man I thought I saw coming out of the flat had been visiting Miss Gilchrist on another occasion, and I happened to mention his name to my mistress afterwards.
>
> She flew into a temper with me and told me that if I ever displayed the slightest curiosity again about any of her visitors she would discharge me. . . .
>
> There were many circumstances to make it easier for me to accept the notion that Slater was the man. . . . Moreover, we were told that he had been caught trying

> to escape to America with some of the property of my mistress. . . .
>
> I am convinced that the man I saw was better dressed and of a better station in life than Slater. The only thing they had in common was that when standing end on the outlines of the faces from the left were very much the same.

"What a story!" Conan Doyle wrote afterward. "What a scandal! She says that the police *made* her say it was Slater. Third degree! What a cess pool it all is! But we have no words of hope from those wooden-headed officials. I shall put on the political screw and I know how to do it. I'll win in the end but it has been a long fight."

Park, meanwhile, was trying to locate Mary Barrowman, who had vanished into the Glasgow slums and was believed to have become a prostitute. "She is in the streets & has been in prison," he wrote to Conan Doyle in the autumn of 1927. "A denial from her would finish the Crown case." Assisted by Palmer and an unnamed ex-convict, Park found her, and on November 5, 1927, the *Daily News* printed her recantation:

> I, Mary Barrowman, who was a witness at the New York proceedings and at the trial in Edinburgh, desire in the interests of justice to make the following statement: . . .
>
> Regarding the proceedings at New York, where I was confronted with the prisoner for the first time . . . I did not feel warranted in then saying after my viewing of him, that Oscar Slater was positively the man I had seen coming down the steps of the house in West Princes Street where Miss Gilchrist was murdered.

I only thought at the time that he was very like the man I had seen, and I did not say in my identification that he positively was the man.

It was when I returned to Glasgow that the question of Slater being positively the man was brought before my notice. This was done by Mr. Hart, the Fiscal.

This gentleman was most severe in his treatment of me as a witness. He made me appear at his office day after day to have a meeting with him.

I should say that I was in attendance at his office for the purpose of going over my evidence on at least 15 occasions. I am positive that is an under- rather than an overstatement of the number of my appearances in his office.

It was the same routine every day. He went over my evidence, himself doing all the talking and I for the most part listening. He was so much the director of the things that were to be said that I had no opportunity or very little to have my say.

It was Mr. Hart who got me to change my statement from being "very like the man" to the emphatic declaration that Slater was the man.

The furthest I wanted to go was to say he was very like the man, and it was Mr. Hart who really used the words "the man," and applied them to my statement.

I want to state most definitely that I thought Mr. Hart's demeanour was not what it should be. He was the party who was laying down what was to be said. . . .

I was just a girl of fifteen years of age then, and I did not fully appreciate the difference between saying that Slater was the man instead of very like the man; and if I had it to say now all I would declare is that he was very like the man—and that is what I said when I first saw him.

The recantations made it impossible for the government to stonewall Slater's supporters any longer. On November 10, Sir John Gilmour issued a statement: "Oscar Slater has now completed more than eighteen and a half years of his life sentence, and I have felt justified in deciding to authorise his release on license as soon as suitable arrangements can be made."

The news reached Slater on the prison bush telegraph. Reverend Eleazar Phillips, his champion from the beginning, was summoned in secret to Peterhead to escort him out. On Monday, November 14, 1927, at 3:00 p.m., the gates that separated the prison from the world swung open, and Oscar Slater passed through them, after eighteen years, four months, and six days, a free man.

## Chapter 20

# MORE LIGHT, MORE JUSTICE

WORD OF SLATER'S IMPENDING RELEASE HAD TRICKled out to the British press and become a sensation. One reporter, posing as the chauffeur, managed to sneak into the car carrying Slater and Reverend Phillips from the prison. Another infiltrated their private compartment on the train to Glasgow. How did it feel, he asked Slater, to have been freed at long last? "The best plan," Slater replied, "is to go to Peterhead and find out!"

At Glasgow's Buchanan Street Station, a throng of pressmen met the train. Whisked by Phillips and his grown daughter into a waiting car, Slater was taken to the minister's house. There, too, a mob of reporters and photographers awaited. How did he feel? Slater was asked again and again. "I am tired," he said. "I have not slept for the last five nights, since I heard I was coming back again. I want rest. I want rest."

He dined with the Phillips family that evening, and stayed the night. Soon afterward, he paid a visit to Glasgow police headquarters, where his odyssey had begun so long ago: as a paroled convict, he was required to report to the police once a month. Now gaunt, grizzled, and nearly bald, Slater was much changed from the dapper, dark-haired, well-built man of two decades before. At headquarters, he asked after many of the principal actors in his case—Chief Inspector Pyper, Superintendent Ord, Sheriff Warnock—and was told that all were retired or dead.

From Conan Doyle, he received a warm, welcoming letter:

*Dear Mr. Oscar Slater,*

*This is to say in my wife's name and my own how grieved we have been at the infamous injustice which you have suffered at the hands of our officials. Your only poor consolation can be that your fate, if we can get people to realise the effects, may have the effect of safeguarding others in the future.*

*We will still work in the hope of getting an inquiry into these iniquities and eventually, as I hope, some compensation for your own undeserved suffering.*

*Yours faithfully,*
*Arthur Conan Doyle*

Slater replied ardently, his English unalloyed by eighteen years in a British prison:

*Sir Conan Doyle, you breaker of my shackels, you lover of truth for justice sake, I thank you from the bottom of my heart for the goodness you have shown towards me.*

*My heart is full and almost breaking with love & gratitude for you [and] your wife dear Lady Conan Doyle and all the upright men and women, who for justice sake (and that only) have helped me, <u>me an outcast.</u>*

*Till my dying day I will love and honor you and the Dear Lady, my dear, dear Conan Doyle, yet that unbounded love for you both, makes me only sign plainly.*

*Yours,*
*Oscar Slater*

SLATER WAS FREE, BUT what remained was to have him exonerated. In 1926, Scotland had established its first court of criminal appeals, partly as a result of the agitation by Conan Doyle and others on Slater's behalf. But as constituted, the new court was of no help to Slater himself: It was empowered to hear only those cases tried after October 31, 1926. It would take a special act of British Parliament to have the Slater case grandfathered in.

Aided by Ramsay MacDonald, Conan Doyle prepared to take Parliament on, writing a pamphlet that pressed for judicial review. It was distributed to every member of the House of Commons. On November 16, 1927, Secretary Gilmour presented to Commons a special bill that would let Slater's case be reheard. It passed into law on November 30.

To represent Slater, supporters hired Craigie Aitchison, one of Scotland's foremost criminal lawyers. "Many lawyers rated [Aitchison] the greatest to have practised at the Scottish bar," the *Guardian* wrote in 2009. "In his many defences in murder trials he never lost a single case." Aitchison did not come cheap, and a public subscription was begun to meet his fees.* The funds

* A record of donors includes the crime novelist Dorothy L. Sayers, who contributed three guineas—three pounds and three shillings.

raised were not enough to cover the expected costs, and Conan Doyle agreed to make up the difference himself, an act of generosity he would come to regret.

THE APPEAL OF OSCAR SLATER against His Majesty's Advocate opened on June 8, 1928, at the High Court of Justiciary in Edinburgh, in the same courtroom in which Slater had been sentenced to hang. Presiding was a five-judge panel headed by the Lord Justice General (Scotland's highest-ranking criminal judge), James Avon Clyde. Representing the Crown was the Lord Advocate, William Watson. Slater, accompanied by Reverend Phillips, sat in the gallery. Conan Doyle was there, returned to the city of his birth to cover the appeal for the *Sunday Pictorial* newspaper. It was the only time that he and Slater met face-to-face.

The judges insisted that the hearing not retry the original case, ruling that no new evidence could be introduced unless it stemmed from newly discovered facts. They also barred testimony from Slater. "In these circumstances," they wrote, "it would be quite unreasonable to spend time over his examination now."

Slater, who did not understand the legal wellsprings of the decision, was incensed. With characteristic hotheadedness, he decided to torpedo the appeal, wiring the participants that he wanted the proceedings called off. This, in turn, incensed Conan Doyle. "I think his brain is about turned by all that he has gone through," he said in an interview. "I told him that he was a very foolish fellow to even think of withdrawing, and insisted that it would go on in any case, whether he liked it or not." (In private, Conan Doyle was far more immoderate, writing to Roughead, "I was in a mood to sign a petition that the original sentence be carried out.") Gradually Slater's supporters prevailed on him, and he agreed to sit quietly in the gallery.

Because the trial would not be reprised, few original witnesses were allowed to testify. As a result, neither Detective Pyper nor Superintendent Douglas, both influential in the murder investigation, would be available for Aitchison to cross-examine. "I am very anxious to get Detective Pyper into the box," Park had told Conan Doyle earlier that year. "This man, I am sure, we can bring to earth as a Liar of the first water." He added: "Slater described to us how he was identified at the . . . police office. Superintendent Douglas took each of the witnesses by the shoulders, went down the line of presented men, pushed the witness towards each man and asked, 'Is that him.' When the witness came to be opposite Slater, Douglas gave a violent push this time & shouted in unmistakable signification, '*Is this him?*' "

Nor would Miss Gilchrist's niece Margaret Birrell, to whom Lambie had run after the crime, be called—though her testimony, Park pointed out, would have been of little help. "This woman will die before she emits the name now," he said. "It involves ruin, the possible hanging of her cousin & other terrible things. No: She will not squeal."

Without these witnesses, it was vital that Helen Lambie give testimony, which, in light of her 1927 recantation, the judges were going to allow. "This woman," Aitchison declared, "holds the secret." But Lambie was nowhere to be found. She had left Pittsburgh, and efforts to trace her had been unsuccessful. She was eventually discovered living in Peoria, Illinois, with her husband, Robert Gillon, who worked in the coal mines there, and their two daughters, Margaret and Marion. In June

1928, the *Peoria Star* published an article under the headline "Slayer's Fate Is in Peorian's Hands."

"Wiping her suds-covered hands on her apron," it read, "Mrs. Gillon, a slender, ruddy faced woman, appeared at the door of her humble little home in the rear of a barber shop in answer to the reporter's long knocking. On the floor of the kitchen were heaps of clothing, ready for the electric washer that was at work some feet away. . . . Each question she answered with a ready, 'That's my business.'"

Lambie refused to become involved. In December 1927, two months after her recantation in the *Empire News*, she issued another statement, recanting the recantation. Written in a huge, childish hand, the original boasts spelling and punctuation to rival Slater's:

> I wish to put a denial to the statement recentaly published in the Newspapers there is no truth in that statement. Connan Doyle used a false statement I would not blame another man Slater is the man that I saw coming out of the house of Miss Gilchrist I am as strong and of the same mind as I was at the trial If Slater would tell the truth he is not an Innocent man
>
> From Helen Lambie now in the USA

In a letter to Conan Doyle, Park dismissed the new statement. "Lambie will go down as a shifty wretch," he wrote. "I suggest that [her] mother was seen by someone at this end who was anxious that Helen should disavow the interview. That would be the Glasgow police or a representative of the Birrell-Charteris conspiracy. . . . Lambie could not steer through a day's severe cross-examination."

Asked to come to Scotland for the appeal, Lambie dug in her heels. She could not legally be compelled to return, and the case went ahead without her.

SLATER'S APPEAL RESUMED ON July 9, 1928. Witnesses testifying on his behalf included William Roughead, who had interviewed John Adams, the first physician on the scene, for his book *Trial of Oscar Slater*. Dr. Adams had died in 1922, and Roughead was allowed to testify to their interview: "He expressed a very strong view that the hammer could have no possible connection with the crime, in view of the injuries that he had observed," Roughead said. "He said he first looked at the head, saw the injuries, and then it occurred to him was there anything in the room likely to cause them. Looking round . . . he noticed this chair, an ordinary Victorian chair, and he saw the back leg 'dripping'—as he described it to me—with blood. . . . He said that leg must manifestly have been in contact with the wounds."

U.S. marshal John W. M. Pinckley came from America to recount what had happened at the extradition hearing, when he led Slater past the witnesses:

Q. Was it possible for either Lambie or Barrowman to be under the impression that the man who was handcuffed to you was not a prisoner in custody?
A. I do not see how it could be. . . .
Q. You are satisfied that [Lambie] did see you coming down the corridor along with the prisoner?
A. She must have.
Q. If she had eyes to see?
A. Yes.

The acknowledged star of the appeal was Slater's lawyer, Craigie Aitchison. Addressing the judges, he spoke for some fourteen hours, dissecting every aspect of the investigation, manhunt, and prosecution. Conan Doyle set the scene in the *Sunday Pictorial*; it bears noting that even in 1928 his description is suffused with the Victorian idea about the link between physiognomy and character:

> For three days I have sat in the well of the court. For three days a dignified row of five Scottish judges have sat at the back of me. For three days my whole vision has consisted of one man in front of me, and of the courtroom crowd behind him. But that one man is worth watching. . . .
>
> It is a Pickwickian figure. His face is as pink as a baby's, and a baby might have owned those eyes of forget-me-not blue. A little heavy the face, but comely and fresh-complexioned withal, redeemed from weakness by the tight, decided lips.
>
> Yes, it is for fourteen hours exactly that he has been talking. He has been untangling the difficulties of a most intricate case.
>
> Deft to the last degree has been that disentanglement. It is a miracle of analysis. What I recall most clearly are those blue eyes, and the little plump, capable hands.
>
> He talks and talks with a gentle melodious voice, clearing up the difficulties. Those little plump hands accentuate points. There comes an objection from the judges. The blue eyes seem pained and surprised. Up fly the little plump hands. Once more the gentle voice takes up the tale. . . .

> And then suddenly one's eyes are arrested. One terrible face stands out amongst all the others. It is not an ill-famed face nor is it a wicked one, but it is terrible none the less for the brooding sadness that is in it. It is firm and immobile and might be cut from that Peterhead granite which has helped to make it what it is. . . . It is Slater. . . .
>
> Scotland may have erred both in administration and in her Judiciary twenty years ago, but it cannot be denied that she has vindicated her civilisation . . . by assembling a court which could have had weight and dignity enough to try the Kaiser in order to expiate an old-time miscarriage of justice to an unknown alien.

After Aitchison sat down, Watson, the Lord Advocate, argued the Crown's case for upholding Slater's conviction. The judges then retired to deliberate. When court reconvened on July 20, 1928, they issued rulings on four points of law. Slater was seen to lean forward, one hand cupping his ear.

The first ruling upheld the original verdict. So did the second. So did the third. Then the judges ruled on the fourth point: whether the conviction should be overturned as a result of misdirection by the trial judge, Lord Guthrie. As the ruling unfolded, Slater's prospects looked darker than ever. "That a man should support himself on the profits of prostitution is regarded by all men as blackguardism, but by many people as a sign of almost inhuman depravity," the judges began. Then, significantly, they continued:

> It cannot be affirmed that any members of the jury were misled by feelings of this kind in weighing the question of the appellant's guilt, *but neither can it be affirmed that*

> *none of them were.* What is certain is that the judge's charge entirely failed to give the jury the essential warning against allowing themselves to be misled by any feelings of the kind referred to. It is manifestly possible that, *but for the prejudicial effect of denying to the appellant the full benefit of the presumption of innocence,* and of allowing the point of his dependence on the immoral earnings of his partner to go to the jury . . . the proportion of nine to five for "guilty" and "not proven" respectively might have been reversed. . . .
>
> The instructions given in the charge amounted to misdirections in law, and . . . the judgment of the Court before whom the appellant was convicted should be set aside.

Peter Hunt described what happened next: "It was some moments before Slater realised that he had won. [Then] the smile of triumph which had, for a moment, flickered across his face, gave way to a dark scowl." Hotheaded, romantic, and impractical as always, Slater had sought nothing less than complete vindication—not on a technicality but because he was neither a murderer nor a pimp, two truths that he burned for the world to acknowledge. He had been exonerated, but he remained, in his view, dishonored. "I Oscar Slater, was not guilty of the terrible charge of murder and, equally not guilty of the infamous life that has been ascribed to me not only at my trial twenty years ago but repeated in the decision of the Court of Appeal," he said in a statement afterward. "I will tell the whole truth and dispel this calumny."

In a letter to Conan Doyle that betrays the deep Victorian concern with reputation, Slater revealed his mixed emotions:

*Dear Sir Arthur,*

*Many thanks for your Congratulations and from the bottom of my heart many, many thanks for your great work.*

*Sir Arthur, they went too far in throwing muck at me in an open Court, yet I don't care—but I care for my relatives and friends and I must do something for their sake.*

*This cruel 5 judges . . . who knew the frame up of my case, should have limited themselves a little and in not doing so, even the layman in the street know now that my character was the staff for the Crown to lean on.*

*I will fight and expose them all. All of them who I know have taken my confidence have betrayed me. I shall fight regardless of consequences.*

*Yours very sincerely,*
*Oscar Slater*

Conan Doyle, who was grateful for the verdict, knew the battle was finished. "My own connection with the case ends now that I have succeeded in establishing Slater's innocence," he told the press. But as he would discover to his disgust, his association with Slater was far from over.

# Chapter 21

## THE KNIGHT AND THE KNAVE

FOR SLATER, THERE WAS STILL THE MATTER OF COMPENSATION for wrongful imprisonment. At first, with typical volatile pride, he declared he would have none. "As far as I, Oscar Slater, am concerned there will never be a bill sent in," he said in a statement to the *Empire News*. "I will choose first to go to my grave than do such a thing."

By mail, Conan Doyle urged him not to act rashly:

> *I can quite understand your feelings, but you may be sure that you will get no compensation, not a penny, if you do not apply for it. . . . I would suggest £10,000.* You won't get it, but still it certainly is not an unjust claim. Any claim above that would alienate sympathy.*
>
> *However, as I have said, this is your affair. What however has to be done in any case is the paying of our just debts. . . . Your lawyers, both in the Chambers and in court, have worked splendidly and left no stone at all unturned.*

* About £560,000, or $800,000, today.

*The legal expenses, which I think are very moderate compared to most big cases which I know of, work out at roughly £1,200. Of this I have raised £700, in round figures, by my efforts. To the £500 which remains to be met there are certain just extra charges. Mr. Park should have a fee (if he will accept it). I would suggest 100 guineas. . . . I will charge you nothing, but I spent £30 on seeking Helen Lambie and £20 in advertisements which should be refunded to me. . . .*

*I think that pending your own claim you should send in a claim for expenses incurred which you may fairly put at £1600 less £700 in order to meet the various items. . . . If you are generous in refusing compensation for yourself (if you really think that is wise) you will agree that you must be just in paying what you owe to those who have worked so long and well.*

*With best wishes,*
*Yours sincerely*
*A.C.D.*

On August 4, of its own accord, the office of the Secretary of State for Scotland offered Slater £6,000, with nothing additional for expenses. Without consulting any of his advisers, Slater accepted. In doing so, he opened a bitter rift with Conan Doyle.

To Slater—so often at loose ends, so long at hard labor—the £6,000 was his due, and he was not prepared to reimburse anyone for anything. Conan Doyle was wealthy, Slater knew, and could readily afford the few hundred pounds he had laid out. But what Slater did not comprehend was that to Conan Doyle the issue was a matter of deep, abiding principle: absolute probity in fiscal matters, as he had taken pains to teach his children, was one of the canonical imperatives of the upright life.

Both men had been reared in poverty. One became a knight, the other a knave, and it was clear, from their bitter exchange of letters in 1928 and 1929, that neither had the capacity to understand the other. Here the story takes on a regrettable *Pygmalion* aspect, for while Conan Doyle had made Slater a free man, he could not, however much he might have wished it, make him a gentleman. He had fought to return Slater to the law's protection, only to have Slater respond like a man ungoverned by law. To Conan Doyle such behavior—which seemed to flout reason and honor, the lodestars of his own life—was simply not cricket.

In the increasingly vitriolic correspondence between them, the central tensions of the late Victorian age—over class, over conduct, over reputation—were played out in discordant duet. When one reads their exchange, it becomes clear that Conan Doyle had long been operating under a sustained misdiagnosis: a deep, unwitting failure of identification. Slater's past had discomforted him from the moment he joined the case—"a disreputable, rolling-stone of a man," he had called him—and for two decades Conan Doyle made sure to hold him at arm's length. As a result, he saw Slater more as an archetype than an individual.

It was not that Conan Doyle damned Slater as foreigner or Jew, as so many of his era had done. A "Liberal Imperialist" to the end, he had managed to resist the least savory aspects of the Victorian mania for group identification. But as for almost anyone navigating the divide between "us" and "them," a measure of the classifying impulse remained. What Conan Doyle did, over time, was to cast Slater as the noble ideal of the wronged innocent, "eating out his heart at Peterhead."

Now Slater's ungentlemanly past seemed to be reasserting itself, giving the lie to that cherished ideal. In constructing the vision of Slater that had made sustained involvement in his case possible, Conan Doyle seems to have slipped unconsciously into "the easy reading, the one toward which the inertia of our prejudices inclines us." For in the end, his treatment of Slater as an abstraction rather than as a fallible, flesh-and-blood human being was simply a benevolent, though no less convenient, way of keeping the convenient Other at bay.

"LEST I DO YOU an injustice I put the question to you again," Conan Doyle wrote to Slater in August 1928. "Do you propose to relieve those who supported you of the costs of your defence in case the Government does not pay them? I should like a direct and clear reply."

Later that month, he wrote again: "You seem to have taken leave of your senses. . . . If you are indeed quite responsible for your actions, then you are the most ungrateful as well as the most foolish person whom I have ever known. Now that I have learned to know you I have no desire for further direct correspondence, but you may rest assured that you will be held accountable for your just debts."

Before long, Conan Doyle took to the newspapers, a time-honored arena for defending one's reputation in public. As he wrote to the *Empire News* in May 1929:

> *Early in the proceedings I had a letter from Oscar Slater in which he declared that no one should be put out of pocket over his defence. That was before he got his verdict. Since then I have written to him several times pointing out the*

*facts, but have received either no reply or an evasive one. The lawyers have now, very properly, applied for the money and of course I have honoured my personal guarantee and have paid in full.*

*Had Slater lost this case I would cheerfully have taken this expense upon myself, but as he has received £6000 compensation it seems a monstrous thing that these charges should be met by me.*

In September 1928, Conan Doyle gave an interview to the *Telegraph*. "'It is a shocking ending to what might have been a very noble story,' was the comment made by Sir Arthur Conan Doyle yesterday regarding his attempt to recover money he had paid towards the expenses of Oscar Slater," the article read. "'I am naturally terribly disappointed and annoyed. . . . It is not so much a question of the money as the principle of the thing.'"

In an interview of his own with the *Daily Mail,* Slater displayed the hotheaded irrationality that had plagued him through the years:

Let him call me ungrateful dog. The abuse he heaps on me now will only rebound on himself. It is beneath my dignity to answer abuse with abuse. . . . I will not even call him a money-maker or a hunter for notoriety. . . .

Poor man! . . . The lawyers are pressing him. Did he not make hundreds of pounds by writing about me when I was in prison? . . .

Then he wrote articles about me when I was released and he was paid £50 for each one of them. It was good business for him. He raised a subscription for me, and people said "How good he is."

Incensed, Conan Doyle shot back in the same edition of the newspaper: "Making money[!] . . . For 18 years I worked for him. I wrote a book about him which was sold at 6d., and never brought me a penny." He was further inflamed by another *Daily Mail* article, in which a reporter caught up with Slater, then living in a hotel in the English seaside resort of Brighton and to all appearances scaling new heights of Continental dandyism. "Oscar Slater shook hands with me at his hotel here to-day, offered me a cigar from an expensive gold-bound case, and drank Italian Vermouth as an appetiser before an excellent luncheon," the reporter wrote. "He is enjoying life. He bathes, golfs, dances and is a regular theatre-goer. His face is tanned a deep brown and health sparkles from his eyes."

Conan Doyle responded in the *Evening News*. "He has behaved disgracefully and nearly everything he says is untrue. . . . I see Slater was found at Brighton smoking a big cigar, and enjoying himself generally. He is doing that partly with my money."

When Slater remained unmoved, Conan Doyle turned to the courts. In the archives of the National Records of Scotland lies a file whose title betrays one of the most painful chapters of the twenty-year saga: a sheaf of papers with the unimaginable heading "Conan Doyle v. Slater." Filed in the autumn of 1929, the suit sought £250 compensation.

Providentially, the case was settled before coming to trial. In October 1929, Slater's representatives persuaded him to offer Conan Doyle the £250, and prevailed on Conan Doyle to accept. "At the time the man's ingratitude hurt me deeply," Conan Doyle wrote in early 1930, "but I have reflected since that one could hardly go through eighteen years of unjust imprisonment and yet emerge unscathed."

And with those words, the Slater saga, begun amid acute

social-class tensions and concluded much the same way, finally drew to a close.

WITH ONLY A FEW months to live, Sir Arthur Conan Doyle—"Big-Hearted, Big-Bodied, Big-Souled Friend Conan Doyle," in the words of the Victorian writer Jerome K. Jerome—had fought his valedictory battle. An ardent spiritualist to the last, he wrote: "I have had many adventures. The greatest and most glorious of all awaits me now."

On July 7, 1930, his health failing badly, Conan Doyle asked to be moved from his sickbed at Windlesham to a chair by the window overlooking the Sussex countryside: it was clear that he wanted to preempt the unmanly fate of dying in bed. His wife, Jean, and their three children helped him to the chair, and it was there that Conan Doyle died that night, at seventy-one. Perhaps it was only then, with the passing of its most emblematic avatar, that the long nineteenth century was well and truly over.

# EPILOGUE: WHAT BECAME OF THEM

WHO DID KILL MARION GILCHRIST ON THAT RAINY December night? Conan Doyle held fast to the belief that it was her nephew Francis Charteris, a view shared by some later writers on the case. (Acutely aware of the rumors, Charteris, who died in 1964 after a distinguished career as a physician and educator, maintained to the end of his life that he had nothing to do with the crime.) Other observers have pointed fingers at various members of Miss Gilchrist's extended family; still others have posited a ring of professional thieves, or a murderous collaboration between Helen Lambie and one of her suitors.

The eminent commentator William Roughead, while refraining from naming names, was of the opinion that more than one man was involved. "Miss Gilchrist must have been killed by *somebody*," he wrote in the 1929 edition of *Trial of Oscar Slater*. "Twenty years' reflection on the facts as proved in Court confirms me in the view . . . that *two* men were concerned in the affair, one of whom either made off between Mr. Adams's visits to the door, or waited—like Raskolnikov—in the empty flat above until the coast was clear. If the reader, when studying the evidence, will keep in mind this hypothesis . . . he may find it helpful, as explaining the many difficulties created by the disparate accounts of the appearance and movements of 'the man.'"

On the subject of who murdered Miss Gilchrist I remain resolutely agnostic. Any "solution" advanced eleven decades after the fact can only be the product of undiluted speculation. I do believe, however, that Lambie took to her grave far more information about the crime than she ever disclosed—including the killer's identity. That was the view of Conan Doyle, who wrote, in 1930, "I see no prospect of getting to the bottom of Miss Gilchrist's death unless Helen Lambie makes a confession. She undoubtedly knows more about the matter than has ever been made public." But Lambie never obliged. She returned to Scotland with her family in the 1930s and later settled in the north of England. She died in Leeds, West Yorkshire, in 1960, at seventy-three.

Mary Barrowman, who later in adulthood worked as a charwoman, married twice. She was believed to have become an alcoholic; her two children were removed from her care by the state. In *Square Mile of Murder*, his 2002 study of four Glasgow killings, including Miss Gilchrist's, the Scottish newspaperman Robert House wrote: "Many years after the trial of Oscar Slater, Mary Barrowman turned up at a certain house in Glasgow. She said she wanted to confess. She had not been in West Princes Street at all on the night of the murder. Her mother, who was an alcoholic, had made her tell the story so that she could share in the reward." Barrowman died in 1934, at forty, from cervical cancer.

Arthur Adams, seventy-three, was found dead of natural

causes on January 3, 1942, at his home at 14 Queen's Terrace, directly below the flat in which Miss Gilchrist had met her end. In a noteworthy turn of fate, his death certificate was signed by Dr. John S. M. Ord, son of Superintendent John Ord of the Glasgow police.

In 1969, a Glasgow magistrate, John Young, began a campaign for the posthumous rehabilitation of Detective Lieutenant John Thomson Trench. After considering the matter, city officials concluded that it was not within their legal power to have the case for his dismissal reopened. In 1999, however, a plaque honoring Trench was installed in the Glasgow Police Museum. Unveiled in the presence of his sole surviving child, eighty-seven-year-old Nancy Stark, it read: "There are now appeal processes for both criminal cases in the courts and police discipline hearings, which neither Mr Trench nor Mr Slater had the benefit of at that time. The fact that these safeguards are now in place and have been for many years, is perhaps a fitting legacy to the hardship that these individuals endured in the spirit of truth and justice."

His Majesty's Prison Peterhead (known under the reign of Queen Elizabeth II as Her Majesty's Prison Peterhead) was by the late twentieth century considered one of the worst penal institutions in Britain—"Scotland's gulag, a prison of no hope," commentators called it in 1991. It closed in 2013 and is now the Peterhead Prison Museum.

Peterhead's most famous inmate, Oscar Slater—dandy, gambler, foreigner, scapegoat, Jew—remained an exotic enough figure that from time to time in later years rumor swirled round him in the newspapers. "Will Wed a Kaffir, Says Oscar Slater," a *New York Times* headline crowed in 1929, the year after his exoneration, adding: "Scot Who Got $30,000 for False Murder Conviction Plans to Live in Africa."

The reality was far more prosaic. Slater remained in Scotland to the end of his life, settling near Glasgow in the seaside town of Ayr. Sociable and well liked by his neighbors, he did a modest business restoring and selling antiques. In 1936, after his estranged first wife died, he married Lina Schad, a Scotswoman of German parentage some thirty years his junior. By all accounts the marriage was a happy one.

Though Slater had long since lost his German citizenship, the outbreak of World War II threw his Germanness into relief once more. At the start of the war, he was briefly interned, along with his wife, as an enemy alien. Afterward, the couple resumed their congenial life in Ayr. Unable to abide the name Oscar Slater, he once again lived as Oscar Leschziner.

"With the war over, a few golden years remained to Oscar," the British writer Richard Whittington-Egan, who interviewed Lina Leschziner before her death in 1992, has written. "Sometimes, for sheer joy of life, he would stand foursquare on Rabbie Burns's Auld Brig and sing at the top of his lungs' bent, the wind carrying his weird-accented song away across the melodious waves. . . . Possessed of a good singing voice, he much enjoyed listening to music. He went frequently, too, to the theatre and the cinema. He was, always had been, a great walker. He was also a great talker. After all the years of enforced silence, he liked nothing better than a good crack. A very generous man, he was forever giving his mite to charities—in particular those concerned with the plight of sick or homeless children."

Oscar Leschziner died of a pulmonary embolism at his home in Ayr on January 31, 1948, at seventy-six, having outlived nearly all the principals in the case against him. He never returned to Germany. That was almost certainly just as well: on July 27, 1942, more than a thousand Jews were deported from

Breslau, in his home region of Silesia, a group out of which barely two dozen would survive. Among the thousand were Slater's sister Phemie, murdered at Treblinka, and his beloved sister Malchen, murdered at Terezin—racialized, identified, apprehended, transported, exterminated.

# ACKNOWLEDGMENTS

*CONAN DOYLE FOR THE DEFENSE* IS IN NO SMALL PART the product of thousands of pages of documents, painstakingly gathered, reproduced, and sent winging across the sea by indefatigable people in a string of archives throughout Britain. They include, at the National Records of Scotland in Edinburgh, Jessica Evershed, Jane Jamieson, Samantha Smart, and Robin Urquhart; at the Mitchell Library in Glasgow, Linda Burke, Michael Gallagher, Patricia Grant, Claire McGugan, Barbara McLean, Peter Munro, Susan Taylor, and Nerys Tunnicliffe; at the Peterhead Prison Museum, Alexander Geddes; and, at the Conan Doyle Archives at Portsmouth City Council, Michael Gunton.

Thanks also to Kirsty Wark for a lovely, long-ago lunch in Glasgow, and to Alan Clements and Caitlin Wark Clements for their assistance with this project. My agents, Katinka Matson and Max Brockman, deserve sustained thanks for their support over many years, as does Michael Healey, also of Brockman Inc.

At Random House, I am privileged to work with an extraordinary editor, Hilary Redmon, who, reading an early draft of this book, glimpsed the heart of the story long before I did. Hilary's assistant, Molly Turpin, has provided able assistance. Other Random House colleagues who have helped bring *Conan Doyle to the Defense* to life include Nancy Delia, Barbara Bachman, Richard Elman, Sharon Propson, Mary Moates, and Jessica Bonet. The manuscript was copyedited by Sue Warga; Cohen Carruth prepared the index.

At my U.K. publisher, Profile Books, thanks are due to Andrew Franklin, the co-founder and managing director, and to my editor, Cecily Gayford. John Davey, who oversaw the U.K. edition of my previous book, *The Riddle of the Labyrinth,* and was to do likewise with *Conan Doyle for the Defense,* died as this book was nearing completion. He was able to comment incisively on an early draft of the manuscript, for which I am deeply grateful, and I hope that the finished product will stand as a small tribute to his memory.

Daniel Stashower, a biographer of Conan Doyle; Leslie S. Klinger, editor of the definitive edition of the Sherlock Holmes canon; and Ben Braber, a historian of Scottish Jewry, have all read the manuscript and made invaluable suggestions and corrections.

At *The New York Times,* colleagues present and past have shown remarkable forbearance by day as I wrestled with this book by night and have made working at the paper a continued source of pleasure and pride. Among them are Barbara Baumgarten, Charlotte Behrendt, Tom Caffrey, the late Janet Elder, Bernadette Espina, Neil Genzlinger, William Grimes, Jack Kadden, Peter Keepnews, William McDonald, Robert D. McFadden, Douglas Martin, Dolores Morrison, Amisha Padnani, Sam Roberts, Jeff Roth, Richard Sandomir, Daniel E.

Slotnik, Charles Strum, Bruce Weber, and Earl Wilson. As he did for *The Riddle of the Labyrinth,* the *Times* graphics editor Jonathan Corum created masterful visual aids for this book.

Laura Otis, a MacArthur Award–winning scholar who studies the fascinating intellectual landscape at the intersection of Victorian science and Victorian literature (and whom I have had the pleasure of calling a friend since the second grade), gave me a much-needed grounding in the era's scientific and literary currents. Teresa Williams and Ira Hozinsky deserve much thanks for their tireless willingness to hear about this project, and for their cherished friendship over the past three decades.

Finally, more thanks, love, and esteem than I can ever convey in print go to the writer, critic, and teacher George Robinson, my boon companion these thirty years and more.

# CAST OF CHARACTERS

**Arthur Adams:** Miss Gilchrist's downstairs neighbor.

**Dr. John Adams:** The first doctor at the murder scene; not related to Arthur Adams.

**Craigie Aitchison:** Slater's barrister in the 1928 rehearing of his case.

**Andrée Junio Antoine ("Madame Junio"):** Slater's mistress; allegedly a prostitute.

**Annie Armour:** Glasgow subway clerk; witness for the prosecution at Slater's trial.

**Mary Barrowman:** Teenage delivery girl who claimed to have witnessed the murderer's flight along West Princes Street.

**Dr. Joseph Bell:** Conan Doyle's medical-school teacher, master diagnostician, and the model for Sherlock Holmes.

**Margaret Birrell:** Miss Gilchrist's niece.

**Hugh Cameron:** Glasgow bookmaker and friend of Slater's; he directed police to the shop where Slater had pawned a diamond crescent brooch.

**Francis Charteris:** Eminent Glasgow physician and nephew of Miss Gilchrist.

**David Cook:** Glasgow lawyer; friend and supporter of Detective Lieutenant Trench.

**William Miller Douglas:** Superintendent, Glasgow police.

**George Edalji:** Anglo-Indian lawyer whose wrongful conviction for animal maiming Conan Doyle helped overturn in 1907 in a case that prefigured Slater's.

**Maggie Galbraith Ferguson:** Miss Gilchrist's former maid, who, with her daughter, Marion Gilchrist Ferguson, was the chief beneficiary of Miss Gilchrist's new will.

**Charles Fox:** Counsel for the British Crown at Slater's extradition hearing in New York.

**Marion Gilchrist:** The victim.

**Sir John Gilmour:** Secretary of State for Scotland, 1924–29.

**John Glaister:** Forensic-medicine expert; witness for the prosecution at Slater's trial.

**William A. Goodhart:** Slater's primary defense lawyer at his New York extradition hearing.

**William Gordon:** Slater's fellow convict; on his release in 1925, he smuggled Slater's urgent message to Conan Doyle.

**Agnes Guthrie:** Helen Lambie's former employer.

**The Hon. Lord Charles John Guthrie:** The judge at Slater's trial.

**James Hart:** Procurator fiscal for Lanarkshire, instrumental in Slater's wrongful conviction.

**Helen (Nellie) Lambie (later Gillon):** Miss Gilchrist's maid.

**Adolf Leschziner:** father of Slater (born Oskar Josef Leschziner).

**Euphemia (Phemie) Leschziner:** Slater's sister.

**Georg Leschziner:** Slater's brother.

**Pauline (or Paula) Leschziner:** Slater's mother.

**Rowena Adams Liddell:** Sister of Arthur Adams.

**Duncan MacBrayne:** Glasgow greengrocer who could have alibied Slater; he was not called at trial.

**Colin MacCallum:** Glasgow bootmaker and employer of Mary Barrowman.

**Alexander Logan McClure:** Slater's barrister; argued his defense at trial.

**Ramsay MacDonald:** British Labour Party leader; British prime minister, 1924, 1929–31, 1931–35.

**Allan McLean:** Glasgow bicycle dealer; informed the police of Slater's pawn ticket.

**Erna Meyer:** Daughter of Slater's sister Phemie.

**James Gardner Millar:** Lawyer and sheriff of Lanarkshire; presided at the 1914 secret inquiry.

**John Ord:** Senior superintendent, Criminal Investigation Department, Glasgow police.

**John Orr:** Chief superintendent, Glasgow police.

**Ernest Clephan Palmer ("The Pilgrim"):** British journalist; author of a 1927 newspaper exposé on the Slater case.

**William Park:** Glasgow journalist, and author of the 1927 book *The Truth About Oscar Slater*, edited and published by Conan Doyle.

**Rev. Eleazar P. Phillips:** Leader of the Garnethill Hebrew Congregation; a Glasgow Jewish clergyman who was Slater's longtime supporter.

**John W. M. Pinckley:** United States deputy marshal at Slater's extradition hearing.

**John Pyper:** Detective inspector, Glasgow police; instrumental in Slater's extradition proceedings in New York.

**William Roughead:** Scottish lawyer, criminologist, and journalist; editor of *Trial of Oscar Slater*, published in four editions between 1910 and 1950.

**Catherine Schmalz:** Slater's maid.

**Alexander Shaughnessy:** Slater's second Glasgow solicitor; succeeded Ewing Speirs.

**John A. Shields:** United States commissioner for the Southern District of New York; presided at Slater's extradition hearing.

**John Sinclair:** Secretary of State for Scotland, 1905–12.

**Ewing Speirs:** Slater's first Glasgow solicitor.

**Amalie (Malchen) Leschziner Tau:** Slater's sister.

**Käthe (Kätel) Tau:** Daughter of Slater's sister Malchen.

**John Thomson Trench:** Detective lieutenant, Glasgow police; his support of Slater in the 1914 inquiry resulted in his own ruin.

**Alexander Ure:** Lord Advocate; chief prosecutor at Slater's trial. Later elevated to the peerage as Baron Strathclyde.

**William Warnock:** Chief criminal officer of the Glasgow sheriff court; instrumental in Slater's extradition proceedings in New York.

**Thomas McKinnon Wood:** Secretary for Scotland, 1912–16.

# GLOSSARY

**Close** (*n., rhymes with "gross"*): The vestibule of a Scottish apartment house, with a staircase leading to the upper floors.

**Donegal cap:** A flat, round, soft tweed cap, traditionally associated with Ireland.

**Gey** (*adv.*): Scottish dialect term meaning "very" or "really." Comparable to the American colloquial term "pretty" in this sense.

**Home Office:** The British ministerial department in charge of domestic affairs, including judicial matters in England and Wales.

**Identity parade:** A lineup.

**Lord Advocate:** The chief prosecutor for the Crown.

**Maindoor house:** The ground-floor flat in a Scottish apartment building; it has its own entrance onto the street, separate from the close door.

**Master of Polworth:** Chairman of the prison commission for Scotland.

**Memorial** (*n.*): In Scottish law, a type of closely argued legal memorandum.

**Not proven:** In Scottish criminal trials, one of the three available verdicts, along with guilty and not guilty, that jurors may render.

**Panel (or Pannell):** The defendant (accused) in Scottish criminal trials.

**Procurator Fiscal:** Scottish judicial office combining investigative and prosecutorial functions; somewhat akin to that of district attorney in the United States.

**Production:** An exhibit in Scottish criminal trials.

**Release on license:** To parole a convict.

**Reset:** Scottish legal term denoting the receipt or resale of stolen goods. It can also denote the illegal harboring of a criminal.

**Secretary of State for Scotland (formerly "Secretary for Scotland"):** The chief British government minister in charge of Scottish affairs.

**Sheriff:** A member of the Scottish judiciary who presides over a local court.

**Wain (or wean):** A child.

# REFERENCES


Accardo, Pasquale, M.D. *Diagnosis and Detection: The Medical Iconography of Sherlock Holmes.* Rutherford, N.J.: Fairleigh Dickinson University Press, 1987.

Adam, Alison. *A History of Forensic Science: British Beginnings in the Twentieth Century.* London: Routledge, 2016.

Asimov, Isaac. "Thoughts on Sherlock Holmes." *Baker Street Journal* 37, no. 4 (1987): 201–4.

Barnes, Julian. *Arthur and George.* London: Jonathan Cape, 2005.

Bell, Dr. Joseph. "Mr. Sherlock Holmes." Introduction to Conan Doyle (1892), 5–13.

Bigelow, S. Tupper. "Fingerprints and Sherlock Holmes." *Baker Street Journal* 17, no. 3 (1967): 131–35.

Booth, Martin. *The Doctor and the Detective: A Biography of Sir Arthur Conan Doyle.* New York: Thomas Dunne Books/St. Martin's Minotaur, 1997.

Boreham, N. C., G. E. Mawer, and R. W. Foster. "Medical Diagnosis from Circumstantial Evidence." *Le Travail Humain* 59, no. 1 (1996): 69–85.

Braber, Ben. *Jews in Glasgow 1879–1939: Immigration and Integration.* London: Vallentine Mitchell, 2007.

———. "The Trial of Oscar Slater (1909) and Anti-Jewish Prejudices in Edwardian Glasgow." *History* 88 (2003): 262–79.

Caplan, Jane. "'This or That Particular Person': Protocols and Identification in Nineteenth-Century Europe." In Caplan and Torpey (2001), 49–66.

Caplan, Jane, and John Torpey, eds. *Documenting Individual Identity: The Development of State Practices in the Modern World.* Princeton, N.J.: Princeton University Press, 2001.

Carroll, Lewis. *Alice's Adventures in Wonderland* and *Alice's Adventures Underground.* Cleveland: World Publishing Company, 1946.

Cole, Simon A. *Suspect Identities: A History of Fingerprinting and Criminal Identification.* Cambridge, Mass.: Harvard University Press, 2001.

Conan Doyle, A. *The Stark Munro Letters: Being a Series of Twelve Letters Written by J. Stark Munro, M.B., to His Friend and Former Fellow-Student, Herbert Swanborough, of Lowell, Massachusetts, During the Years 1881–1884.* New York: D. Appleton & Company, 1895.

———. *The War in South Africa: Its Cause and Conduct.* New York: McClure, Phillips & Company, 1902.

Conan Doyle, Adrian. *The True Conan Doyle.* New York: Coward-McCann, 1946.

Conan Doyle, Arthur. *The Case of Oscar Slater.* New York: Hodder & Stoughton/George H. Doran Company, 1912.

———. Introduction to Park (1927).

———. *Memories and Adventures.* Oxford: Oxford University Press, 1924; 2nd ed., London: John Murray, 1930.

———. *Through the Magic Door.* Pleasantville, N.Y.: Akadine Press, 1999.

Conan Doyle, Sir A. *A Study in Scarlet.* London: Ward, Lock & Company, 1892.

Conan Doyle, Sir Arthur. *The Case of Mr. George Edalji.* London: T. Harrison Roberts, 1907. In Conan Doyle (1985), 34–78.

———. *The Penguin Complete Sherlock Holmes.* New York: Penguin Books, 1981.

———. *The Story of Mr. George Edalji.* Edited by Richard and Molly Whittington-Egan. London: Grey House Books, 1985.

———. *Strange Studies from Life and Other Narratives: The Complete True Crime Writings of Sir Arthur Conan Doyle.* Selected and edited by Jack Tracy. Bloomington, Ind.: Gaslight Publications, 1988.

Costello, Peter. *The Real World of Sherlock Holmes: The True Crimes Investigated by Arthur Conan Doyle.* New York: Carroll & Graf Publishers, 1991.

Crowther, M. Anne, and Brenda White. *On Soul and Conscience: The Medical Expert and Crime. 150 Years of Forensic Medicine in Glasgow.* Aberdeen, U.K.: Aberdeen University Press, 1988.

Dickens, Charles. *A Christmas Carol: And Other Christmas Books.* New York: Vintage Classics, 2012.

*Dictionary of the Scottish Language* (an online database comprising two major historical dictionaries, *A Dictionary of the Older Scottish Tongue* and *The Scottish National Dictionary*), http://www.dsl.ac.uk.

Doyle, Georgina. *Out of the Shadows: The Untold Story of Arthur Conan Doyle's First Family.* Ashcroft, B.C.: Calabash Press, 2004.

Duff, Peter. "The Scottish Criminal Jury: A Very Peculiar Institution." *Law and Contemporary Problems* 62, no. 2 (Spring 1999): 173–201.

Eco, Umberto, and Thomas A. Sebeok, eds. *The Sign of the Three: Dupin, Holmes, Peirce.* Bloomington: Indiana University Press, 1983.

Ellis, Havelock. *The Criminal.* Memphis, Tenn.: General Books, 2012.

Ferrero, Gina Lombroso. *Criminal Man: According to the Classification of Cesare Lombroso, Briefly Summarised by His Daughter Gina Lombroso Ferrero.* New York: G. P. Putnam's Sons, 1911.

Frank, Lawrence. *Victorian Detective Fiction and the Nature of Evidence: The Scientific Investigations of Poe, Dickens, and Doyle.* London: Palgrave Macmillan, 2009.

Freeman, R. Austin. *The Best Dr. Thorndyke Stories*. Selected by E. F. Bleiler. New York: Dover Publications, 1973.

———. "The Case of Oscar Brodski." In Freeman (1973).

Garavelli, Dani. "Insight: The Jury's Still Out on 'Not Proven' Verdict." *Scotsman*, Feb. 13, 2016.

Gay, Peter. *The Cultivation of Hatred: The Bourgeois Experience, Victoria to Freud*. Vol. 3. New York: W. W. Norton & Company, 1993.

Gibson, John Michael, and Richard Lancelyn Green, eds. *The Unknown Conan Doyle: Letters to the Press.* London: Secker & Warburg, 1986.

Grant, Douglas. *The Thin Blue Line: The Story of the City of Glasgow Police.* London: John Long, 1973.

Gross, Hans. *Criminal Investigation: A Practical Handbook for Magistrates, Police Officers and Lawyers*. Translated and edited by John Adam and John Collyer Adam. New Delhi: Isha Books, 2013.

Hardwick, Michael, and Mollie Hardwick. *The Man Who Was Sherlock Holmes.* Garden City, N.Y.: Doubleday & Company, 1964.

Higgs, Edward. *Identifying the English: A History of Personal Identification, 1500 to the Present.* London: Continuum, 2011.

Hines, Stephen. *The True Crime Files of Sir Arthur Conan Doyle.* New York: Berkley Prime Crime, 2001.

House, Jack. *Square Mile of Murder.* Edinburgh: Black & White Publishing, 2002.

Hunt, Peter. *Oscar Slater: The Great Suspect.* London: Carroll & Nicholson, 1951.

Huxley, Thomas Henry. *Science and Culture: And Other Essays.* New York: D. Appleton, 1882.

Jann, Rosemary. *The Adventures of Sherlock Holmes: Detecting Social Order.* New York: Twayne Publishers, 1995.

Jeffrey, Robert. *Peterhead: The Inside Story of Scotland's Toughest Prison.* Edinburgh: Black & White Publishing, 2013.

Jones, Dr. Harold Emery. *The Original of Sherlock Holmes.* Windsor, U.K.: Gaby Goldscheider, 1980.

Joseph, Anne M. "Anthropometry, the Police Expert, and the Deptford Murders: The Contested Introduction of Fingerprinting for the Identification of Criminals in Late Victorian and Edwardian Britain." In Caplan and Torpey (2001), 164–83.

Julius, Anthony. *Trials of the Diaspora: A History of Anti-Semitism in England.* Oxford: Oxford University Press, 2010.

Kirsch, Adam. *Benjamin Disraeli.* New York: Schocken Books, 2008.

Klinefelter, Walter. *The Case of the Conan Doyle Crime Library.* La Crosse, Wis.: Sumac Press, 1968.

Klinger, Leslie S., ed. *The New Annotated Sherlock Holmes.* 3 vols. New York: W. W. Norton & Company, 2005–6.

Knepper, Paul. "British Jews and the Racialisation of Crime in the Age of Empire." *British Journal of Criminology* 47 (2007): 61–79.

Liebow, Ely. *Dr. Joe Bell: Model for Sherlock Holmes.* Madison, Wis.: Popular Press, 2007.

Lillo, Antonio. "Nae Barr's Irn-Bru Whit Ye're oan Aboot: Musings on Modern Scottish Rhyming Slang." *English World-Wide* 33, no. 1 (2012): 69–102.

Loftus, Elizabeth, and Katherine Ketcham. *Witness for the Defense: The Accused, the Eyewitness, and the Expert Who Puts Memory on Trial.* New York: St. Martin's Press, 1991.

Lycett, Andrew. *The Man Who Created Sherlock Holmes: The Life and Times of Sir Arthur Conan Doyle.* New York: Free Press, 2007.

McConnell, Frank D. "Sherlock Holmes: Detecting Order amid Disorder." *Wilson Quarterly* 11, no. 2 (1987): 172–83.

MacLean, John. *Accuser of Capitalism: John MacLean's Speech from the Dock, May 9th 1918.* London: New Park Publications, 1986.

———. "Life in Prison." *The Red Dawn* 1, no. 1 (March 1919): 8–9; republished at www.scottishrepublicansocialistmovement.org/Pages/SRSMJohnMacLeanLifeinPrison.aspx.

McNay, Michael. "Craigie Aitchison Obituary." *Guardian*, Dec. 22, 2009.

Markovits, Stefanie. "Form Things: Looking at Genre Through Victorian Diamonds." *Victorian Studies* 52, no. 4 (2010): 591–619.

Miller, Russell. *The Adventures of Arthur Conan Doyle: A Biography.* New York: Thomas Dunne Books/St. Martin's Press, 2008.

Murch, A[lma] E[lizabeth]. *The Development of the Detective Novel.* New York: Philosophical Library, 1958.

Nordon, Pierre. *Conan Doyle: A Biography*. Translated by John Murray. New York: Holt, Rinehart & Winston, 1967.

O'Brien, James F. *The Scientific Sherlock Holmes: Cracking the Case with Science and Forensics.* Oxford: Oxford University Press, 2013.

"Oscar Slater's Own Story: Specially Compiled from Private Documents." *Empire News*, April 13, 1924.

Otis, Laura. *Membranes: Metaphors of Invasion in Nineteenth-Century Literature, Science, and Politics.* Baltimore: Johns Hopkins University Press, 1999.

Park, William. *The Truth About Oscar Slater [with the Prisoner's Own Story]*. London: Psychic Press, 1927.

Peckham, Robert, ed. *Disease and Crime: A History of Social Pathologies and the New Politics of Health.* New York: Routledge, 2014.

———. "Pathological Properties: Scenes of Crime, Sites of Infection." In Peckham (2014), 56–78.

Pellegrino, Edmund D. "To Look Feelingly: The Affinities of Medicine and Literature." *Literature and Medicine* 1 (1982): 19–23.

Piel, Eleanor Jackson. "The Death Row Brothers." *Proceedings of the American Philosophical Society* 147, no. 1 (2003): 30–38.

Poe, Edgar Allan. "The Murders in the Rue Morgue." In Poe (1984), 397–431.

———. "The Mystery of Marie Rogêt." In Poe (1984), 506–54.

———. *Poetry and Tales*. New York: Library of America, 1984.

Pollock, Sir Frederick, and Frederic William Maitland. *The History of*

*English Law Before the Time of Edward I* 2nd ed. 2 vols. Cambridge: Cambridge University Press, 1911.

Ramsey, Ted. *Stranger in the Hall.* Glasgow: Ramshorn Publications, 1988.

Rapezzi, Claudio, Roberto Ferrari, and Angelo Branzi. "White Coats and Fingerprints: Diagnostic Reasoning in Medicine and Investigative Methods of Fictional Detectives." *BMJ: British Medical Journal* 331, no. 7531 (2005): 1491–94.

Roughead, William, ed. *Trial of Oscar Slater.* Notable British Trials Series. Edinburgh and London: William Hodge & Company, 1910; 2nd ed., 1915; 3rd ed., 1929; 4th ed., 1950.

Saxby, Jessie M. E. *Joseph Bell: An Appreciation by an Old Friend.* Edinburgh: Oliphant, Anderson & Ferrier, 1913.

Scraton, Phil, Joe Sim, and Paula Skidmore. *Prisons Under Protest.* Milton Keynes, U.K.: Open University Press, 1991.

Sebeok, Thomas A., and Jean Umiker-Sebeok. "You Know My Method: A Juxtaposition of Charles S. Peirce and Sherlock Holmes." In Eco and Sebeok (1983), 11–54.

Siegel, Jack M. "The First Citizen of Baker Street." *Chicago Review* 2, no. 2 (1947): 49–55.

Sims, Michael. *Arthur and Sherlock: Conan Doyle and the Creation of Holmes.* New York: Bloomsbury, 2017.

Smith, Alexander Duncan, ed. *The Trial of Eugène Marie Chantrelle.* Notable Scottish Trials Series. Glasgow: William Hodge & Company, 1906.

Smith, Sir Sydney. *Mostly Murder.* New York: Dorset Press, 1988.

Stashower, Daniel. *Teller of Tales: The Life of Arthur Conan Doyle.* New York: Owl/Henry Holt, 1999.

Tilstone, William J., Kathleen A. Savage, and Leigh A. Clark. *Forensic Science: An Encyclopedia of History, Methods, and Techniques.* Santa Barbara, Calif.: ABC-CLIO, 2006.

Toughill, Thomas. *Oscar Slater: The "Immortal" Case of Sir Arthur Conan Doyle.* Stroud, U.K.: Sutton Publishing, 2006.

Truzzi, Marcello. "Sherlock Holmes: Applied Social Psychologist." In Eco and Sebeok (1983), 55–80.

Van Dover, J. K. *You Know My Method: The Science of the Detective.* Bowling Green, Ky.: Bowling Green State University Popular Press, 1994.

Voltaire, M. de. *Zadig*. New York: Rimington & Hooper, 1929.

Wade, Stephen. *Conan Doyle and the Crimes Club: The Creator of Sherlock Holmes and His Criminological Friends.* Oxford: Fonthill Media, 2013.

Whittington-Egan, Richard. *The Oscar Slater Murder Story: New Light on a Classic Miscarriage of Justice.* Glasgow: Neil Wilson Publishing, 2001.

Whittington-Egan, Richard, and Molly Whittington-Egan. Introduction to Conan Doyle (1985).

"Will Wed a Kaffir, Says Oscar Slater." *New York Times,* Nov. 28, 1929, 21; reprint of Associated Press article datelined London, Nov. 27, 1929.

Wilson, Philip Whitwell. "But Who Killed Miss Gilchrist?" *North American Review* 226, no. 5 (1928): 531–44.

Wistrich, Robert S. "Antisemitism Embedded in British Culture." Online interview by Manfred Gerstenfeld, Jerusalem Center for Public Affairs, 2008, http://jcpa.org/article/antisemitism-embedded-in-british-culture.

Womack, Steven. Introduction to Hines (2001).

# NOTES

ABBREVIATIONS

| | |
|---|---|
| ACD | Arthur Conan Doyle |
| AMA | Arthur Montague Adams |
| AT | Amalie (Malchen) Leschziner Tau |
| DC | David Cook |
| ES | Ewing Speirs |
| EL | Euphemia (Phemie) Leschziner |
| HL | Helen Lambie |
| HMPP | His Majesty's Prison Peterhead |
| JTT | Det. Lt. John Thompson Trench |
| LF | Leschziner family |
| MB | Margaret Birrell |
| ML | Mitchell Library, Glasgow |
| MP | Master of Polworth |
| NRS | National Records of Scotland, Edinburgh |
| OS | Oscar Slater |
| PL | Pauline Leschziner |
| REP | Reverend Eleazar Phillips |
| WAG | William A. Goodhart |
| WG | William Gordon |
| WP | William Park |
| WR | William Roughead |

AUTHOR'S NOTE

xiii **"given the compound surname":** Russell Miller, *The Adventures of Arthur Conan Doyle: A Biography* (New York: Thomas Dunne Books/St. Martin's Press, 2008), 24.

xiii ***The True Conan Doyle***: Adrian Conan Doyle, *The True Conan Doyle* (New York: Coward-McCann, 1946).

INTRODUCTION

xv **"as brutal and callous a crime"**: Arthur Conan Doyle, *The Case of Oscar Slater* (New York: Hodder & Stoughton/George H. Doran Company, 1912), 79–80.

xv **"remain immortal in the classics"**: ACD letter to the *Spectator*, July 25, 1914. In John Michael Gibson and Richard Lancelyn Green, eds., *The Unknown Conan Doyle: Letters to the Press* (London: Secker & Warburg, 1986), 205.

xvi **"See you Oscar"**: *Dictionary of the Scottish Language*, www.dsl.ac.uk/entry/snd/sndns2758. Though less well known than its Cockney counterpart, Glasgow rhyming slang likewise arose during the nineteenth century and has remained at least as robust as its London cousin. Contemporary examples include "the Tony Blairs" ("stairs"), "Andy Murray" ("curry"), "Gregory Pecks" ("specs"), and "Marilu Henner" ("tenner"—a ten-pound note). These examples are from Antonio Lillo, "Nae Barr's Irn-Bru Whit Ye're oan Aboot: Musings on Modern Scottish Rhyming Slang," *English World-Wide* 33, no. 1 (2012): 69–102.

xvi **"disgraceful frame-up"**: Arthur Conan Doyle, *Memories and Adventures*, 2nd ed. (London: John Murray, 1930), 445.

xvi **"Scotland's gulag"**: Quoted in Phil Scraton, Joe Sim, and Paula Skidmore, *Prisons Under Protest* (Milton Keynes, U.K.: Open University Press, 1991), 65.

xvi **Had he passed the twenty-year mark:** WP to ACD, Dec. 1, 1927, ML.

xvii **"I was up against a ring of political lawyers"**: Letter, marked "Private," from ACD to unknown recipient, n.d., ML; also quoted in Miller (2008), 299.

xvii **"a cat would scarcely be whipped"**: Andrew Lang letter to WR. Quoted in Peter Hunt, *Oscar Slater: The Great Suspect* (London: Carroll & Nicholson, 1951), 142.

xvii **"The Slater affair"**: Pierre Nordon, *Conan Doyle: A Biography*, trans. John Murray (New York: Holt, Rinehart & Winston, 1967), 115.

xvii **"that paladin of lost causes":** William Roughead, ed., *Trial of Oscar Slater*, 4th ed., Notable British Trials Series (Edinburgh and London: William Hodge & Company, 1950), xxviii.

xviii **very likely the most famous character:** In 1987, the eminent science-fiction writer and impassioned rationalist Isaac Asimov went this appraisal one better, writing, "Indeed, it is quite possible to maintain that Sherlock Holmes is the most famous fictional creation *of any sort* and of all time." Isaac Asimov, "Thoughts on Sherlock Holmes," *Baker Street Journal* 37, no. 4 (1987): 201.

xviii ***Arthur and George*:** Julian Barnes, *Arthur and George* (London: Jonathan Cape, 2005).

xviii **"a disreputable, rolling-stone of a man":** Conan Doyle (1912), 43.

xix **"reason backward":** "A Study in Scarlet," in Sir Arthur Conan Doyle, *The Penguin Complete Sherlock Holmes* (New York: Penguin Books, 1981), 83.

xix **"I have a turn":** Ibid., 23–24.

xx **the moving series of letters:** In accordance with prison regulations, Slater was normally obliged to write to his family in English; their German-language replies, on reaching Scotland, had to be translated into English before they could be passed on to him. Slater's English was not the best, and his writing in the language reflects as much. Correspondingly, the texts of the letters from his family that have been preserved in Scottish archives are rendered in the English of a series of translators of varying abilities. The situation is not ideal, but it is the best we have, and the letters in both directions are no less valuable for it, and no less moving. In the quotations from Slater's letters that appear in this book, I have occasionally, for ease of reading, made minute changes to the unorthodox punctuation and paragraphing that he, and some of the translators, used throughout; I have also standardized the various English spellings of certain German names.

xx **"the long nineteenth century":** Peter Gay, *The Cultivation of Hatred: The Bourgeois Experience, Victoria to Freud* (New York: W. W. Norton & Company, 1993), 3: fn.

xxii **"a painful and sordid aftermath":** Conan Doyle (1930), 445.

xxii **"the racialization of crime":** Cf. Paul Knepper, "British Jews and the Racialisation of Crime in the Age of Empire," *British Journal of Criminology* 47 (2007): 61–79.

PROLOGUE: PRISONER 2988

xxiii **On January 23, 1925:** Gordon's release date and prisoner number per HMPP internal memorandum, Feb. 17, 1925.

xxiii **would culminate nearly three years later:** OS was released in November 1927.

xxiii **during a meeting:** Hunt (1951), 187.

xxiii **a regimen of enforced silence:** John MacLean, "Life in Prison," *Red Dawn* 1, no. 1 (March 1919): 8–9; republished at www.scottishrepublicansocialistmovement.org/Pages/SRSMJohnMacLeanLifeinPrison.aspx.

xxiii **supervised round the clock by armed guards:** Robert Jeffrey, *Peterhead: The Inside Story of Scotland's Toughest Prison* (Edinburgh: Black & White Publishing, 2013), 19.

xxiii **Slater had already been disciplined:** HMPP disciplinary record, Sept. 1, 1912, NRS.

xxiv **Gordon my boy:** OS to WG, n.d., ML.

xxiv **Just a few lines:** Suppressed anonymous letter to OS, most likely from WG, Feb. 14, 1925. Attached to HMPP internal memorandum, Feb. 17, 1925, NRS.

xxv **"a case of murder":** Douglas Grant, *The Thin Blue Line: The Story of the City of Glasgow Police* (London: John Long, 1973), 54.

xxv **"Circumstantial evidence is a very tricky thing":** "The Boscombe Valley Mystery," in Conan Doyle (1981), 204–5.

CHAPTER I: A FOOTFALL ON THE STAIR

3 **population of more than three-quarters of a million:** www.bbc.co.uk/bitesize/ks3/history/industrial_era/the_industrial_revolution/revision/3.

3 **the second-largest city in Britain:** Ibid.

4 **"Now an alien breed":** Quoted in Ben Braber, "The Trial of Oscar Slater (1909) and Anti-Jewish Prejudices in Edwardian Glasgow," *History* 88 (2003): 273–74.

4 **"has cast a lurid light":** Quoted in ibid., 274.

4 **She was born in Glasgow:** County of Lanark, Register of Births and Baptisms, NRS.

5 **"Miss Gilchrist was not on good terms":** MB to JTT, December

1908; document preserved by him for use in 1914 Slater case inquiry, ML.

5 **On November 20, 1908:** Marion Gilchrist, Trust Disposition and Deed of Settlement and Codicil, May 28 and Nov. 20, 1908. Books of Council and Sessions, NRS.

5 **The previous version:** Ibid.

5 **valued at more than:** Richard Whittington-Egan, *The Oscar Slater Murder Story: New Light on a Classic Miscarriage of Justice* (Glasgow: Neil Wilson Publishing, 2001), 71.

5 **"a likeable, high-spirited, superficial":** Hunt (1951), 17.

6 **"a very good domestic worker":** Agnes Guthrie letter to WP, quoted in Whittington-Egan (2001), 156.

6 **the "maindoor house":** Ibid., 7.

7 **she amassed an extensive collection:** List adapted from Roughead (1950), 248–49.

7 **At her death, the collection:** William Park, *The Truth About Oscar Slater [with the Prisoner's Own Story]* (London: Psychic Press, 1927), 46.

7 **"She seldom wore her jewelry":** Conan Doyle (1912), 9.

7 **forgoing the safe in her parlor:** Hunt (1951), 17.

7 **"a detachable pocket":** Ibid.

7 **She pinned other pieces:** Jack House, *Square Mile of Murder* (Edinburgh: Black & White Publishing, 2002), 143.

8 **"Against . . . unwelcome intrusion":** Hunt (1951), 17.

8 **"The back windows were kept locked":** Ibid.

8 **If she were ever in distress:** Ibid.

9 **New York, London, Paris, and Brussels:** Hunt (1951), 69–70.

9 **he married a local woman:** Register of marriages, Oscar Leschziner (Slater) and Mary Curtis Pryor, July 12, 1901, NRS.

9 **an alcoholic who was constantly after him:** Hunt (1951), 69.

9 **He was known to have lived briefly again:** Ibid., 73.

9 **Slater arrived in Glasgow:** Ibid., 75.

9 **known professionally as Madame Junio:** Ibid., 39.

9 **On November 10:** Roughead (1950), lxi.

9 **an initial loan of £20:** Ibid. Slater pawned the brooch on Nov. 18.

10 **her Irish terrier:** Hunt (1951), 18.

10 **during the first three weeks of December:** Ibid.

10 **"The 'watcher' was seen":** Ibid., 19.
10 **"I was informed by her":** AG to WP, 1927. Quoted in Whittington-Egan (2001), 157.
10 **which Lambie implied in a later conversation:** Ibid.
10 **and confirmed outright:** MB to JTT, December 1908.
11 **returning at about four-thirty:** HL, Slater trial testimony, May 3, 1909. In Roughead (1950), 51.
11 **a rainy evening:** Hunt (1951), xi.
11 **"Before I reached the door":** Rowena Adams Liddell, Slater trial testimony, May 4, 1909. In Roughead (1950), 85–86.
11 **At a minute or two before seven:** Conan Doyle (1912), 10.
12 **a penny for the newspaper:** Ibid., 20.
12 **"Lambie took the keys with her":** Ibid., 10.
12 **a forty-year-old flutist:** Hunt (1951), 17; House (2002), 140. Adams was born on April 21, 1868; www.scotlandspeople.gov.uk.
12 **"I rang hard":** AMA, Slater trial testimony. Quoted in Roughead (1950), 78.
12 **"breaking sticks in the kitchen":** Ibid.
12 **"like to crack":** Quoted in Park (1927), 22.
13 **she noticed a footprint:** HL, Slater trial testimony. Quoted in Roughead (1950), 51.
13 **"He was never a visitor":** Ibid.
13 **"Oh, it would be the pulleys":** Ibid.
13 **in her recollection, she remained:** Hunt (1951), 21.
13 **a well-dressed man come toward her:** HL, Slater trial testimony. Quoted in Roughead (1950), 51.
13 **the gaslight in that room:** Ibid.
13 **his clothing bore no visible traces:** Hunt (1951), 24.
13 **"I did not suspect anything wrong":** AMA, Slater trial testimony. Quoted in Roughead (1950), 79.
14 **"Where is your mistress?":** Ibid.
14 **"The spectacle in question":** Conan Doyle (1912), 13.
14 **autopsy photographs depict:** Thomas Toughill, *Oscar Slater: The "Immortal" Case of Sir Arthur Conan Doyle* (Stroud, U.K.: Sutton Publishing, 2006).
14 **Adams rushed downstairs:** Park (1927), 25.
14 **"Dr. Adams surmised":** Hunt (1951), 24.
15 **who arrived at 7:55:** Ibid., 24.

15 **who arrived later that night:** Ibid., 25.
15 **The half sovereign:** Ibid., 24.
15 **There was no sign of a struggle:** Ibid., 27.
15 **trade name Runaway:** Ibid., 25.
15 **Adams, who was nearsighted:** Conan Doyle (1912), 14.
16 **"well featured and clean-shaven":** Ibid., 15.
16 **a three-quarter-length gray overcoat:** Conan Doyle (1912), 15.
16 **At 9:40 that night:** Glasgow police internal report, Dec. 21, 1909, ML.
16 **"An old lady was murdered":** Ibid.
16 **In 1908, Glasgow:** Braber (2003), 273.
16 **a letter from an old American crony:** Park (1927), 171.
17 **told the barber of his travel plans:** Hunt (1951), 94.
17 **On Wednesday, December 23:** Toughill (2006), 150; Roughead (1950), 88.
17 **"not merely as an honest man":** Conan Doyle (1930), 445.
17 **a local woman, Barbara Barrowman:** Hunt (1951), 30; Toughill (2006), 250.
17 **Encouraged by her mother:** Hunt (1951), 31.
18 **"He looked towards St. George's Road":** Ibid., 31–32.
18 **known as a Donegal cap:** Mary Barrowman testimony, Slater extradition hearing transcript, Jan. 26, 1909, 36, NRS.
18 **a second internal bulletin:** Quoted in Hunt (1951), 32–33; italics in original.
19 **That day, Superintendent Ord:** Ibid., 33.
19 **Glasgow soon blazed with rumor:** Ibid.
19 **"News of the dastardly outrage":** Park (1927), 36–37.
20 **On the evening of December 25:** Hunt (1951), 34.

## CHAPTER 2: THE MYSTERIOUS MR. ANDERSON

21 **answered to the name Anderson:** Hunt (1951), 36.
22 **It weighs barely an ounce:** The wrapper, weighed by me on a postal scale at the National Records of Scotland in 2017, registers 0.7 ounce.
22 **"marginal clubs, peopled by marginal characters":** Hunt (1951), 36.
22 **a bookmaker's clerk named Hugh Cameron:** Ibid.
22 **On the morning of December 26:** Park (1927), 78.

23 **Miss Gilchrist's brooch was set:** Ibid., 78–79.

23 **Slater had left the brooch there:** Hunt (1951), 78.

23 **should have been a "fiasco":** Sir Arthur Conan Doyle, *Memories and Adventures* (Oxford: Oxford University Press, 1924), 223.

23 **"Already the very bottom of the case":** Conan Doyle (1912), 22–23; italics added.

23 **"The trouble . . . with all police prosecutions":** Ibid., 61.

23 **One of four children:** Hunt (1951), 131.

23 **on January 8, 1872:** A letter from LF to OS dated Jan. 7, 1912, NRS, refers to Jan. 8 of that year as Slater's fortieth birthday.

24 **"I was educated very inadequately":** "Oscar Slater's Own Story: Specially Compiled from Private Documents," *Empire News*, April 13, 1924.

24 **Oskar lighted out for Berlin:** Whittington-Egan (2001), 49–50.

24 **"two or three well-kept rooms":** Hunt (1951), 130.

24 **"decayed tenement house":** Ibid.

24 **an invalid with spine disease:** Ibid.

24 **Pauline was partly blind:** Ibid.

24 **"I could not wish a better son":** Quoted in ibid., 131.

24 **first visited England in about 1895:** Whittington-Egan (2001), 30.

25 **"underworld, peopled by strange denizens":** Ibid., 57.

25 **two prior arrests:** HMPP intake form, May 28, 1909, NRS.

25 **"the marginal world":** Hunt (1951), 123.

25 **"men who, without being criminals":** Ibid.

25 **a world in which many Jewish immigrants:** See, e.g., Ben Braber, *Jews in Glasgow 1879–1939: Immigration and Integration* (London: Vallentine Mitchell, 2007), 29.

26 **the act was widely understood:** Ibid., 25.

26 **In 1190, in the deadliest:** Anthony Julius, *Trials of the Diaspora: A History of Anti-Semitism in England* (Oxford: Oxford University Press, 2010), 118ff.

27 **"the first ejection":** Robert S. Wistrich, "Antisemitism Embedded in British Culture," online interview by Manfred Gerstenfeld, Jerusalem Center for Public Affairs (2008), http://jcpa.org/article/antisemitism-embedded-in-british-culture.

27 **Only in the mid-seventeenth century:** Ibid.

27 **"The lay Englishman":** Sir Frederick Pollock and Frederic Wil-

liam Maitland, *The History of English Law Before the Time of Edward I*, 2nd ed. (Cambridge: Cambridge University Press, 1911), 1:407.

27 **"and I make this Declaration":** Jews Relief Act (1858). Text at www.legislation.gov.uk/ukpga/Vict/21–22/49/contents/enacted.

28 **the only person of Jewish birth:** Born to a Jewish family in 1804, Disraeli was baptized in 1817, at his father's insistence, in the interest of assimilation and social advancement. As an adult, he considered himself religiously intermediate, "the blank page between the Old Testament and the New," as he famously said. Quoted in Adam Kirsch, *Benjamin Disraeli* (New York: Schocken Books, 2008), 32. As Kirsch points out, the imagery was not original to Disraeli, coming from the playwright Richard Brinsley Sheridan.

28 **between the early 1880s:** Braber (2007), 4.

28 **In 1914, London had:** Ibid., 184.

28 **Glasgow's the same year:** Ibid., 4.

28 **"Following the discovery":** Knepper (2007), 63.

28 **first taken up formally in 1887:** Ibid.

29 **"Crime had become":** Ibid., 63–65; italics added.

29 **"Scottish Protestants put great emphasis":** Braber (2007), 18.

29 **The first Jews settled:** Ibid., 8.

30 **about four dozen strong:** Ibid.

30 **an optician, a quill merchant:** Ibid.

30 **"A small group of Jews":** Ibid., 21.

30 **the supposed involvement:** Ibid., 23.

30 **"was of a Jewish type":** Ibid., 25.

30 **one of his few early champions:** Ibid., 29.

31 **one of the first in Britain:** Grant, (1973), 15.

32 **"Poor devils":** Conan Doyle (1924), 296.

33 **the "convenient Other":** Gay (1993), 35 and passim.

33 **"Wanted for identification":** Quoted in Hunt (1951), 39.

## CHAPTER 3: THE KNIGHT-ERRANT

35 **"the individual's traces":** Rosemary Jann, *The Adventures of Sherlock Holmes: Detecting Social Order* (New York: Twayne Publishers, 1995), 67.

35 **"social pathology":** See, e.g., Robert Peckham, ed., *Disease and Crime: A History of Social Pathologies and the New Politics of Health* (New York: Routledge, 2014).

35 **"Liberal Imperialist":** Laura Otis, *Membranes: Metaphors of Invasion in Nineteenth-Century Literature, Science, and Politics* (Baltimore: Johns Hopkins University Press, 1999), 98.

36 **"depicts British society":** Ibid., 6.

36 **The First Citizen of Baker Street:** See, e.g., Jack M. Siegel, "The First Citizen of Baker Street," *Chicago Review* 2, no. 2 (1947): 49–55.

36 ***Beeton's Christmas Annual*:** The annual's founder, Samuel Orchart Beeton, was the husband of the tastemaker and author Isabella Beeton, whose instructional book on cooking and homemaking, *Mrs. Beeton's Book of Household Management,* first published in 1861, was a lodestar for generations of bourgeois Victorian women.

37 **"Marshall McLuhan . . . once observed":** Frank D. McConnell, "Sherlock Holmes: Detecting Order amid Disorder," *Wilson Quarterly* 11, no. 2 (1987): 181–82.

37 **"It often annoyed me":** Quoted in J. K. Van Dover, *You Know My Method: The Science of the Detective* (Bowling Green, Ky.: Bowling Green State University Popular Press, 1994), 90.

37 **Readers requested his autograph:** For all these things, see, e.g., Miller (2008), 158, 465; Jann (1995), 12; Michael Hardwick and Mollie Hardwick, *The Man Who Was Sherlock Holmes* (Garden City, N.Y.: Doubleday & Company, 1964), 9.

38 **"Occasionally," a biographer has written:** Daniel Stashower, *Teller of Tales: The Life of Arthur Conan Doyle* (New York: Owl/Henry Holt, 1999), 132.

38 **"It was easy to get people into scrapes":** Conan Doyle (1924), 13.

39 **suffered from epilepsy, alcoholism:** E.g., ibid.

39 **"We lived," Conan Doyle later wrote:** Conan Doyle (1924), 11.

39 **"Charles possessed":** Miller (2008), 16–17.

39 **the series of Scottish institutions:** Ibid., 18–21.

39 **To honor a childless great-uncle:** Jann (1995), xv.

40 **who had married Charles in 1855:** Ibid., 15.

40 **"Diminutive Mary Doyle":** Ibid., 24, and A. Conan Doyle, *The Stark Munro Letters: Being a Series of Twelve Letters Written by J. Stark Munro, M.B., to His Friend and Former Fellow-Student,*

*Herbert Swanborough, of Lowell, Massachusetts, During the Years 1881–1884* (New York: D. Appleton & Company, 1895), 60.

40 **"I will say for myself":** Conan Doyle (1924), 12.

41 **"I can speak with feeling":** Ibid., 16–17.

41 **"I was wild, full-blooded":** Ibid., 22.

41 **He had already begun to part company:** Ibid., 20.

41 **"Judging . . . by all the new knowledge":** Ibid., 31.

42 **"Bell was a very remarkable man":** Ibid., 25–26.

42 **"my father's health":** Ibid., 30.

42 **a pastiche of Poe and Bret Harte:** Miller (2008), 58.

43 **with its crew of fifty:** Conan Doyle (1924), 36.

43 **he was thrown overboard:** Ibid., 40.

43 **"Its instinct urges it":** Ibid., 43.

43 **"Who would swap that moment":** Ibid.

43 **In 1881, Conan Doyle:** Ibid., 47.

43 **helped subdue an out-of-control fire:** Ibid., 56–57.

43 **"The germ or the mosquito":** Ibid., 52.

44 **"There were . . . some unpleasant":** Ibid., 49.

44 **"more on affection and respect":** Jann (1995), xvi.

44 **"I made £154":** Conan Doyle (1924), 70.

44 **Though her legal name:** Georgina Doyle, *Out of the Shadows: The Untold Story of Arthur Conan Doyle's First Family* (Ashcroft, B.C.: Calabash Press, 2004), 55.

45 **"Poe's masterful detective":** Ibid., 74–75.

45 **Sherrinford Holmes:** Leslie S. Klinger, ed., *The New Annotated Sherlock Holmes* (New York: W. W. Norton & Company, 2005–6), 3:847. (Some sources erroneously give the name as Sherringford.)

45 **"Often, physicians who become":** Edmund D. Pellegrino, "To Look Feelingly: The Affinities of Medicine and Literature," *Literature and Medicine* 1 (1982), 20; italics added.

45 **Ormond Sacker:** Andrew Lycett, *The Man Who Created Sherlock Holmes: The Life and Times of Sir Arthur Conan Doyle* (New York: Free Press, 2007), 121.

46 **"Please grip this fact":** Quoted in Jann (1995), 15; accent mark added for scansion.

46 **"I have often been asked":** Conan Doyle (1924), 100.

46 **"I . . . have several times solved":** Ibid., 101.

47 **"In travelling through":** Adrian Conan Doyle (1946), 19.

47 **"I always regarded him":** Quoted in Ely Liebow, *Dr. Joe Bell: Model for Sherlock Holmes* (Madison, Wis.: Popular Press, 2007), 175.
48 **"Undaunted," his biographer Russell Miller wrote:** Miller (2008), 125.
48 **"Observing the patients":** Otis (1999), 109.
48 **Koch's remedy, he wrote:** ACD to *Daily Telegraph*, Nov. 20, 1890. Quoted in Gibson and Lancelyn Green (1986), 36.

## CHAPTER 4: THE MAN IN THE DONEGAL CAP

50 **On December 21, 1908:** Hunt (1951), 85.
50 **Slater had already been planning:** Ibid., 84ff.
50 **Slater promptly gave Schmalz:** Ibid., 85–86.
50 **It was during his last days in Glasgow:** Ibid., 86.
50 **By 7:00 p.m. on December 21:** Ibid.
51 **their ten pieces of luggage:** Ibid., 95.
51 **Arriving at 3:40 a.m.:** Roughead (1950), 294.
51 **"the chambermaid had a conversation":** Quoted in ACD letter to the *Spectator*, July 25, 1914. In Gibson and Lancelyn Green (1986), 205.
51 **two second-class tickets:** Park (1927), 83.
51 **Mr. and Mrs. Otto Sando:** Ibid.
51 **"The pawned brooch":** Conan Doyle, introduction to Park (1927), 7–8.
52 **ARREST OTTO SANDO:** Quoted in Park (1927), 83.
52 **On January 2, 1909:** Hunt (1951), 44ff.
52 **"Dear Friend Cameron!":** OS to Hugh Cameron, Feb. 2, 1909, NRS. Also quoted in Toughill (2006), 53–54.
53 **"It is a measure of Cameron's friendship":** Toughill (2006), 54.
53 **On January 13, 1909:** Hunt (1951), 45.
54 **"At the time of the arrest of Slater":** William A. Goodhart to Ewing Speirs, Slater's Glasgow attorney, April 17, 1909, NRS.
54 **Glasgow officials showed Slater's photograph:** Hunt (1951), 46.
54 **One marshal:** Ibid., 215 n. 1.
55 **As Marshal Pinckley would testify:** John W. M. Pinckley, testimony in the appeal of Oscar Slater, 1928. Quoted in ibid., 215.
55 **"Do you see the man here":** HL testimony, Slater extradition hearing transcript, Jan. 26, 1909, 17, NRS.

55 **she had not seen the intruder's face:** Hunt (1951), 26.
55 **"he was sort of shaking himself":** Ibid., 19.
55 **"Is that man in this room?":** Ibid., 19–20.
56 **"That man here":** Barrowman testimony, ibid., 37.
56 **"had a slight twist":** Barrowman testimony, ibid.
56 **admitted having been shown:** Barrowman testimony, ibid., 38.
56 **"not at all unlike":** Arthur Adams testimony, ibid., 51.
56 **"I never doubted his innocence":** William A. Goodhart to ACD, May 28, 1914, ML.
57 **on February 6, 1909:** Hunt (1951), 56.
57 **Another was almost certainly a concern:** Ibid., 55–56.
57 **A trial, he felt certain:** This position is confirmed by his lawyer Goodhart, who in 1909 wrote, "Slater's willingness to go back is certainly indicative of innocence." William A. Goodhart to Ewing Speirs, April 17, 1909, NRS.

## CHAPTER 5: TRACES

61 **"The foreteller asserts":** Thomas Henry Huxley, "On the Method of Zadig: Retrospective Prophecy as a Function of Science," in Thomas Henry Huxley, *Science and Culture: And Other Essays* (New York: D. Appleton, 1882), 139–40.
62 **"retrospective prophecy":** Ibid., 135.
62 **"From a drop of water":** Arthur Conan Doyle, "A Study in Scarlet," in Conan Doyle (1981), 23.
63 **his fictional "scientific detective":** Conan Doyle (1924), 26.
63 **therein lies a basic challenge:** The literary critic Lawrence Frank, in *Victorian Detective Fiction and the Nature of Evidence: The Scientific Investigations of Poe, Dickens, and Doyle* (London: Palgrave Macmillan, 2009), 19, also makes this point.
64 **"Throughout the 18th century":** Claudio Rapezzi, Roberto Ferrari, and Angelo Branzi, "White Coats and Fingerprints: Diagnostic Reasoning in Medicine and Investigative Methods of Fictional Detectives," *BMJ: British Medical Journal* 331, no. 7531 (2005): 1493.
64 **"look feelingly":** Pellegrino (1982), 19–23.
64 **"It has long been an axiom":** Conan Doyle (1981), 194.
64 **"The importance of the infinitely little":** Dr. Joseph Bell, "Mr. Sherlock Holmes," introduction to Sir A. Conan Doyle, *A Study*

*in Scarlet* (London: Ward, Lock & Company, 1892), 9–10; italics added.

65 **an acknowledged influence on Conan Doyle:** A[lma] E[lizabeth] Murch, *The Development of the Detective Novel* (New York: Philosophical Library, 1958), 177.

65 **"One day, when he was walking":** M. de Voltaire, *Zadig* (New York: Rimington & Hooper, 1929), 16–19.

67 **"ratiocination," Poe calls it:** E.g., Edgar Allan Poe, "The Mystery of Marie Rogêt," in Edgar Allan Poe, *Poetry and Tales* (New York: Library of America, 1984), 521.

67 **"You were remarking to yourself":** Edgar Allan Poe, "The Murders in the Rue Morgue," in Poe (1984), 402–4.

68 **"The scientific method":** Van Dover (1994), 10.

68 **"The detective offered himself":** Ibid., 1.

68 **"medico-legal practice":** R. Austin Freeman, "The Case of Oscar Brodski," in *The Best Dr. Thorndyke Stories*, selected by E. F. Bleiler (New York: Dover Publications, 1973), 15.

68 **"only a foot square":** Ibid., 16.

68 **"rows of little re-agent bottles":** Ibid., 17.

68 **"Dupin was a very inferior fellow":** Conan Doyle (1892), 49.

69 **"The narrative of the detective story":** Van Dover (1994), 30; italics added.

## CHAPTER 6: THE ORIGINAL SHERLOCK HOLMES

70 **His grandfather Sir Charles Bell:** Michael Sims, *Arthur and Sherlock: Conan Doyle and the Creation of Holmes* (New York: Bloomsbury, 2017), 17.

70 **"For some reason":** Conan Doyle (1924), 25.

71 **He said to a civilian patient:** Ibid.

71 **"He greeted her politely":** Stashower (1999), 20.

72 **"Use your eyes, sir!":** Dr. Harold Emery Jones, *The Original of Sherlock Holmes* (Windsor, U.K.: Gaby Goldscheider, 1980), iv–v.

72 **a classmate of Conan Doyle's:** Ibid., i.

73 **"Gentlemen, a fisherman!":** Ibid., v–vi.

73 **"Cultivate absolute accuracy":** Quoted in Liebow (2007), 116.

73 **"Nearly every handicraft":** Quoted in ibid., 177.

74 **"Is there any system":** Quoted in Jessie M. E. Saxby, *Joseph Bell: An Appreciation by an Old Friend* (Edinburgh: Oliphant, Anderson & Ferrier, 1913), 23–24.

75 **"For twenty years or more":** "The Original of 'Sherlock Holmes': An Interview with Dr. Joseph Bell," *Pall Mall Gazette,* Dec. 28, 1893. Quoted in Saxby (1913), 19.

75 **he married one of his pupils:** Alexander Duncan Smith, ed., *The Trial of Eugène Marie Chantrelle*, Notable Scottish Trials Series (Glasgow: William Hodge & Company, 1906), 2.

75 **"My dear Mama":** Quoted in Liebow (2007), 120.

75 **Chantrelle insured his wife's life:** Ibid.

75 **on the bedside table:** Ibid.

75 **Returning, she saw:** Ibid.

75 **"Bell and Littlejohn found evidence":** Ibid., 120–21.

76 **An investigation by the gas company:** Ibid., 121.

76 **discovered a pipefitter:** Ibid.

76 **Chantrelle was hanged:** Ibid.

76 **Conan Doyle had long admired:** See, e.g., Arthur Conan Doyle, *Through the Magic Door* (Pleasantville, N.Y.: Akadine Press, 1999), 259ff.

77 **who suffered from tuberculosis:** Sims (2017), 197.

77 **"blended the praise":** Ibid.

77 **"Dear Sir," Stevenson wrote:** Ibid.; italics added.

## CHAPTER 7: THE ART OF REASONING BACKWARD

78 **"To-day criminal investigation":** Sir Sydney Smith, *Mostly Murder* (New York: Dorset Press, 1988), 30.

78 **Many of the methods invented:** *Illustrated London News*, Feb. 27, 1932. Quoted in Nordon (1967), 211.

80 **he left a written legacy:** "Charles Sanders Peirce," *Stanford Encyclopedia of Philosophy* (2001; revised 2014), http://plato.stanford.edu/entries/peirce.

80 **"A given object":** Charles Sanders Peirce, unpublished manuscript. Quoted in Thomas A. Sebeok and Jean Umiker-Sebeok, "You Know My Method: A Juxtaposition of Charles S. Peirce and Sherlock Holmes," in Umberto Eco and Thomas A. Sebeok, eds.,

*The Sign of the Three: Dupin, Holmes, Peirce* (Bloomington: Indiana University Press, 1983), 17.

80 **"*Abduction* makes its start":** Peirce, unpublished manuscript. Quoted in ibid., 24–25; italics added.

81 **Fact C is observed:** N[ick] C. Boreham, G. E. Mawer, and R. W. Foster, "Medical Diagnosis from Circumstantial Evidence," *Le Travail Humain* 59, no. 1 (1996): 73.

81 **"In solving a problem":** *A Study in Scarlet,* in Conan Doyle (1981), 83.

81 **All serious knife wounds:** Adapted from Marcello Truzzi, "Sherlock Holmes: Applied Social Psychologist," in Eco and Sebeok (1983), 69.

82 **"We are coming now":** Conan Doyle (1981), 687; italics added.

82 **"*the scientific use of the imagination*":** Holmes is quoting the physicist John Tyndall, author of the 1870 essay "Scientific Use of the Imagination," whom Conan Doyle acknowledged as a deep influence.

82 **"the whole thing is a chain":** *A Study in Scarlet,* in Conan Doyle (1981), 85.

83 **"who had such a hatred":** Ibid., 583.

83 **"considering," Holmes points out:** Ibid., 584.

83 **"Holmes pointed":** Ibid., 587.

83 **"by a connected chain":** Ibid., 594.

83 **"Holmes . . . operates like a semiotician":** Jann (1995), 50; italics added.

## CHAPTER 8: A CASE OF IDENTITY

85 **On February 11, 1909:** Hunt (1951), 60ff.

85 **To avoid the throng:** Park (1927), 37.

85 **As he disembarked:** Hunt (1951), 61.

85 **neatly folded, carefully packed:** Ibid., 62.

85 **Nor did police find:** Ibid., 61.

86 **"In the fierce popular indignation":** Sir Arthur Conan Doyle, *Strange Studies from Life and Other Narratives: The Complete True Crime Writings of Sir Arthur Conan Doyle*, selected and ed. Jack Tracy (Bloomington, Ind.: Gaslight Publications, 1988), 33.

86 **the inherent unreliability of eyewitness testimony:** See, e.g., Eliza-

beth Loftus and Katherine Ketcham, *Witness for the Defense: The Accused, the Eyewitness, and the Expert Who Puts Memory on Trial* (New York: St. Martin's Press, 1991).

86 **another wrongful conviction:** E.g., Toughill (2006), 115–16.

87 **"It is notorious":** Conan Doyle (1912), 27.

87 **On February 21, 1909:** Hunt (1951), 61ff.

87 **those who made an identification chose Slater:** Ibid., 63.

87 **"To expect a row":** Park (1927), 116.

87 **common practice at the time:** WP to ACD, Feb. 2, 1927, ML.

88 **"Slater impressed everyone":** Hunt (1951), 66.

88 **"The more I see of Slater":** Quoted in ibid., 67.

88 **On April 6:** Ibid.

89 **that would come to be called *criminalistics*:** For an extended discussion of the ideological and methodological differences between criminalistics and criminology, see, e.g., Alison Adam, *A History of Forensic Science: British Beginnings in the Twentieth Century* (London: Routledge, 2016).

89 **the Age of Identification:** See, e.g., Anne M. Joseph, "Anthropometry, the Police Expert, and the Deptford Murders: The Contested Introduction of Fingerprinting for the Identification of Criminals in Late Victorian and Edwardian Britain," in Jane Caplan and John Torpey, eds., *Documenting Individual Identity: The Development of State Practices in the Modern World* (Princeton, N.J.: Princeton University Press, 2001), 164–83.

90 **the very concept of a "crime scene":** Robert Peckham, "Pathological Properties: Scenes of Crime, Sites of Infection," in Peckham, ed. (2014), 58.

90 **did not begin to come into its own:** Adam (2016), 3.

91 **think of Hester Prynne:** Although Cain was also marked after killing Abel, the purpose of that mark, as Genesis 4:13–15 makes clear, was not to protect other people from Cain but to protect Cain from reprisals at the hands of other people. God, who had condemned Cain to wander the earth, deemed that to be sufficient punishment.

91 **"Branding and ear-boring":** Edward Higgs, *Identifying the English: A History of Personal Identification, 1500 to the Present* (London: Continuum, 2011), 89.

91 **criminal suspects were routinely strip-searched:** Ibid.

92 **"Outlawry was the capital punishment":** Pollock and Maitland (1911), 2:450.

92 **"To pursue the outlaw":** Pollock and Maitland (1911), 1:476.

92 **"Who are you, with whom I have to deal?":** Jeremy Bentham, *Principles of Penal Law* (CreateSpace Independent Publishing Platform, 2016), 248. Quoted in Jane Caplan, "'This or That Particular Person': Protocols and Identification in Nineteenth-Century Europe," in Caplan and Torpey (2001), 51.

92 **a "waived" woman:** www.nationalarchives.gov.uk.

93 **In the 1870s, Alphonse Bertillon:** See, e.g., Simon A. Cole, *Suspect Identities: A History of Fingerprinting and Criminal Identification* (Cambridge, Mass.: Harvard University Press, 2001), 33ff. Bertillon did his professional reputation considerable damage when he testified as a handwriting analyst—a field in which he had no expertise—in the 1894 trial of Captain Alfred Dreyfus. Dreyfus was convicted of treason partly as a result of Bertillon's testimony, later discredited, that he was the author of an anonymous memorandum disclosing French military secrets to the Germans.

95 **"This was not merely an idea":** Gina Lombroso Ferrero, *Criminal Man: According to the Classification of Cesare Lombroso, Briefly Summarised by His Daughter Gina Lombroso Ferrero* (New York: G. P. Putnam's Sons, 1911), xii.

95 **the writings of Havelock Ellis:** See, e.g., reprint of Havelock Ellis, *The Criminal* (Memphis, Tenn.: General Books, 2012).

95 **the work of Francis Galton:** See, e.g., Adam (2016), 52ff.; Cole (2001), 25ff.

96 **"the racialization of crime":** Knepper (2007).

97 **His handbook ranged over such subjects:** Hans Gross, *Criminal Investigation: A Practical Handbook for Magistrates, Police Officers and Lawyers*, trans. and ed. John Adam and John Collyer Adam (New Delhi: Isha Books, 2013), ix–xix.

97 **scarcely more than half a dozen references:** S. Tupper Bigelow, "Fingerprints and Sherlock Holmes," *Baker Street Journal* 17, no. 3 (1967): 133. As more than one student of literary forensics has pointed out, the sagacious Mark Twain (1835–1910) homed in early on the utility of fingerprints: in both *Life on the Mississippi* (1883)

and *Pudd'nhead Wilson*, first published in book form in 1894, murderers are identified by means of them.

98 **on the workbox:** Hunt (1951), 26.

99 **"Sentence first—verdict afterwards":** Lewis Carroll, *Alice's Adventures in Wonderland* and *Alice's Adventures Underground* (Cleveland: World Publishing Company, 1946), 147.

99 "available and disposable": Eleanor Jackson Piel, "The Death Row Brothers," *Proceedings of the American Philosophical Society* 147, no. 1 (2003): 30.

100 **"For some time *before the murder*":** WP to ACD, Nov. 25, 1927, ML; italics added.

101 **"virtually hypnotized by class":** Gay (1993), 429.

## CHAPTER 9: THE TRAP DOOR

105 **At 10:00 a.m.:** Roughead (1950), 1.

105 **On his right:** Toughill (2006), 71ff.

105 **the Georgian courtroom:** Whittington-Egan (2001), 79.

105 **among them a warehouseman:** Roughead (1950), 8.

105 **known in Scottish law as "productions":** Whittington-Egan (2001), 79.

105 **planned to introduce sixty-nine of them:** Roughead (1950), 2–3.

105 **We know the physical arrangement:** Toughill (2006), 71.

106 **"like a pantomime genie":** Whittington-Egan (2001), 79.

106 **"Evidence of this kind":** Conan Doyle (1912), 40.

107 **planned to present ninety-eight of them:** Roughead (1950), 4–5.

107 **just thirteen names:** Ibid., 7–8.

107 **"It is one of the new points":** Quoted in Park (1927), 184–85.

107 **"Helen Lambie's evidence":** Conan Doyle (1912), 31–32.

108 **Was it only his walk and his height:** Roughead (1950), 55–56.

109 **The hat presented to her:** Hunt (1951), 89.

109 **"You were shown a photograph":** Quoted in ibid., 93.

110 **she took pains to say:** Ibid., 89–90.

110 **a man "closely resembling":** Ibid., 80.

110 **"It is too serious a charge":** Ibid., 81.

110 **She testified that on the night:** Ibid., 97–100.

110 **Two months later:** Ibid., 98.

110 **she, too, had been shown:** Ibid., 91.

110 **weaving up and down:** Park (1927), 147–48.

111 **At the Crown's request:** Roughead (1910), 108ff.

111 **"Over his 33 years":** M. Anne Crowther and Brenda White, *On Soul and Conscience: The Medical Expert and Crime. 150 Years of Forensic Medicine in Glasgow* (Aberdeen, U.K.: Aberdeen University Press, 1988), 42–44.

111 **"The body was that":** Quoted in Roughead (1910), 110ff. Glaister conducted the autopsy with a colleague, Dr. Hugh Galt.

112 **Glaister went on to state:** Ibid., 108–21.

112 **eight-ounce hammer:** Hunt (1951), 99.

112 **"I did not find in the dining-room":** Quoted in Roughead (1950), 112.

112 **Glaister identified twenty-five stains:** Ibid., 114ff.

112 **"more of gravy than of grave":** Charles Dickens, *A Christmas Carol: And Other Christmas Books* (New York: Vintage Classics, 2012), 21.

113 **"In the absence":** Crowther and White (1988), 47.

113 **"The case later provided":** Ibid.

113 **Among them was McLean:** Roughead (1950), 135–37.

113 **"Did you find out":** Quoted in ibid., 104; italics added.

114 **"McClure would have scored":** Hunt (1951), 124–25.

114 **"When you first knew him":** Quoted in Roughead (1950), 156.

115 **"The treasured and conspicuous emblems":** Gay (1993), 496.

115 **At this point:** Ben Braber, personal communication.

116 **"Who engaged you?":** Quoted in Roughead (1950), 182–83.

117 **"The public careers":** Jann (1995), 111.

117 **Antoine, too, alibied Slater:** Roughead (1950), 187.

118 **"I have no questions to ask":** Quoted in ibid., 188.

118 **"never heard of a case":** WP to ACD, Dec. 5, 1927, ML.

118 **In February 1909:** Roughead (1950), xlviii.

118 **working his way stealthily home on foot:** ACD to the *Spectator*, July 25, 1919. In Gibson and Lancelyn Green (1986), 206.

118 **material that was never shared:** Hunt (1951), 145–46.

## CHAPTER 10: "UNTIL HE BE DEAD"

119 **"crushing the while":** Quoted in ibid., 103.

119 **Speaking for nearly two hours:** Ibid., 103.

119 **"Up to yesterday":** Quoted in ibid., 198–99.
120 **"a house situated":** Quoted in ibid., 199.
120 **"We shall see":** Quoted in ibid., 199.
120 **"I come now":** Quoted in ibid., 213–14.
121 **"Gentlemen, I have done":** Quoted in ibid., 217.
121 **"That, however":** Quoted in ibid., 220.
122 **"Can you lay":** Quoted in ibid., 235.
122 **"Clarence Darrow could have done it":** Hunt (1951), 109.
122 **His father, the Rev. Thomas Guthrie:** Braber (2007), 24.
122 **the elder Mr. Guthrie had helped found:** Ibid.
122 **a temperance crusader:** Ibid.
123 **"You have heard a good deal":** Quoted in Roughead (1950), 329–38; italics added.
123 **The jury retired at 4:55 p.m.:** Ibid., 245.
124 **"not guilty, and don't do it again":** See, e.g., Dani Garavelli, "Insight: The Jury's Still Out on 'Not Proven' Verdict," *Scotsman*, Feb. 13, 2016.
124 **to preempt hung juries:** Peter Duff, "The Scottish Criminal Jury: A Very Peculiar Institution," *Law and Contemporary Problems* 62, no. 2 (Spring 1999): 187.
124 **At 6:05:** Roughead (1950), 245.
124 **the most painful utterance:** Toughill (2006), 119.
124 **"My lord":** Quoted in Roughead (1950), 245.
125 **"The said Oscar Slater":** OS death sentence, May 6, 1909, NRS.
125 **"whereby a prisoner":** Park (1927), 38.
125 **On May 17:** Roughead (1950), 264.
125 **requesting the commutation:** Reprinted in ibid., 257ff.
126 **"The Memorialist thinks":** Reprinted in ibid., 264.
126 **signed by more than twenty thousand:** Ibid., 257.
126 **Mary Barrowman received half:** Hunt (1951), 140.
126 **on loan to Inverness:** Ibid., 132.
126 **"somewhat to the astonishment":** Ibid.
127 **he had just arranged:** Ibid., 137.
127 **"It was a curious compromise":** Philip Whitwell Wilson, "But Who Killed Miss Gilchrist?," *North American Review* 226, no. 5 (1928): 536.
127 **"Should you visit":** OS to REP, March 11, 1911 (letter suppressed by prison officials), NRS.

## CHAPTER II: THE COLD CRUEL SEA

128 **"Through my small window":** OS to LF, June 4, 1914, NRS.

128 **"It was, I find by my log":** Conan Doyle (1924), 37–38.

129 **opened in 1888:** Jeffrey (2013), 5.

129 **"We are always being told":** PL to OS, Dec. 27, 1910, NRS.

130 **"I would rather be":** John MacLean, *Accuser of Capitalism: John MacLean's Speech from the Dock, May 9th 1918* (London: New Park Publications, 1986), 26.

130 **"just a little box":** MacLean (1919).

130 **The only furniture:** Jeffrey (2013), 14.

130 **"Each cell is heated":** MacLean (1919).

130 **"The endless dreary days":** Gerald Newman, two-part handwritten ms., n.d., ML.

131 **Convicts' hair:** MacLean (1919).

131 **"kept clean and sanitary":** Ibid.

131 **From the prison's earliest days:** Jeffrey (2013), 18–19.

131 **"The blades were no ornamental":** Ibid., 18.

131 **on July 8, 1909:** Roughead (1950), lxi.

131 **Prisoner 1992:** LF to HMPP, March 27, 1913, NRS: "The old parents of the prisoner Oscar Slater Pr. No. 1992 long greatly for a sign of life from their son and beg you kindly to allow him to write to them."

131 **Slater's prison intake sheet:** Enquiry Form, completed by Detective Superintendent John Ord, May 28, 1909, NRS.

132 **At five each morning:** MacLean (1919).

132 **"to break great granite blocks":** OS to MP, Dec. 17, 1912, NRS.

133 **"He was a quiet, well-spoken man":** William Gordon newspaper clipping, n.d. [c. 1925], newspaper unknown, ML.

133 **"a pint of broth":** MacLean (1919).

133 **The sleeping hammock could be used:** Ibid.

133 **"My innocent Oscar":** PL to OS, postmarked Dec. 15, 1909, NRS.

134 **"In your last letter":** OS to PL, April 11, 1914, NRS.

134 **"You need not get anxious":** PL to OS, Dec. 30, 1913, NRS.

134 **"You would hardly know Beuthen":** PL to OS, Dec. 30, 1913, NRS.

134 **"Electric light is very convenient":** OS to LF, Dec. 13, 1913. NRS.

134 **"Yes! It is quite correct":** PL to OS, April 28, 1914, NRS.

134 **"You were always a good child":** PL to OS, Aug. 21, 1913, NRS.

135 **"We were very much rejoiced":** PL to OS, Sept. 18, 1909, NRS.
136 **"My beloved and good son":** PL to OS, March 14, 1910, NRS.
136 **"I should like to give you":** OS to LF, Jan. 1, 1912, NRS.
137 **"When I was sitting":** OS to LF, Sept. 13, 1913, NRS.
137 **"This is a very deep business":** OS to Dr. Mandowsky [first name not recorded], May 27, 1910, NRS.
137 **scant correspondence with their lawyers:** An undated letter, written c. 1922, from an official of HMPP to a Dr. Mamroth, a German lawyer known to Slater's family, reads, "As it is against the Commissioners' practice to permit Law Agents to have access to convicted prisoners with a view to preparing petitions for their release, and there does not seem to be any reason for setting this practice aside in favour of Slater, I have to inform you that letters from you cannot be forwarded to him."
138 **"The question of visiting you":** PL to OS, July 17, 1910, NRS.
138 **"Unfortunately I have to confess":** OS to LF, Oct. 24, 1912, NRS.

## CHAPTER 12: ARTHUR CONAN DOYLE, CONSULTING DETECTIVE

139 **died in December 1909, at thirty-seven:** Ewing Speirs death record, scotlandspeople.gov.uk.
139 **"For them the bullets":** Conan Doyle (1924), 175.
139 **an account of the conflict:** A. Conan Doyle, *The War in South Africa: Its Cause and Conduct* (New York: McClure, Phillips & Company, 1902).
140 **"At a time in history":** Steven Womack, introduction to Stephen Hines, *The True Crime Files of Sir Arthur Conan Doyle* (New York: Berkley Prime Crime, 2001), 13; italics in original.
140 **"I lunched that day":** Conan Doyle (1924), 386–87.
141 **"from the embraces of drunkards":** Quoted in Miller (2008), 279–81.
141 **"When I shot a crocodile":** Adrian Conan Doyle to Pierre Nordon, Dec. 7, 1959. Quoted in Nordon (1967), 192; italics in original.
141 **"Two white lies":** Conan Doyle (1924), 153.
141 **"Mr. Adrian Conan Doyle":** Nordon (1967), 174 n. 4.
142 **"There was a breadth of mind":** Adrian Conan Doyle (1946), 15.
143 **"This is the very individual":** Ibid., 16.
143 **some fifteen years his junior:** Leckie was born on March 14, 1874.

143 **"Even among writers":** Womack (2001), 15.
144 **Among the titles in his collection:** Walter Klinefelter, *The Case of the Conan Doyle Crime Library* (La Crosse, Wis.: Sumac Press, 1968).
144 **Though Conan Doyle acquired most:** Ibid., 6–7.
144 **three were published posthumously:** Conan Doyle (1988).
144 ***Strange Studies from Life*:** Conan Doyle (1988).
144 **In 1904, he became:** Stephen Wade, *Conan Doyle and the Crimes Club: The Creator of Sherlock Holmes and His Criminological Friends* (Oxford: Fonthill Media, 2013), 9.
144 **Other members included:** Ibid., 10.
144 **The cases they analyzed:** Peter Costello, *The Real World of Sherlock Holmes: The True Crimes Investigated by Arthur Conan Doyle* (New York: Carroll & Graf Publishers, 1991), 52; Wade (2013), 41ff.
145 **"We have the epitome":** Adrian Conan Doyle (1946), 16.
145 **Camille Cecile Holland:** Costello (1991), 46ff.
146 **"What about the moat?":** Ibid., 48.
146 **He confessed his guilt:** Ibid., 49.
146 **from the Langham Hotel:** Ibid., 104.
146 **"A few of the problems":** Conan Doyle (1924), 110–12.

## CHAPTER 13: THE STRANGE CASE OF GEORGE EDALJI

150 **George Ernest Thompson Edalji:** Richard and Molly Whittington-Egan, introduction to Sir Arthur Conan Doyle, *The Story of Mr. George Edalji*, ed. Richard and Molly Whittington-Egan (London: Grey House Books, 1985), 11.
150 **Charlotte Elizabeth Stuart Stoneham:** Ibid., 12.
150 **"Placed in the exceedingly difficult":** Conan Doyle (1985), 36.
151 **In 1888, when George:** Ibid., 37.
151 **Then, in 1892:** Ibid.
151 **"Before the end of this year":** Quoted in ibid., 41.
151 **objects stolen from around the village:** Ibid., 42ff.
151 **bogus advertisements:** Miller (2008), 259.
151 **Some of the letters identified:** Nordon (1967), 118.
151 **He was arrested in August 1903:** Ibid.
152 **an expert witness identified:** Sir Arthur Conan Doyle, *The Case of*

*Mr. George Edalji* (London: T. Harrison Roberts, 1907), in Conan Doyle (1985), 58.

152 **"He is 28 years of age":** Quoted in Miller (2008), 261–62.

152 **"Many and wonderful":** Quoted in ibid., 262.

152 **Tried in October 1903:** Costello (1991), 77.

152 **garnered ten thousand signatures:** Miller (2008), 262.

152 **In October 1906:** Ibid.

153 **He had read the Sherlock Holmes stories:** Ibid., 263.

153 **"As I read":** Conan Doyle (1924), 216–18.

153 **his 1907 pamphlet:** Conan Doyle (1907), reprinted in Conan Doyle (1985), 34–78.

153 **"The first sight":** Conan Doyle (1985), 35; italics added.

154 **"So bad was this defence":** Conan Doyle (1924), 218.

154 **"My own sight":** ACD to the *Daily Telegraph*, Jan. 15, 1907, in Gibson and Lancelyn Green (1986), 125.

155 **"Now the police try":** Conan Doyle (1985), 57–58.

155 **"England soon rang":** Conan Doyle (1924), 217.

155 **Conan Doyle, too, began receiving:** Ibid., 220.

156 **"a fact," he wrote:** Ibid.

156 **published fully only in 1985:** Womack (2001), 19.

156 **the Home Secretary, Herbert Gladstone:** Herbert Gladstone was the youngest son of William Ewart Gladstone, a prime minister under Queen Victoria.

156 **In May 1907:** Nordon (1967), 123.

156 **"The conclusions it came to":** Ibid.

156 **"It was a wretched decision":** Conan Doyle (1924), 219.

157 **Edalji was reinstated:** Nordon (1966), 126.

157 **Edalji was a guest:** Miller (2008), 273.

157 **"Conan Doyle claimed":** Stashower (1999), 260.

157 **helped spur the establishment:** Womack (2001), 20.

## CHAPTER 14: PRISONER 1992

159 **"The convict is somewhat excited":** Report from HMPP governor to prison commissioners, April 8, 1910, NRS.

159 **"Conduct somewhat indifferent":** Ibid., Sept. 2, 1910.

159 **"Conduct very indifferent":** E.g., ibid., May 4, 1911.

159 **Entries during his first years:** HMPP disciplinary record, NRS.
159 **"As regards Georg":** PL to OS, April 16, 1913, NRS.
160 **"Fanny's girls":** PL to OS, Sept. 22, 1913, NRS.
160 **"My beloved innocent Oscar"** PL to OS, July 18, 1911, NRS.
160 **"I am most unhappy":** OS to PL, April 3, 1913, NRS.
161 **"I have appealed":** OS to LF, April 19, 1913, NRS.
161 **"Dear parents, do not grieve":** OS to LF, Nov. 13, 1913, NRS.
161 **"I don't likely satisfy":** OS to MP, Dec. 17, 1912, NRS.
162 **"I did not consider him":** Unsigned memorandum, HMPP, Dec. 19, 1912, NRS.
162 **"I hope to get my liberty":** Suppressed letter from OS to REP, March 11, 1911, NRS.
162 **"Master of Polworth":** OS to MP, March 24, 1911, NRS.
163 **"On Saturday last":** OS to MP, March 25, 1911, NRS.
164 **"an intractable hell":** MacLean (1919).
164 **"When I was in Peterhead":** MacLean (1986), 25–26.
165 **"What is not in question":** Ibid., 25 n. 29.
165 **"With respect to prisoner's":** HMPP internal memorandum, June 4, 1911, NRS.
165 **"Since I was generally":** Conan Doyle (1924), 222.
166 **"It is impossible to read":** Conan Doyle (1912), 7–8.

## CHAPTER 15: "YOU KNOW MY METHOD"

169 **"It is an atrocious story":** Conan Doyle (1924), 225.
169 **"I have been in touch":** Arthur Conan Doyle, introduction to Park (1927), 14.
170 **Peterhead's correspondence log:** The log is in the archives of the NRS.
170 **it offered a welcome distraction:** Conan Doyle (1924), 215.
170 **"Some of us still retain":** ACD to *Spectator*, Oct. 12, 1912. In Gibson and Lancelyn Green (1986), 176.
170 **without leaving his rooms:** "The Mystery of Marie Rôget," in Poe (1984).
170 **"Insurance companies are":** Pasquale Accardo, M.D., *Diagnosis and Detection: The Medical Iconography of Sherlock Holmes* (Rutherford, N.J.: Fairleigh Dickinson University Press, 1987), 109.

171 **"Data! data! data!"**: Arthur Conan Doyle, "The Adventure of the Copper Beeches," in Conan Doyle (1981), 322.
171 **"That his opinion"**: Hunt (1951), 141.
172 **"The Iserbach"**: PL to OS, March 5, 1914, NRS.
172 **"On working with my granite-stones"**: OS to LF, Dec. 13, 1913, NRS.
172 **"No doubt you would realise"**: OS to LF, April 11, 1914, NRS.
172 **"Your letter has been handed"**: OS to LF, June 4, 1914, NRS.
172 **"My most beloved good son"**: PL to OS, June 15, 1914, NRS.
173 **"You know my method"**: E.g., Conan Doyle, "The Boscombe Valley Mystery," in Conan Doyle (1981), 214.
173 **"Never trust to general impressions"**: Conan Doyle, "A Case of Identity," in Conan Doyle (1981), 197.
174 **"Is there any point"**: Conan Doyle, "Silver Blaze," in Conan Doyle (1981), 347.
174 **"The actions of Helen Lambie"**: Conan Doyle (1912), 16–17; italics added.
176 **"In Edinburgh Barrowman"**: Ibid., 34.
176 **"The Lord Advocate made"**: ACD to *Spectator*, July 15, 1914. In Gibson and Lancelyn Green (1986), 205–6; italics added.
177 **"Consider the monstrous"**: Conan Doyle (1912), 59.
177 **"What the police never"**: Ibid., 27.
178 **"No further reference"**: Ibid., 50.
178 **"How did the murderer"**: Ibid., 64–66; italics added.
179 **He has planned out:** Ibid., 66–67; italics added.
179 **"Presuming that the assassin"**: Ibid., 62–63; italics added.
180 **"It will be observed"**: Ibid., 44; italics added.
180 **"the three important points"**: Ibid., 26.
180 **"The Lord-Advocate spoke"**: Ibid., 45–48.
181 **"Some of the Lord-Advocate's"**: Ibid., 48–49.
181 **"that answers to the prisoner"**: Quoted in ibid., 51.
182 **"'That answers to the prisoner'"**: Ibid., 51.
182 **"The Lord-Advocate said"**: Ibid., 52–53.
182 **"Where so many points"**: Ibid., 55–56.
183 **"What clue could you have"**: Conan Doyle, "The Adventure of the Blue Carbuncle," in Conan Doyle (1981), 246–47.
185 **"What so often leads"**: Sebeok and Sebeok (1983), 23.

186 **"One question which has to be asked":** Conan Doyle (1912), 61–63; italics added.

186 **Diamonds were objects:** See, e.g., Stefanie Markovits, "Form Things: Looking at Genre Through Victorian Diamonds," *Victorian Studies* 52, no. 4 (2010): 591–619.

187 **"It might be said":** Conan Doyle (1912), 63; italics added.

187 **published on August 21, 1912:** Roughead (1950), lxii.

187 **went on sale for sixpence:** Miller (2008), 295.

187 **"Since the publication":** Sept. 2, 1912; quoted in Gibson and Lancelyn Green (1986), 175.

187 **"I may seem to have stated":** Conan Doyle (1912), 45; italics added.

188 **"When you have eliminated":** Conan Doyle, *The Sign of Four*, in Conan Doyle (1981), 111; italics in original.

188 **"I do not see":** Conan Doyle (1912), 58.

188 **"each clue against Slater":** Conan Doyle, introduction to Park (1927), 8.

188 **"As to my case":** OS to LF, Aug. 21, 1912.

188 **"I am happy to say":** OS to LF, Aug. 9, 1913.

## CHAPTER 16: THE RUIN OF JOHN THOMSON TRENCH

190 **In November 1912:** House (2002), 164.

190 **all five identified Warner:** Ibid., 164.

190 **"One of them wept":** Hunt (1951), 167.

191 **There, twelve more witnesses:** Ibid.

191 **she had been killed several weeks earlier:** House (2002), 164–65.

191 **"Warner found that":** Hunt (1951), 167.

191 **The son of a Scottish plowman:** Whittington-Egan (2001), 101.

191 **he had joined the force:** Hunt (1951), 158.

192 **"conspicuous for gallantry":** Whittington-Egan (2001), 113.

192 **"His manners were easy":** Hunt (1951), 159.

192 **the father of six:** Ibid.

193 **"If the constable mentioned":** Quoted in ibid., 168.

193 **Trench appeared to interpret this:** Hunt (1951), 168.

193 **"You will be good enough":** DC to ACD, March 26, 1914, ML; italics added.

194 **Before the end of March 1914:** Hunt (1951), 168.

194 **the following five points:** Quoted in ibid., 168.

195 **"The convict named":** H. Ferguson Watson to HMPP officials, Feb. 2, 1914, NRS.
196 **"Sheriff Gardner Millar is":** DC to ACD, April 24, 1914, ML; italics added.
196 **not with the conduct of the trial:** Toughill (2006), 149.
196 **"suggest to me that the Enquiry":** DC to ACD, April 17, 1914, ML.
197 **"I had particular instructions":** JTT, statement to 1914 inquiry, quoted in Toughill (2006), 150.
197 **"This is the first real clue":** Hunt (1951), 161.
197 **"I am niece":** Glasgow police internal report, Dec. 23, 1908, ML.
198 **"I have been ringing up":** Hunt (1951), 161.
198 **"Although I had not":** Quoted in Roughead (1950), 271.
199 **named Elizabeth Greer:** Toughill (2006), 154.
199 **James died in 1870:** Ibid., 213, 154.
199 **The couple had three sons:** Ibid., 154.
199 **their forebears included:** Ibid., 153.
199 **Francis Charteris further cemented:** Whittington-Egan (2001), 19.
200 **whose wedding Miss Gilchrist attended:** Ibid., 20.
200 **it was from him:** Ibid., 19.
200 **"Miss Gilchrist stated to me":** Glasgow police internal report, Dec. 23, 1908, ML.
200 **Conan Doyle privately believed:** Costello (1991), 117.
200 **"I intend to deal delicately":** DC to ACD, May 9, 1914, ML.
200 **from April 23 to 25, 1914:** Roughead (1950), lxii.
200 **some twenty witnesses:** Hunt (1951), 171.
200 **who now held the rank:** Ibid.
201 **now chief detective inspector:** Ibid., 172.
201 **denied having mentioned:** HL, testimony before 1914 inquiry. Quoted in Roughead (1950), 282–83.
201 **MacBrayne testified:** Ibid., 289.
201 **MacCallum testified:** Ibid., 285.
201 **Last to testify:** DC to ACD, April 24, 1914, ML.
201 ***"The Inquiry as you are aware":*** DC to ACD, April 24, 1914, ML.
202 **"With regard to the manner":** Quoted in Toughill (2006), 175.
202 **"I am satisfied":** Quoted in Hunt (1951), 180; italics added.
202 **"This inquiry was held *in camera*":** ACD to *Spectator*, July 25, 1914, in Gibson and Lancelyn Green (1986), 204–6; italics in original.
202 **"we could do no more":** Conan Doyle (1924), 226.

203 **On July 14, 1914:** Hunt (1951), 182.
203 **the Royal Scots Fusiliers:** Toughill (2006), 178.
203 **In May 1915:** Ibid.
203 **Cook was arrested:** Ibid.
203 **The trial of Cook and Trench:** Toughill (2006), 179.
203 **The jury complied:** Ibid.
203 **Trench went on to serve with distinction:** Roughead (1950), xxxi.
203 **discharged from the military in October 1918:** Toughill (2006), 180.
203 **Trench in 1919:** Death record, scotlandspeople.gov.uk. The cause was heart trouble and pernicious anemia.
203 **Cook in 1921:** Death record, scotlandspeople.gov.uk. The cause was bronchitis and heart failure.
204 **"I got weary":** ACD to unnamed recipient, n.d., marked "Private," ML. The letter clearly postdates the prosecution of Trench and Cook: in a postscript, Conan Doyle writes, "The faked police prosecution of their own honest Inspector . . . was a shocking business."
204 **"It is a curious circumstance":** Conan Doyle (1924), 226.

## CHAPTER 17: CANNIBALS INCLUDED

205 **"It is a recognised thing":** William Gordon newspaper clipping, n.d. [c. 1925], newspaper unknown, ML.
205 **"Dearest Parents":** OS to LF, July 24, 1919, NRS.
206 **"I need not hide from you":** AT to OS, April 16, 1919, NRS.
206 **"I can imagine, dear Oskar":** AT to OS, Feb. 24, 1920, NRS. The earlier letter, informing Slater of the deaths of his parents, has not survived.
207 **"It is a pity":** AT to OS, Oct. 7, 1920, NRS.
208 **"Good Malchen":** OS to AT, n.d., NRS.
208 **"Certainly I will write you":** AT to OS, March 20, 1922, NRS.
208 **"We often think of you":** EL to OS, Aug. 15, 1922, NRS.
209 **"My beloved Oscar":** PL to OS, Aug. 3, 1914, NRS.
209 **from the lining of his coat:** Hunt (1951), 187.
210 **Years later, Adrian Conan Doyle:** Hardwick and Hardwick (1964), 75.
210 **An expansive Victorian villa:** Miller (2008), 272.
210 **"a butler . . . a cook":** Ibid., 381.

210 **"The importance of the infinitely little":** Bell (1892), 10.

210 **where he came under fire:** Miller (2008), 331ff.

210 **"From time to time":** Conan Doyle (1927), 13–14.

211 **"It was not very difficult":** Conan Doyle (1924), 337–38.

211 **"A dear friend":** Ibid., 338.

212 **The authorities declined:** Miller (2008), 322.

212 **a nationwide network of two hundred thousand:** Conan Doyle (1924), 331.

212 **"Our drill and discipline":** Ibid., 331–33.

212 **In 1914, after:** Miller (2008), 323.

213 **"Those who, in later years":** Ibid., 356.

213 **"How thorough and long":** Conan Doyle (1924), 396–401.

214 **By the 1920s, he had come to believe:** E.g., Arthur Conan Doyle, *The Coming of the Fairies* (New York: George H. Doran, 1922). The evocative telegraph address of the Psychic Bookshop and Museum, an enterprise Conan Doyle established to disseminate spiritualist beliefs, was ECTOPLASM, SOWEST, LONDON. ACD to unknown recipient, n.d., 1929, on letterhead of the Psychic Book Shop, Library & Museum, ML.

214 **At Windlesham, Conan Doyle:** Miller (2008), 381.

215 **But even in the opinion:** Whittington-Egan (2001), 161.

215 **"In vain I have waited":** AT to OS, Nov. 28, 1923, NRS.

215 **"You write me in your letters":** OS to AT, Jan. 12, 1926, NRS.

215 **"Max speaks often":** EL to OS, March 12, 1924, NRS.

215 **"I have just come from the grave":** EL to OS, Sept. 8, 1924, NRS.

216 **now worked in the prison carpentry shop:** In a letter to his sister Malchen in early 1926, Slater wrote that he had been working as a joiner at Peterhead "for the last eighteen months." OS to AT, Jan. 12, 1926, NRS.

216 **"I don't know if there is a Being":** OS to Samuel Reid, July 5, 1924, NRS.

## CHAPTER 18: THE PURLOINED BROOCH

217 **"After a careful analysis":** Quoted in Hunt (1951), 188.

217 **"The big atmosphere":** Adrian Conan Doyle (1946), 29–30.

218 **Conan Doyle got no answer:** Hunt (1951), 188.

218 **with whom he had been corresponding:** Correspondence between

Conan Doyle and Park is in the collection of the ML. The first known letter between them, from WP to ACD, is dated Sept. 25, 1914.

218 **"You may take it":** Quoted in Hunt (1951), 188; italics in original.

218 **On February 28, 1925:** Ibid.

218 **"I am directed":** Quoted in ibid., 188–89.

218 **"I need not say":** Quoted in ibid., 189.

218 **"You will be astonished":** Erna Meyer to OS, Sept. 15, 1925, NRS.

219 **"I was astonished":** OS to Erna Meyer, Dec. 5, 1925, NRS.

220 **"We have received":** Käthe Tau to OS, Jan. 24, 1926, NRS.

220 **"Among other things":** OS to Käthe Tau, June 21, 1926, NRS.

221 **As a series of government memorandums:** E.g., British government memorandums, May 27, 1924; May 28, 1924; July 8, 1924; July 14, 1924, NRS.

221 **"Apparently we cannot":** Ibid., July 14, 1924.

222 **"Poor Slater told us":** WP to ACD, Dec. 1, 1927, ML. Park had met with Slater shortly after his release.

222 **exchange of letters with Conan Doyle:** The WR-ACD correspondence has been preserved at ML.

222 **"This strange, self-tortured fanatic":** Hunt (1951), 190.

222 **"Park was a remarkable man":** Ibid., 166.

223 **he sent Park money:** E.g., WP to ACD, Nov. 25, 1927, ML. Park's letter reads in part: "I have your cheque for £25. You personally cannot be bled in this fashion. What you have done is incalculable; one of the finest things in British history. Personally, my chief trouble is the collapse of shares held by me in the best Mexican mines which have gone down. . . . I shall not desert you, come what may, although I am struggling for existence now. The public, I hope, will come to the rescue & do its belated duty to you & Slater."

223 **appeared in July 1927:** Roughead (1950), lxii.

224 **As Park pointed out:** Park (1927), 90ff.

224 **"Now that the whole world":** Ibid., 90.

224 **The answer, he explained:** Though Park did not quote directly from this document in his book, he did so in his correspondence with Conan Doyle.

224 **Before he died:** Toughill (2006), 189–90.

224 **As originally worded:** Ibid., 190–91; italics added.
224 **"It is certain":** Conan Doyle (1927), 5.
225 **"There is not one point":** Ibid., 6.
225 **"Who is to blame":** Ibid., 10.
225 **"Finally, we may ask":** Ibid., 14–15; italics in original.
225 **"It is indeed":** Ibid., 18.

## CHAPTER 19: THE GATES OF PETERHEAD

226 **had begun to attach themselves:** See, e.g., Jann (1995), 125.
226 **In September 1927:** Hunt (1951), 193.
227 **"I have been going further":** Quoted in ibid., 193.
227 **"Each day Palmer attacked":** Ibid., 193–94.
227 **On October 23:** Ibid., 195.
227 **"one of the most dramatic":** Quoted in ibid., 195.
227 **was widely presumed dead:** In Conan Doyle (1927), 13, ACD erroneously includes Lambie's name in a list of principals in the Slater case who had since died.
228 **"It has been said and denied":** Quoted in Hunt (1951), 195–96.
229 **"What a story!":** ACD postcard to the writer J. Cuming Walters, n.d., ML.
229 **"She is in the streets":** WP to ACD, Oct. 31, 1927, ML.
229 **Assisted by Palmer:** Hunt (1951), 196.
229 **"I, Mary Barrowman":** Quoted in ibid., 197–98.
231 **"Oscar Slater has now":** Quoted in ibid., 199.
231 **summoned in secret to Peterhead:** Ibid., 199.
231 **at 3:00 p.m.:** Ibid.

## CHAPTER 20: MORE LIGHT, MORE JUSTICE

232 **"The best plan":** Quoted in ibid., 199.
232 **"I am tired":** Quoted in ibid., 200.
233 **At headquarters, he asked:** Ibid., 201.
233 **"Dear Mr. Oscar Slater":** Quoted in ibid., 200.
233 **"Sir Conan Doyle":** OS to ACD, n.d. [autumn 1927], ML.
234 **It was empowered to hear:** Hunt (1951), 202.
234 **On November 16, 1927:** Ibid., 203.

234 **It passed into law:** Ibid.

234 **supporters hired Craigie Aitchison:** In 1929, Aitchison (1882–1941) became the first socialist to be appointed Lord Advocate for Scotland, the post held during Slater's original trial by Alexander Ure. Aitchison's son and namesake (1926–2009) was a distinguished painter.

234 **"Many lawyers rated":** Michael McNay, "Craigie Aitchison Obituary," *Guardian*, Dec. 22, 2009. (The subject of the obituary from which the quotation is drawn was Aitchison's son and namesake.)

235 **The appeal of Oscar Slater:** Ibid., 208–9.

235 **in the same courtroom:** Ibid., 208.

235 **a five-judge panel:** Ibid.

235 **the *Sunday Pictorial* newspaper:** Ibid., 217.

235 **"In these circumstances":** Quoted in Hunt (1951), 212.

235 **wiring the participants:** Ibid., 213.

235 **"I think his brain":** Quoted in ibid., 213.

236 **"I was in a mood":** Quoted in ibid., 213.

236 **"I am very anxious":** WP to ACD, Jan. 27, 1928, ML. Italics added.

236 **"This woman will die":** WP to ACD, n.d., ML.

236 **"This woman":** Quoted in WP to ACD, Dec. 5, 1927, ML.

237 **"Wiping her suds-covered hands":** Quoted in Whittington-Egan (2001), 176.

237 **"I wish to put a denial":** HL open letter, Dec. 18, 1927, NRS.

237 **"Lambie will go down":** WP to ACD, Dec. 19, 1927, ML.

238 **Slater's appeal resumed:** Hunt (1951), 213.

238 **Dr. Adams had died:** Roughead (1950), 312.

238 **"He expressed a very strong":** Ibid., 315.

238 **John W. M. Pinckley:** Ibid., 319–22.

238 **"Was it possible":** Quoted in ibid., 320–22.

239 **"For three days":** Quoted in Hunt (1951), 216–17.

240 **rulings on four points of law:** Ibid., 220–26.

240 **Slater was seen:** Ibid., 220.

240 **"It cannot be affirmed":** Ibid., 226; italics added.

241 **"It was some moments":** Ibid.

241 **"I Oscar Slater":** Quoted in ibid., 226.

242 **"Dear Sir Arthur":** Quoted in ibid., 226–27; italics in original.

242 **Conan Doyle, who was grateful:** Ibid., 227.

242 **"My own connection":** Quoted in ibid., 227.

## CHAPTER 21: THE KNIGHT AND THE KNAVE

243 **"I can quite understand":** Quoted in Hunt (1951), 231–32.
244 **On August 4:** Ibid., 232.
245 **"a disreputable, rolling-stone of a man":** Conan Doyle (1912), 43.
245 **"A Liberal Imperialist":** Otis (1999), 98.
245 **"eating out his heart":** Conan Doyle (1924), 226.
246 **"the easy reading":** Van Dover (1994), 30.
246 **"Lest I do you":** ACD to OS, Aug. 9, 1928, ML.
246 **"You seem to have taken leave":** ACD to OS, Aug. 14, 1928, quoted in Hunt (1951), 233.
246 **"Early in the proceedings":** ACD to the *Empire News*, May 5, 1929, quoted in Hunt (1951), 235–36.
247 **In September 1928:** *Telegraph*, Sept. 14, 1929, ML.
247 **"Let him call me":** *Daily Mail*, autumn 1929 [precise date illegible], ML. Also quoted in part in Hunt (1951), 236–37.
248 **"Making money[!]":** *Daily Mail*, autumn 1929 [precise date illegible], ML. Also quoted in Hunt (1951), 237.
248 **"Oscar Slater shook hands":** *Daily Mail*, autumn 1929 [precise date illegible], ML.
248 **Conan Doyle responded:** *Evening News*, Sept. 13, 1929.
248 **In October 1929:** Hunt (1951), 238.
248 **"At the time":** Conan Doyle (1930), 445.
249 **"Big-Hearted, Big-Bodied":** Quoted in Martin Booth, *The Doctor and the Detective: A Biography of Sir Arthur Conan Doyle* (New York: Thomas Dunne Books/St. Martin's Minotaur, 1997), 170.
249 **"I have had many adventures":** Quoted in Adrian Conan Doyle (1946), 7.
249 **On July 7, 1930:** Miller (2008), 476.

## EPILOGUE: WHAT BECAME OF THEM

250 **a view shared by some later writers:** E.g., Costello (1991).
250 **Other observers have pointed:** E.g., Toughill (2006).
250 **a ring of professional thieves:** E.g., Whittington-Egan (2001).
250 **a murderous collaboration:** E.g., Ted Ramsey, *Stranger in the Hall* (Glasgow: Ramshorn Publications, 1988).
250 **"Miss Gilchrist must have been killed":** Roughead (1929), lix; italics added.

251 **"I see no prospect":** Conan Doyle (1930), 446.
251 **She returned to Scotland:** Whittington-Egan (2001), 179.
251 **She died in Leeds:** Ibid.
251 **Mary Barrowman, who:** Ibid., 316–17.
251 **"Many years after the trial":** House (2002), 180.
251 **Barrowman died in 1934:** Whittington-Egan (2001), 316.
251 **Arthur Adams, seventy-three:** Ibid., 314. Adams was found dead, of natural causes, in his home on Jan. 3, 1942. He had last been seen alive on Dec. 31.
252 **In a noteworthy turn of fate:** Ibid., 315.
252 **In 1969, a Glasgow magistrate:** Grant (1973), 58.
252 **In 1999, however:** Whittington-Egan (2001), 266.
252 **"Scotland's gulag":** Quoted in Scraton et al. (1991), 65.
252 **"Will Wed a Kaffir":** "Will Wed a Kaffir, Says Oscar Slater," *New York Times,* Nov. 28, 1929, 21; reprint of Associated Press article datelined London, Nov. 27, 1929.
253 **after his estranged first wife died:** Whittington-Egan (2001), 195.
253 **he was briefly interned:** Ibid., 197.
253 **Unable to abide the name:** Ibid., 198.
253 **"With the war over":** Ibid., 197.
253 **on July 27, 1942:** www.ushmm.org/online/hsv/source_view.php?SourceId=7133.
254 **Slater's sister Phemie:** Database of Holocaust victims, www.holocaust.cz.
254 **his beloved sister Malchen:** Ibid.

# INDEX

## ABOUT THE AUTHOR

MARGALIT FOX is a senior writer at *The New York Times*. As a member of the paper's celebrated Obituary News department, she has written the Page One send-offs of some of the best-known cultural figures of our era, including the pioneering feminist Betty Friedan, the writer Maya Angelou, and the children's author Maurice Sendak. For her work at the *Times,* she received Front Page Awards from the Newswomen's Club of New York in 2011 and 2015.

Fox is also the author of *Talking Hands: What Sign Language Reveals About the Mind* (Simon & Schuster, 2007) and *The Riddle of the Labyrinth: The Quest to Crack an Ancient Code* (Ecco, 2013). That book, which chronicles the decipherment of the mysterious Bronze Age script known as Linear B, was selected by *The New York Times Book Review* as one of the best books of the year and received the 2014 William Saroyan Prize for International Writing.

Her work is prominently featured in *The Sense of Style* (2014), the bestselling guide to writing well by Steven Pinker. In 2016, the Poynter Institute named Fox one of the six best writers in the history of *The New York Times.*

Fox holds bachelor's and master's degrees in linguistics from Stony Brook University and a master's degree from the Columbia University Graduate School of Journalism. She lives in Manhattan with her husband, the writer and critic George Robinson.

Facebook.com/conandoyleforthedefense
Twitter: @margalitfox